THE LOOK OF THE OLD WEST

William Foster-Harris

With Illustrations by Evelyn Curro

Skyhorse Publishing

To Jill

Who had to Look for me
On much of this book
How blessed and kind she was!

Skyhorse Publishing books may be purchased in bulk at special discounts for sales promotion, corporate gifts, fund-raising, or educational purposes. Special editions can also be created to specifications. For details, contact the Special Sales Department, Skyhorse Publishing, 555 Eighth Avenue, Suite 903, New York, NY 10018 or info@skyhorsepublishing.com.

www.skyhorsepublishing.com

10 9 8 7 6 5 4 3 2

Library of Congress Cataloging-in-Publication Data

Foster-Harris, William.
  The look of the old West / William Foster-Harris ; with illustrations by Evelyn Curro.
     p. cm.
Originally published: New York : Viking Press, 1955.
Includes bibliographical references and index.
  ISBN-13: 978-1-60239-024-9 (pbk. : alk. paper)
  ISBN-10: 1-60239-024-X (pbk. : alk. paper) 1. Frontier and pioneer life--West (U.S.)
2. Frontier and pioneer life--West (U.S.)--Pictorial works. 3. West (U.S.)--Social life and customs. 4. West (U.S.)--Social life and customs--Pictorial works. 5. Cowboys--West (U.S.)--History. 6. Cowboys--West (U.S.)--History--Pictorial works. 7. Frontier and pioneer life--Collectibles--West (U.S.) 8. West (U.S.)--Collectibles. 9. Cowboys--Collectibles--West (U.S.) I. Title.

F596.H34 2007
978'.01--dc22
2007000008

Printed in Canada

CONTENTS

THE WAYBILL OF THIS BOOK

"Perfection," said great old Michelangelo, "is made up of trifles. But perfection is no trifle." Well, here is a book of Western ingredients, the little things which the historians, darn them, generally leave out.

This book tries to cover the real glory years of the Old West, from the Civil War to the Spanish-American conflict and the turn of the century. It tries both to tell you and to show you what the details looked like, what they were named, how they worked, what you did with them—from pistols to pants buttons, from sabers to soup spoons. As you'll appreciate, this is a tall order we've given ourselves, and we've probably made some mistakes, even doing our best. If you catch any, we'd appreciate it if you wrote and told us.

Because, in good part, this is a labor of love. There are worlds and worlds of vital statistics about the West, but just try and visualize a vital statistic! How does it hold its pants up? Does it pack a gun, smoke, chew, wear its hair long, smell sort of peculiar? Sure, this sounds silly, maybe, to a scholar, but when something is really alive in your mind, when you can see it, hear it, and even smell it, these are the tall trifles that perfect the picture. They make it real. And that is the main intent and purpose of this book.

We'll also say it sure took a lot of digging on our part and we hope you like it.

FOSTER-HARRIS
EVELYN CURRO

I

SOLDIERS INTO CIVILIANS

WHEN General Robert E. Lee at Appomattox turned from shaking hands with his weeping men, struck his gauntleted fist grimly into his palm, and rode off into immortality, when the blue-clad conquerors converted to Indian fighters, as some of them did, and the defeated grays were about to be civilians again—just what did these seasoned warriors look like?

What did they wear? What kind of weapons did they carry? How about their saddles, wagons, books, suspenders, cigars, and all the other details of their paraphernalia? When they went West, as thousands of them did, what did they take with them, and what were the Westerners wearing when they got there? By the eternal, as old Andy Jackson used to say, I like to know!

Here in the spring of 1865 was the supreme turn of American history, the rebirth of a great nation. Here, released, were army corps of some of the fiercest fighting men the world had ever bred. And ready and waiting for them was the wide, wild, and woolly West! The years from 1865 to the turn of the twentieth century were the time of the trail driver, the homesteader, the Indian fighter, the railroad builder. They were the great days that have inspired at least three-fourths of our Western legends and songs, and a multitude of novels, motion pictures, and plays.

Yellowleg sergeant

The epoch begins with soldiers. The flavor of the military, Yank and Reb, and the ways of the war are part and parcel of our tale. Soldiers, shedding their blue and gray uniforms (but not all their old Army habits and enmities) to turn back to civilian pursuits; other soldiers still in uniform—or part of a uniform— swinging out to chase Indians, guard emigrants, watch over railroad builders, supervise land rushes, man lonely frontier outposts. At the end of the era it was just the other way around: probably there was never a more civilian American army than that rounded up—one can scarcely say mobilized—for the brief war with Spain in 1898.

Let's take a look at this human seed stock of the fighting West in 1865. Suppose we start with the cavalry, and, first, the Union cavalryman. The Yellow-leg, so called because of the yellow cavalry-color stripes down his breeches seams, was a far cry from his prewar predecessor. He hadn't been too good at first, but four years of furious fighting against the born horsemen of Jeb Stuart, Nathan Bedford Forrest, and such, had made him into a superb warrior, fit match for the red raiders waiting out West.

The 1865 cavalryman had two kinds of headgear: a big black "Kossuth" hat; and a forage or fatigue cap, a type that was to characterize our Army for more than forty years. Our trooper had a quaint habit of getting this forage cap a little too small and wearing it right on the top of his head. It had a chin strap to hold it on, a wide leather affair a little different from our modern ones in that it had a brass slide-buckle instead of a leather keeper

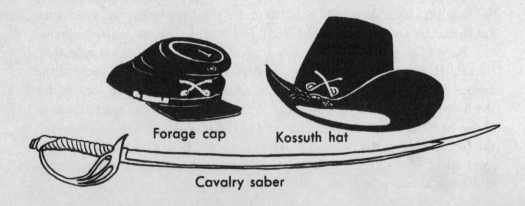

Forage cap   Kossuth hat

Cavalry saber

Zouaves

where the pieces join. And there was quite a bit of history behind this piece of Army headgear.

Napoleon and the great days of the First Empire had greatly influenced American military matters. At the beginning of the war there were entire Union regiments dressed in French uniforms, particularly in the flashy attire of the Zouaves, the French Algerian troops who wore baggy pants, sashes, and braided jackets. These didn't last too long, but the frock coats worn by officers on both sides, the shell jackets, the forage caps, the sleeve insignia worn by Southern officers (*galons*), even the Union pup tent (*tente d'abri*) were all very, very Gallic.

The forage cap was the American version of the French *kepi*, which in turn had developed from the Napoleonic and earlier shako. A shako (there were some on both sides in the war, by the bye, and the U. S. Infantry returned to them for a while in the seventies) is a stiff, high-crowned cap of leather, felt, or stiffened cloth; and it has a round, flat, hard top, and a cap vizor usually sticking straight out in front. Take the stiffening out of the sides of a shako so that the top flops down toward the front, and you have a kepi. The American Civil War forage caps were made of soft dark blue cloth-finished flannel. They had either a flat or a sloping leather vizor. The cap had a wide leather sweatband and was lined with black drill. The troopers were likely to have the down-sloping, rounded style of vizor, which, along with much cloth in the sides of the cap, made up what was popularly known as a "Bummer's cap," the contract style of 1864 that was worn by Sherman's "Bummers" on their march through Georgia. Officers usually had the flat-vizored cap, and the round top of the crown ordinarily was braided, something like a modern Marine officer's cap.

Incidentally, Army caps and hats, like other military clothing, came in numbered sizes 1 to 4, going up; there were no supplied sizes by eighths, as there are today, which may explain those too-small caps. A Number 3 was about our modern size 7¼, and a Number 1 about size 6⅞.

Regulations prescribed that insignia should be worn on the wrinkled and floppy front, with the top of the device level with the top of the crown. But, very often, for officers and men alike, the insignia was on the top of the cap itself, which, slanting forward, was easily visible.

For cavalry the insignia was two crossed sabers of stamped brass, with loops on the back for sewing to the cap. It was considerably larger than modern insignia, about 1½ inches high and 3½ wide. The number of the regiment in silver was worn above the sabers, and the letter of the company, also in silver, below. (Cavalry was organized in companies in Civil War days; although the units were often referred to as troops, the designation "troop" was not adopted officially for a cavalry unit until 1880.) Officers might have the entire device—sabers, number, letter—embroidered on black velvet and sewn to the cap.

There might also be a corps badge, pinned somewhere on the hat, probably in the front. General Philip Kearny, that lean, distinguished veteran who had lost an arm in the Mexican War, was responsible for establishing corps badges during the Civil War. He gave his division a scarlet cloth badge, known as the "Kearny patch," usually shaped like a diamond. From this start the Northern Army developed a bewildering plethora of badges for different organizations.

These badges were either cloth or—a bit fancier—large brass enameled pins. They could be had in silver and gold—real jewelry. They were worn on the top of the cap or in front of the hat or sometimes, by officers, on the left breast. The First Corps had a circle; the Second a trefoil or "three-leaf clover," as the soldiers preferred to call it; the Third Corps sported a diamond, and so on, through crosses, hearts, stars, acorns, cartridge boxes, and what not; for there had been twenty-five army corps in the Union forces.

In addition there were badges for Signal Corps, Engineers, and Miners Corps, Hancock's Veteran Corps, and two cavalry corps, Philip H. Sheridan's and James H. Wilson's. Sheridan's Cavalry Corps had a white badge shaped like a Vauban fortification, or a sunburst with squared ends on the rays, if

CORPS BADGES

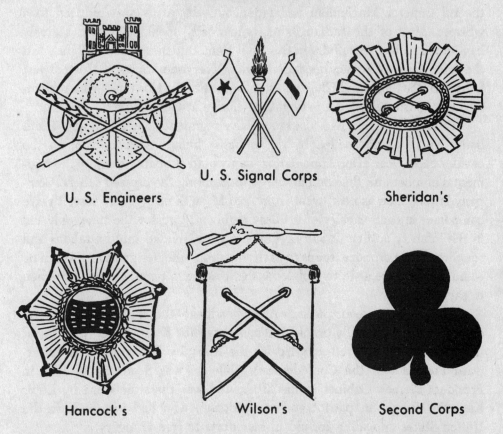

U. S. Engineers

U. S. Signal Corps

Sheridan's

Hancock's

Wilson's

Second Corps

you prefer. It had a blue oval center on which were crossed sabers in gold. Wilson's Cavalry Corps had a red banner badge, a flag with a swallow-forked end carrying gold crossed swords, suspended from a gold cavalry carbine by a cord with tassels.

These ornate cavalry corps emblems, presumably, did not change color for smaller units. But other corps badges did, the shape distinguishing the corps and the color identifying the division. Each Civil War corps numbered its divisions, and the First Division had a red badge, the Second a white, the Third a blue. If the corps was a big one, the Fourth Division had an orange badge, and the Fifth a green. The Signal Corps had a device much like today's, a torch and crossed flags, with a red star on the left flag and a blue rectangle on the right flag. These corps badges persisted through the Spanish-American War, when again they were either cloth, felt, or large brass pins, worn on the campaign hat or the left breast (if one was an officer).

But corps, and even divisions, didn't worry the Indian-fighting Army much. After Appomattox, and after the prospect of a war with Mexico over the tin emperor Maximilian had faded out, the Army was reduced to a whisper. Most of the Indian fights, numerically speaking, would scarcely have rated as outpost affairs in the Civil War. But these are the fights, just the same, that we remember individually. Everyone knows of Custer's last fight with the Sioux and Cheyennes at the Little Big Horn, but who remembers that Custer also led a very gallant charge at Gettysburg?

In 1866 the Army had just ten cavalry regiments, the Ninth and Tenth being Negro outfits, called by the Indians "buffalo soldiers." So, on the cavalry cap a year after Appomattox, you would probably see just the regimental number and the company letter decorating the crossed sabers. Company letters, then as now, went from A to M, with no J. There were twelve companies in each cavalry or artillery regiment, but, for the time, only ten in the infantry outfits. Cavalry regiments were divided into battalions and squadrons, two or more troops to each squadron—the designation was elastic—and, while we're at it, two platoons to a company, twenty-five to fifty men to each platoon.

The really gorgeous piece of Army headgear—the one, so help me, you can still see occasionally on old Indians—was the "Kossuth" or "Jeff Davis" hat. It had been ordered adopted for the Army by Jefferson Davis (afterward President of the Confederacy) while he was Secretary of War in President Pierce's Cabinet in the fifties, and was the style worn by Louis Kossuth, Hungarian patriot and revolutionist, who had just been in the United States appealing for aid in his efforts to free Hungary.

For enlisted men, it was a black wool-felt affair, with a flat, raw-edged (three rows of stitching), 3¼-inch brim and a crown 6¼ inches high, shaped like an upside-down flowerpot. It had a poor-quality, ½-inch, ribbed grosgrain ribbon band, which faded to a sort of funereal purple on exposure to

KOSSUTH HATS

Field officer's   Cavalry lieutenant's   Staff officer's
("looped up")

the elements, and a wide leather sweatband; the inside of the flat, round top was heavily varnished, for added stiffening. On the inside top was stamped a gold eagle, surmounted by "U. S. Army," and below, "Extra Manufacture," whatever you care to assume that means. There was also the size number, 1 to 4.

Decorating this chapeau was a whole millinery stock of bright doodads. First came a hatcord (yellow for cavalry), and double-looped, much like the hatcords used on the Army campaign hats up until World War II, and ending in 2-inch tassels. Curiously, original regulations seem to have intended these tassels to be worn on the side of the hat, like a cowboy's horsehair hatband, rather than straight in front. But straight in front everybody wore 'em, when they wore any cord at all. For enlisted men the cords were worsted.

The hat was usually "looped up," which means the brim was pinned to the crown on the side like a modern Australian Army hat, with a small brass U. S. eagle coat of arms. The top of this badge was fastened to the hat, but it had a small hook to the brim on the bottom, so that the hat brim could be unhooked when the wearer wanted more shade. Mounted men, employing the saber right-handed, looped up the right side of the hat to get it out of the way, while the infantryman, with many support arms and such on his left side, pinned up the left brim.

In front, set midway between brim and top, was the brass device of the arm—the brass crossed sabers for cavalry—with the number of the regiment ⅝ inch high, and the letter of the company 1 inch high, also in brass. And for a finishing touch, there was an 18-inch black ostrich-feather plume, worn slanted jauntily upward and to the rear, on the side opposite the loop.

Officers' hats, of better fur felt and with bound edges on the brim, usually had the insignia embroidered on patches of black velvet sewn to the hat. For officers the hatcords were gold and black silk, for generals gold silk. Officers' cords ended in acorns. General and staff officers had a silver U. S. in a gold embroidered wreath on the front; engineers sported a silver turreted castle in a gold wreath of laurel and palm, and ordnance officers a gold shell and flame. Generals and field officers had three ostrich plumes for their bonnets, captains and lieutenants, two. By regulations at least, all officers' hats looped on the right side. Line officers' hats—cavalry, infantry, artillery—carried the device of their arm, crossed sabers for cavalry, crossed cannon for artillery, and, for infantry, not crossed rifles as you'd suppose, but instead a bugle, a chasseur's hunting horn! The crossed rifles for infantry were not adopted until 1875, and before that time the infantry device was a bugle, silver from 1834 to 1851, and gold from 1851 to 1875. The badge was 3½

General officers

Engineering officers

Topographical Engineers

Infantry

Artillery

Riflemen

Ordnance

Emblem on velvet
(reduced)

Cavalry

Emblem on velvet (reduced)
Number of regiment,
letter of company

inches wide and 2 inches high and was worn with the bell and mouthpiece up, with the regimental number inside the round loop.

Much as it must have needed one, with its many trappings and its casual fit, this hat did not have a chin strap. It was dress gear, far from practical for campaigns; and in field service, stiffening or not, it soon got dented and creased and lost its fine feathers. But the cavalryman did like the wide brim. About 1873 another version was issued, the brim of which could be folded up on both sides to look very much like a pirate's headpiece or a Navy officer's chapeau; it was called the Custer hat, after General George Armstrong Custer. This is the hat you see folded flat in the hands of cavalry officers in photographs of the period. It must have flopped like the very devil in fast riding, because often it was pinned up in front with the crossed sabers.

General Custer, by the way, was much given to freakish apparel and often wore a wide light-colored "planter's hat," so called because it had been a favorite of Southern planters before the war. It, too, had a flat plug crown, like the Army hat, but much lower. It was worn undented. The regulation color of Army hats during this period, however, was black.

The just-postwar trooper, so soon to try his mettle against Red Cloud, Black Kettle, Cochise, and the rest, had several bits of gear, in addition to the hat, that certainly could have been improved upon for campaigning in the sometimes red-hot West. The cavalry jacket was one of them. As to cut it wasn't too bad. It was waist-length, snug-fitting so far as the fit went, fine for an active horseman. In the Confederate service its gray counterpart was often called a "shell jacket," and it reminds one of the Eisenhower jacket that came out of World War II. But in material and detail it was something else. It was made of cloth-finished flannel, dark blue woolen and astoundingly heavy, and usually lined with dark blue flannel to boot. It was worn summer and winter. A man fighting in that on a nice July day must have got hot in a hurry! Scant wonder you see so many old photographs with the Army all unbuttoned (which was strictly against regulations, except for "officers in bureaus"!) and scratching their tummies. The jacket was single-breasted, with a high standing collar fastened in front at the bottom with a large hook and eye. The corners of the collar were cut away at about a 30-degree angle, giving room for the Adam's apple and throat. Under this collar, the troopers were supposed to wear an atrocity of a stock, of black leather. This is where the name "leatherneck" came from, since the Marines also had to wear these dog-collar affairs and evidently did. And "raw recruit" no doubt stemmed from the same galling source. But in no Civil War or later picture have I been able to make certain that any soldier is actually wearing such a stock. Hanged if I blame them!

The jacket was piped with yellow braid, the buttonhole edge down the front, around the bottom, the top and bottom of the collar all around, and the two seams in back. In addition there were two 4-inch bars of yellow braid on each side of the collar, running horizontally from the front and ending at the rear in small brass buttons. More braid defined the pointed cuff on each sleeve. Down the front was a single row of twelve small, "vest-size" eagle buttons.

Musicians—trumpeters as well as bandsmen—boasted still more bright braid in the color of the arm, seven to nine rows of it, set horizontally across the chest. And sometimes there'd be two additional rows of buttons at the ends of the braid, instead of just one. Two or three more buttons adorned each cuff—a Prussian idea to keep brave soldiers from wiping their noses on their fancy cuffs, no fooling; and if you'll look at your own civilian coat sleeve you'll discover you're still being discouraged from the nasty habit, too!

So a frontier cavalryman had at least twenty buttons, and a musician maybe forty-four, to polish every day, in addition to all the other metal. But at least he had, or could improvise, a button cleaner, a wooden board with slots in it, often hinged, like a pair of scissors, which he could clamp under the buttons and so keep his uniform clean while he scrubbed industriously with a mixture of vinegar and salt. For steel, the old Army used sand for

UNION CAVALRY

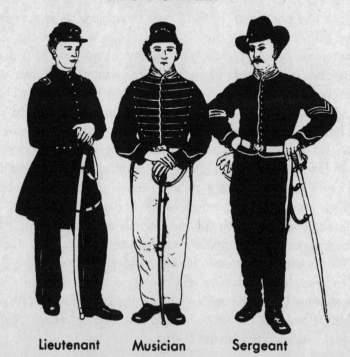

Lieutenant   Musician   Sergeant

UNION UNIFORMS

Corporal,   Ordnance   Cavalry trumpeter
Light Artillery sergeant

bad rust and then moistened wood ashes to get the high polish—plus untold elbow grease, never doubt it!

In the rear of the jacket, at the bottom of the two seams, were two belt supporters, weird little cloth-covered bolsters, like miniature pillows. The jacket had one pocket inside the breast, opening vertically to the left about opposite the third and fourth buttons.

Now those buttons, as long as we're polishing them up. Brass, rounded, and rimless, they carried an eagle looking very much like the bird on our modern Army button, except that this Civil War variety lacked the field of stars above his head, had stubbier wings, and the shield on the breast showed a three-pointed top, instead of being flat, as now.

For all enlisted men this shield carried only the United States coat of arms. But for officers it was fancier, with a C for cavalry, I for infantry, and A for artillery. Staff officers' buttons were rimmed, with a circle of stars. Ordnance officers' buttons had a wreath, crossed cannons, and bombshell with the words Ordnance Corps. For the Topographical Engineers, a specialist corps combined with the engineers in the changes of 1863, the buttons

UNION ADORNMENTS

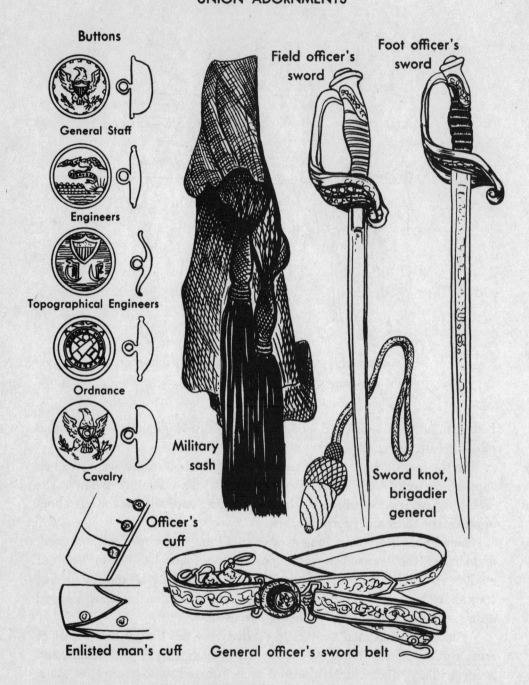

Buttons

General Staff

Engineers

Topographical Engineers

Ordnance

Cavalry

Military sash

Field officer's sword

Foot officer's sword

Sword knot, brigadier general

Officer's cuff

Enlisted man's cuff

General officer's sword belt

had a shield and the letters T E. Engineers, top dogs in the Army setup (they got first crack at West Point graduates, and Robert E. Lee, graduating second in the class of 1829, went into the engineers), were particularly gorgeous with so-called "essayons" buttons bigger than anybody else's, %10 of an inch in diameter. The button's name came from the motto on the ribbon in the eagle's beak, and in addition to the valiant bird there was a bastion with embrasures, surrounded by water, and topped by a rising sun!

But to get back to our cavalryman. Under the jacket he wore a gray flannel shirt. In summer it would often be a loudly striped "hickory" or checked calico or gingham shirt, scrounged from somewhere. But the benevolent government issued him just the flannel shirt and drawers, no undershirt; and if in summer he wore nothing at all under that jacket you have only to remember the thickness of the thing to understand why. Not until January 1881 was the gray flannel shirt discontinued, blue woolen shirts piped in the color of the arm substituted, and an issue of three knitted undershirts a year provided to go with the drawers.

This is one of many details on which Western storytellers often go wrong. True, the frontier Army had often only the sketchiest regard for uniform, and some of the officers did provide themselves with heavy blue double-breasted miner's or lumberman's shirts from civilian stocks. But it is hardly likely that a private making $13 a month would spend much of his magnificent stipend enhancing his government issues. 'Twas a stout heart, but little else, he wore under that jacket of blue. Permission for the enlisted man to shed his blouse and appear in shirt sleeves, with his suspenders right out in the open, came only with the blue shirts in 1881, and the drab-colored campaign hat, as we noted, was not officially allowed until 1885. So, strictly speaking, only stories and plays dealing with the later Indian troubles, those with Geronimo and the Chiricahua Apaches in Arizona in the eighties, and the final flurry of Ghost Dance unrest, and the brief, brutal battle of Wounded Knee in 1889-90, should have cavalrymen all neatly got up in blue shirts, white undershirts showing at rolled-up sleeves and open collars, web suspenders, drab campaign hats.

Shirts of the period, incidentally, all pulled on over the head, and the collar, if any, was an atrocity, merely a foldover of the material at the neckband. The truly natty soldier, trying to do something about the ghastly expanse of bare neck, experimented at first with the prevailing civilian cravat or stock, which was simply a length of black ribbon wound around the throat and usually tied in a bow. But out West the bandanna was much easier come by and more convenient. And I have no doubt that those horrible shirt collars, both military and civilian, were the real and indeed about the only reason for the cavalry and cowboy neckerchief.

Troopers, when they wore neckerchiefs, usually had a red or blue cotton bandanna, the ordinary farm work handkerchief. Officers, however, often sported silk, and again in the color of the arm, yellow for cavalry, red for artillery, and blue for infantry.

The trooper's jacket, as noted, was dark blue. His "trowsers," in contrast, were a light sky blue, usually of stout kersey cloth. At the beginning of the war they had been dark blue, except for light artillery. But in 1863 the sky-blue color had been adopted, and it would continue until the blue uniforms were abolished. The trousers were built with more waistband than we generally see on pantaloons today, and either were fitted tightly enough to stay up of their own accord or were worn with braces or suspenders. There was often a small tightening strap in back. The pockets were much like those in modern riding breeches, the openings nearly horizontal and to the front, rather than vertical along the side seams.

Down the outer seam of the trouser leg, coming up to but not crossing the waistband, officers and noncommissioned officers added a welt, or stripe, in the color of the arm. By wartime regulations this was a welt ⅛ inch wide for officers, a stripe 1½ inches for sergeants and ½ inch for corporals. Privates wore no stripe. In 1872 this was changed to give officers the 1½-inch stripe, sergeants 1-inch, and corporals ½-inch, and here, save for a change in 1884 from blue to white as the facing color for infantry, the trouser-stripe situation stayed until the end of the blue uniform.

Regulations prescribed that the trousers be full, without pleats, and that they spread well over the boot. But in the mounted service, where the trouser was ordinarily worn inside the boot, the lower part of the leg would often be narrowed and sometimes a slit left along the side. A wadded pants leg inside a tough boot can be horribly uncomfortable.

Now the footgear. Before the Civil War, boots and shoes were pretty much handmade or custom made by the cobbler to the individual customer's requirements. Curiously, it was only during the war that the shoe factories began mass production of paired shoes, rights and lefts. With prewar store-bought brogans it was often hard to decide which shoe was meant for a right and which for a left. But as the war ended, the North had this all pretty well straightened out; and the South was just about barefooted. You could almost say that shoes, or the lack of them, had been a significant contributing cause of the Confederacy's defeat. Henry Heth's ragged and shoeless Confederates had heard there was a shoe factory and a stock of shoes in Gettysburg, and that was one of the reasons they had headed that way, to stub their toes on Buford's blue troopers and so start the decisive Battle of Gettysburg.

But authorized by regulation in both armies, and actually available in the Union quartermaster stores, were shoes much like ours of today, an

UNION UNIFORMS

Cavalry uniforms,
showing boots, belts, hats, swords, spurs, and hickory shirt

Infantry frock coat   Cavalry   Infantry fatigue coat and
jacket and vest   full marching equipment

ordinary low or "ankle" tie shoe—you see this shoe on General Lee in Brady photographs taken in Richmond right after the Surrender—and a high laced "Jefferson" shoe, so called because President Thomas Jefferson had introduced and popularized it. For fatigue and such, the blue trooper wore these Jefferson shoes in rough brogan style, very much like our modern work shoe.

Usually, though, he had been issued at least one pair of boots. And these, even for the enlisted man, were right fancy footwear. Way back, they had been jack boots, huge affairs reaching high above the knees, and, incidentally, lasting just about forever. Jack-boot owners actually bequeathed their boots to their sons. You've probably seen pictures of Colonel William F. Cody, Buffalo Bill, wearing these monstrosities. But they were heavy and hot and expensive, and by the end of the war there was a reduced version—the cavalry boot, with the leg reaching just under the bend of the knee behind, but arched higher in front to cover the kneecap. There was also a straight boot, 14 to 17 inches high, cut straight across the top under the knee, like a modern riding boot. Both of these had somewhat wider legs than our modern boot, since bulky trouser legs had to be stuffed into them. They were black, and usually of grain or calfskin leather, had low flat leather heels and, typically, square toes.

Brass spurs were secured to the boots with a single spur strap, laced through loops in the spur and going around the instep. The spurs were goose-necked—that is, the shank was curved upward. This was necessary, because ordinarily the spur was worn very low, actually on the heel or thereabouts, in sharp contrast with the later fashion for wearing it practically around the ankle. There was a sharp-toothed steel rowel, about the size of a nickel. How they kept from cutting the tripe out of their mounts with these merciless cutters I don't know. But troop horses weren't usually clipped in those days, as they were in the later Army with its humane no-rowel type spur.

Under the boots were gray or natural-colored socks, usually home knitted for the soldier by his womenfolks, since the Army issued him only four pairs a year. They were referred to as stockings, not socks. And he did not wear hose supporters!

On his shoulders, if he wore anything, the Yankee trooper would have a pair of heavy brass epaulettes, big ones, 6 inches long and 3½ wide, with a half-moon at the outer end and a scaled strip toward the neck. These fastened to the jacket by a loop and turnbutton, a steel spring under the epaulette that slid through the loop, then caught the button at the inner end. They were right gaudy, those brass bindings. But they were not as entirely senseless as one might think. Cavalry combat was still, at times, a hand-to-hand affair. If an enemy whacked you on the shoulder with a saber

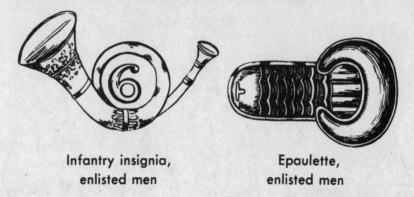

Infantry insignia,
enlisted men

Epaulette,
enlisted men

or spear, that brass epaulette could save you an ugly wound, perhaps even the loss of an arm. But even so, save for dress parades, balls, and such, the brass epaulettes soon disappeared from the American Army frontier uniform. They were too much to polish, and too glittering a mark for the Indian to shoot at.

Now for the cavalry greatcoat. For my money, that old Army overcoat was one handsome garment, and I suspect modernized copies would sell today if some enterprising firm would only put them on the market. It was of sturdy sky-blue kersey cloth, with a stand-and-fall collar about 5 inches high; double-breasted, it had two rows of large eagle buttons in front, and its skirt reached 6 to 8 inches below the knee. The plain slit in back for riding was 15 to 17 inches, and had concealed flap and buttons for closing if desired.

The really characteristic feature of these overcoats was the cape, attached with hooks and eyes under the overcoat collar and reaching down to the cuff of the sleeve. This cape, wide and semicircular, was lined with flannel in the color of the arm—yellow for cavalry, and so on. It had a single row of buttons up the front. Tossed back over the shoulders, it made a very gallant display, while in wet or extra-cold weather it provided additional protection for shoulders and chest, or could be thrown over the head as an impromptu hood.

The infantry greatcoat was single-breasted by Civil War regulation, had one row of buttons down the front and a cape reaching only to the elbow. It was also shorter than the cavalry greatcoat. In the early seventies this coat was abolished and the double-breasted mounted overcoat prescribed for all troops. In the Confederate service, horse and foot alike had double-breasted greatcoats, the principal difference being that the infantry had shorter elbow-length capes. At least Confederate regulations said Johnny Reb was due an overcoat. There was also ordered for both sides, and duly

GREATCOATS

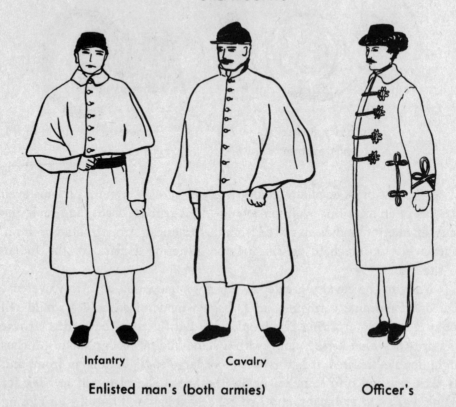

Infantry   Cavalry

Enlisted man's (both armies)   Officer's

provided by the Union quartermasters, a talma for mounted men, a kind of loose waterproof cape made with sleeves, waterproofed with gutta-percha (a substance something like rubber, made from the latex of certain Malaysian trees). Quite a few Confederates had this also, by capture.

Noncommissioned officers in both armies wore large chevrons on the sleeves of both uniform jacket and overcoat, the stripes being of silk or worsted binding, ½ inch wide, in the color of the arm. Chevrons were worn

Sleeve insignia, Union NCO's

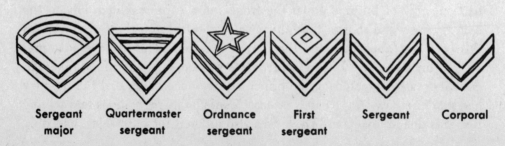

Sergeant major | Quartermaster sergeant | Ordnance sergeant | First sergeant | Sergeant | Corporal

points down, midway between shoulder and elbow. A sergeant major had three bars and an arc of silk, a quartermaster sergeant three bars and a tie of silk, an ordnance sergeant three silk bars and a star, a first sergeant three bars and a lozenge of worsted, a sergeant three bars, a corporal two bars, also worsted.

Pioneers (a special sort of working soldier provided with saws, axes, augers, and the like, to repair roads, erect defenses, and generally spearhead the construction necessary for troops in the field) wore two crossed hatchets, in the color of the arm. Farriers—a farrier, attached to each mounted outfit, was a horseshoer, blacksmith, and on occasion veterinary—had a horseshoe on each sleeve. In the Union Army, for each five years' service (the enlistment period for cavalry was for five years in this era, as it had been, with some fluctuations, since the conflict with Mexico) the enlisted trooper could wear a "half-chevron," which was a diagonal stripe, ½ inch wide, in the color of his arm, extending from seam to seam on his sleeve below the elbow, the front end nearest the cuff. War service was indicated by a red stripe ⅛ inch wide on each side of the half-chevron, except in the artillery, which already had a scarlet stripe, and used light blue for war-service trim.

Medal of Honor, 1862

There were no campaign ribbons and no medals, with a single exception. The Congressional Medal of Honor, the nation's highest award, was authorized by Congress on July 12, 1862, and it was first awarded to six Ohio enlisted men, "Mitchell's Raiders," for the daredevil feat of capturing a Confederate locomotive, The General, and trying, though not successfully, to upset the rebel railroad system. Tom Custer, brother of the general, won two Congressional Medals during the war and sometimes wore both. They looked remarkably like Grand Army of the Republic (G. A. R.) membership medals, in case you ever see them in old photographs. But there were no other Army decorations until January 1918, when President Woodrow Wilson established the Distinguished Service Cross and the Distinguished Service Medal. Campaign medals (which are not "decorations") were eventually authorized for the Civil War, the Indian campaigns, the Spanish-American War, the Philippine Insurrection, the Boxer Rebellion, and so forth, but Congress did not pass this act until 1905.

Until about the turn of the century, our government had a habit of granting special commemorative medals to victorious commanders. These were not intended to be worn, being, typically, big hunks of metal, 3 inches or so across, in bronze, silver, or gold. But one variety of these medals was worn, not by soldiers, but by Indians.

These were the Presidential Medals, so called, issued by the United States Mint at Philadelphia. Each president since Washington has had his face duly immortalized in bronze on one of these medals. On the back are a tomahawk, pipe of peace, and clasped hands; Army officers gave them to the Indians on the conclusion of peace treaties. Under Grant, Hayes, Garfield, Arthur, Cleveland, and Harrison, special Indian Peace Medals also were struck, in addition to the Presidential ones. The Presidential Medal is round and 3 inches in diameter; most of the Indian Peace Medals are 3 by 2⅜ inches, oval. Handed one of these, the red man promptly

Presidential Medals

punched a hole in the rim, ran a thong of rawhide through it, and hung it around his neck. And that's what you see in the old-time Injun pictures.

You can still buy Presidential Medals and some of the Indian Peace Medals from the Philadelphia mint, if you are interested, at very modest prices. Handsome and historical trinkets they are, too.

A "wagon soldier," an artilleryman, in the U.S. Army at the close of the Civil War, was dressed much like the trooper, with the exception of artillery scarlet facings and trimmings in place of cavalry yellow. He had the same waist-length jacket, but trimmed in scarlet; the same forage cap, with crossed cannons, big brass ones; the same light blue trousers. For an NCO the trouser stripe was scarlet. He had a cavalry-type belt with an eagle plate (a rectangular buckle bearing a spread eagle in relief), a shoulder strap like a Sam Browne, and sword slings, because, amusingly enough, he was armed with a saber, a big one with a deeply curved blade like a Turkish scimitar, a brass hilt with only one bow, and a steel scabbard.

He had a stable frock—as did the cavalry, for that matter—a long canvas coat to protect his other garments while he was engaged in stable or fatigue duty. But at the close of the war another style was also well launched, one that presently all the fighting Army would adopt—wearing the infantry blouse, the fatigue coat, for practically all events and occasions except full dress.

The infantry, by regulations, had a single-breasted dress frock coat, with nine large eagle buttons, stand-up collar hooking at the bottom, skirts extending halfway to the knee, collar and cuffs edged with sky-blue welt, two buttons on each cuff, two buttons in back to hold up the belt, back slit, and pockets in the folds of the skirts. They must have just loved to sit on things in the Civil War! But this was dress gear, parade-ground stuff. It had all but vanished during the war, to be replaced by a far more practical garb, the fatigue coat, "a sack coat of dark blue flannel, extending halfway down the thigh and made loose," as the regulations defined it, with a folding collar, one inside pocket on the left side, and four or five large eagle buttons closing the single-breasted front. It was made much like the civilian suit coat of the times, the top button at about the hollow of the throat and the collar folding down much like a modern shirt collar. For ordinary purposes it was unlined. But for recruits it had body and sleeve lining of heavy blue or black flannel. This was the coat the whole frontier Army would speedily adopt; and, please note, it was officially a "coat," sometimes referred to as a "blouse" but never as a "tunic." "Tunic" is a British Army term.

The jaunty cavalryman clung to his short, braided jacket longer than anyone else, both because it looked snappier and because, for a horseman, a short coat is much more convenient. I have no doubt that the vests the later frontier cowboys loved to wear, loose and flapping, the denim jumpers, the leather jerkins and windbreakers (which last is a trademark name, by the way) are descendants, at least in part, of this cavalry jacket. But by the seventies the troopers, too, would be riding and fighting in fatigue coats.

Pantaloons, as we've noted, were sky blue by the end of the war for practically everybody but generals. Since it was considered very unmilitary for a soldier to have a lot of lumpy guesswhats in his pockets the usual remedy was to give him as few pockets as possible. So the trousers usually had only front pockets and, of course, no cuffs on the trouser bottoms. Pants were held up either by the tightness of their fit or by suspenders, which by regulation were supposed to be worn only under the coat. Sometimes the black leather waistbelt, supposed to be worn over the coat, was worn as a trouser belt under the jacket instead. But this was not regulation, even though some generals did it too!

The infantry soldier, in the sixties and seventies, wore the Jefferson shoe, and had a neat trick of tucking the bottoms of his pantaloons into the tops of his heavy gray woolen socks, thus making a very serviceable legging. Leggings were called "gaiters" in the Civil War period, and buttoned or buckled up the side, and sometimes came clear over the knee, like the top of a jack boot. Horsemen sometimes wore them in lieu of the heavier boots. But you seldom saw them on the frontier. The infantryman used his sock instead, and quite often he carried his mess spoon or knife in the top of his sock, too.

Now let's see what the officers looked like. For formal dress, in the sixties and early seventies, the U. S. officer wore a frock coat of dark blue cloth, usually broadcloth, the skirts extending from two-thirds to three-fourths the distance from top of hip to knee. The coat was single-breasted for lieutenants and captains, the so-called company officers. All other officers, including generals, had double-breasted frock coats.

Above the rank of colonel, the spacing of the buttons on the front was one of the indications of the rank of the wearer. Brigadier generals had their buttons spaced in groups of two, with eight buttons in each row. Major generals had groups of three, lieutenant generals (of whom the frontier Army was allotted one) presumably sported groups of four, and a full general (Grant, Sherman, and Sheridan in succession for the Indian-fighting days) should have had groups of five. There is at least one photo-

Ulysses S. Grant

Philip Kearny

UNION GENERALS
Showing buttons, hats, sword
belts, sashes, gloves, dress cape,
swords, dress coats

George Custer
(in his personal uniform)

Stonewall Jackson

Jeb Stuart

Robert E. Lee

CONFEDERATE GENERALS
Showing button arrangements,
collar insignia, gloves, sword,
belts, vest, silk stocks

graph showing Grant with such a brass band on his coat, but it looks so top-heavy that you can understand why the high brass ordinarily just stopped with the major general's three-group, no matter how much higher their rank.

Generals can determine their own uniforms and insignia, and General Custer ordered himself a lulu when he got his first star at the advanced age of twenty-three. A sailor collar with stars, a fireman's red tie, a black velvet sack coat with side pockets, plus a cowboy hat!

But the Confederacy already had set the example of modesty, at least in the matter of brass buttons on the frock coat. Confederate general officers for the most part, even including General Lee, just wore two-group button arrangements. They look neater, to say the least. But sometimes, especially in fancy paintings, you see Confederate generals with three-group buttons.

Colonels, lieutenant colonels, and majors, on both sides, had their buttons evenly spaced, seven buttons in each row. For them, in the Union service, coat collars and cuffs were of the same material as the coat. Union general officers had collars and cuffs of dark blue velvet as another distinguishing mark, while the Confederates, including enlisted men, were supposed to have cuffs and collars in the color of the arm. Often as not they didn't. There were three small buttons on the 2½-inch cuffs. The skirts were full behind, and slit, with a pocket in each skirt, one small button at the opening of each pocket, and a button on each hip, to support the sword belt. As in the enlisted men's version, the stand-up collar hooked at the bottom, then slanted away at a 30-degree angle on each side to accommodate the full whiskers which were Civil War style.

The collar was supposed to be worn hooked. But when you note the choking, stifling thickness of that wool coat, you can see why the collar was very often folded down and the lapels rolled back, like a civilian suit collar. In which event the officer presented an expanse of neck, ordinarily covered with a starched white collar and a black silk stock or cravat, tied in a bow! It wasn't regulation for the bow to show, either, if you care any more than they did. The coat was lined, usually with black silk.

Yankee captains and lieutenants, on their single-breasted frock coats, had one row of nine buttons, equi-spaced; higher-ranking officers two rows. Officers serving with mounted troops could wear "for stable duty" (which was frequently interpreted to mean practically anything) a plain dark blue jacket, with either one or two rows of buttons down the front, according to rank, and no other trimmings at all except the shoulder straps. This, I think, is the garment you sometimes see replaced in the movies by a double-

UNION OFFICERS' UNIFORMS

Colonel   Brigadier general   Captain or lieutenant

breasted blue miner's shirt, which wasn't regulation at all, but was some-times worn on campaigns in the West.

But an officer could wear a vest, if he wanted to and by regulation. In the Union Army it could be blue, white, or buff, with nine small brass buttons. It, too, had a standing or rolling collar (standing, it made the wearer look like some kind of military priest). Both Grant and Lee wore them (Lee's was gray, of course), while Grant even sported a nice fancy watch chain across the weskit to boot. Boy, they were military!

Around their middles, over the frock coat and under the sword belt, Union officers wore a sash (see page 14) of silk net and with silk bullion fringe ends, long enough to go twice around the body, tie at the left hip, and still leave up to 18 inches (more was forbidden by regulations) dangling below the tie. For general officers this sash was buff-colored, for other officers, crimson; except for medical officers, who had emerald green. Some of the noncommissioned officers also had sashes, of red worsted, to wear beneath their sword belts. These included sergeant majors, quartermaster sergeants, ordnance sergeants, first sergeants, chief musicians, yes, and buglers, all armed with trick NCO or musician's swords, straight-bladed affairs with a single bow, brass guard, worn in a sword frog, rather than on slings. Hospital stewards, too, had swords and sashes.

The sash was supposed to be worn under the sword belt on all occasions except stable and fatigue. The Officer of the Day wore his sash over his right shoulder and spread across his breast, as a badge of office. The one useful purpose the sash served was to protect the coat from the dyes in the sword belt and from being tarnished by the buckle.

Sword belts for Union generals were Russia leather (a superior sort in which birch oil is used as part of the tanning process), 2 inches wide and decorated with three horizontal stripes of gold embroidery. All other officers, including NCO's, wore plain black. Officers had slings for their swords, usually attaching with brass studs to rings on the belt, the short front sling having also a hook for the saber ring, while the long lower sling attached to the belt almost in the center of the back. Afoot, an officer always carried his saber hooked up, guard to the rear. When he was mounted, it was always unhooked, to dangle at the ends of its slings— although the movies often violate this rule. The sword-belt plate, for everyone equipped with a sword or saber, was a rectangular brass plate, 2 inches wide, 3 long, with a silver laurel wreath encircling the spread-eagle arms of the United States. Officers' belt plates were often gold-plated, or at least fire gilt, and the stars above the eagle were silvered, as well as the *E Pluribus Unum* motto on the scroll in the eagle's mouth. They were exceedingly handsome buckles.

Now the rank badges for officers. During the Civil War, and until the drastic changes were made in the Army uniforms in 1872, there were elaborate gold dress epaulettes with a large gold crescent on the tip of the shoulder, from which dangled gold bullion fringe, ranging from 3½ inches long for generals to 2½ for lieutenants. The rank devices, stars for generals, eagles for colonels, leaves for lieutenant colonels, two bars for captains, one bar for first lieutenants, all of silver, were on the strap of the epaulette. Inside the loop of the crescent, engineer officers had a turreted silver castle, ordnance a silver shell and flame, the Medical Department a wreath with the Old English letters M S, pay department a P D. Regimental officers had a circular patch in the color of the arm, carrying the number of the regiment in gold, the circle 1¼ inches in diameter and rimmed with silver. Topographical Engineers (consolidated with the engineers in 1863) had a gold shield with the letters T E below it in silver.

Majors and second lieutenants, you'll notice, had no rank devices on these epaulettes. The poor second louie wouldn't get one until World War I, while the major's gold leaf, of course, wouldn't show on a gold field. But

Union officers' epaulettes and saber-belt plate

Union officers' shoulder straps

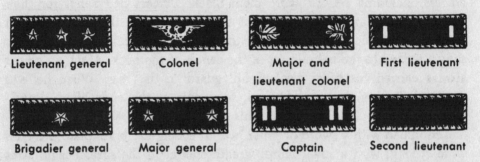

| Lieutenant general | Colonel | Major and lieutenant colonel | First lieutenant |
| Brigadier general | Major general | Captain | Second lieutenant |

both majors and second lieutenants wore epaulettes, and you could tell the difference by the bullion fringe, which for majors was the 3½-inch-long, ½-inch-in-diameter hang-rope stuff the generals wore, while second louies had only 2½-inch, ¼-inch-diameter sash-cord trimmings. All this was dress stuff, seldom seen in the field.

For field service "undress" the U. S. officer wore shoulder straps, a rank device that characterized the American Army from 1836, when it was adopted, until World War I, when most of the dress gear went permanently into the discard. The slang term for officers in the Civil War and frontier Army days was "shoulder straps," just as we now call them "the brass." Our term would have fitted just as well then, for the shoulder strap was even brassier than anything the officer wears today. In this immediate post-Civil-War day it was a cloth pad, 1⅜ by 4 inches, sometimes smaller on the field-service gear, sometimes larger, on the outer edge of the shoulder, parallel with the shoulder-sleeve seam—running, that is, from front to back, and not from the sleeve to the neck, as did the epaulette, and as does our shoulder strap today. The edge of this strap was bordered with gold embroidery, ¼ inch wide. The field inside the border was of velvet or other fine cloth, dark blue for generals and staff officers, scarlet for artillery, sky blue for infantry, and yellow for cavalry. On this field were embroidered the rank devices.

A full general had four stars, evenly spaced in a line on the strap. A lieutenant general had three, a major general two, and a brigadier one, placed in the exact center of the strap. The stars were silver and five-pointed. A colonel had a silver spread eagle on the center of the strap, 2 inches from wingtip to wingtip, the head of the eagle pointing toward the wearer's neck. Lieutenant colonels had two silver leaves, one at each end of the strap. And from here on down there is an important difference between the rank badges then and those of today. The leaves of a major, the twin bars of a captain, and the single bar of a first lieutenant were gold on Civil War shoulder straps, not silver, as now. Although the second lieutenant had no device, his epaulettes or shoulder straps marked him clearly enough as a commissioned officer until the Spanish-American War period, when the American Army, under British influence, adopted khaki. Then you couldn't tell a second louie from an enlisted man—that is, unless you failed to salute him. So in 1917 the Army finally got around to giving him a gold bar—something the Confederacy had done for its shavetails just fifty-five years earlier!

Finally, a medical cadet had a strap of green cloth, 3¾ inches long by 1¼ wide, with a 3-inch strip of gold lace, ½ inch wide, down the middle of it.

The change to silver was made in 1872, when epaulettes were abolished for regimental officers and replaced by shoulder knots. There was no bullion fringe on a shoulder knot, so now there had to be something to distinguish a major from a second louie, and the major's shoulder-strap gold leaf was placed on his shoulder knot also. At the same time the bars of captains and lieutenants were changed from gold to silver.

The shoulder straps, in genuine gold embroidery, or even gilt wire, were expensive darn things, even the ones a second lieutenant wore. They faded, tarnished, and discolored with dismaying haste in field service, too. So, even during the Civil War, many officers wore straps whose "gold" work, border, insignia, and so on, was made of stamped brass, gilded or silvered as required. These mass-production jobs were not only far more serviceable, they were much cheaper. Where a hand-embroidered gilt-wire set of straps would cost $5 or $6, the stamped metal variety was maybe 50 cents to $1. It looked as good and was quite a saving for a young subaltern whose total pay was around $120 a month. The pay of a private in the Civil War was $13 a month, the munificent government withholding $2 until the end of enlistment and deducting 12½ cents more for old soldiers' homes. So you see where withholding and social-security taxes got started.

Officers' hats we've described already. The officer's forage cap was similar to the enlisted man's, plain dark blue cloth, usually with the flat

SOME CHANGES THAT OCCURRED IN THE 1870s

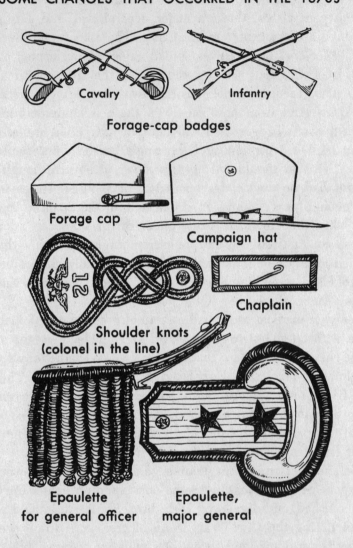

Cavalry   Infantry

Forage-cap badges

Forage cap

Campaign hat

Chaplain

Shoulder knots
(colonel in the line)

Epaulette
for general officer

Epaulette,
major general

platform bill, with the regimental or corps ornament on the front. The overcoat for officers, somewhat similar in cut to the mounted trooper's greatcoat, was a "cloak coat," so called, double-breasted, of dark blue cloth, and closing with four frog buttons and loops of black silk across the breast, with another loop at the throat. Around each frog button on the breast was a 2½-inch knot, also black silk. The coat was edged with black silk braid, ½ inch wide, had a cape falling to the cuff, and on each sleeve, extending from cuff up toward elbow, an elaborate braiding to indicate rank: five braids in a double knot for generals, five in a single knot for colonels, four for lieutenant colonels, three for majors, two for captains, one for first lieutenants—and, as usual, nothing for the poor second lieutenants.

Cavalry officers often had cloaks for rainy wear, and there was even an oilcloth rain cap—little used, I judge, since I can find it only in military purveyors' catalogues. Ponchos, talmas, and cavalry surtouts—the current name for a long, close-fitting overcoat—also were worn by officers in bad weather. For dress wear officers and enlisted men alike had white Berlin gloves—"Berlin" was a kind of worsted, woven from merino wool—and mounted officers and men had also fawn-colored buckskin gauntlets, dashing affairs with large flared cuffs 6 inches or more long, often made partially open at the sides to accommodate the huge uniform cuffs.

Article LI in the *Revised Regulations for the Army of the United States, 1861,* covered all these uniform details, incidentally. In the *Regulations for the Army of the Confederate States, 1862,* the similar uniform section was Article 47, where poor Johnny Reb could read about what he was supposed to have but probably didn't.

Now let's clothe the rebels. The po' Confederate was nowhere near as well provided for by his impoverished and struggling government as was his Northern opposite number. But an American, North or South, is nothing if not resourceful. Practically everything useful the Yank was issued, except General U. S. Grant, presently found its way by capture into the hands of Johnny Reb. It was estimated that two-thirds of the artillery of the Army of Northern Virginia, Lee's outfit, was obtained by capture from the North. As for smaller stuff—shoes, for example, cartridge boxes, or the squares of oilcloth some Union regiments were issued for mixing their flour rations into dough—they were easy pickin's! At least they were for a while.

The South's official Army color was cadet gray. Both North and South, at the onset of the great conflict, had some military organizations in blue uniforms and some in gray. It took several months for the blue-versus-gray distinction to shake down.

It is a curious thing that the South, officially a Confederacy, behaved, at least in military matters, much more like a strongly centralized government than did the North, which, fighting for a dominant Union, acted like a loose confederation, calling sloppily for short-term volunteers, allowing the states to raise, equip, and officer troops, creating a host of unnecessary differences and difficulties. So in the South by dire necessity, in the North often by whim, what the troops actually wore or used often differed widely from regulation. But what I am trying to describe here, for both sides, is regulation paraphernalia, noting, when I know them, the unauthorized departures from the books.

For my money, the South had the North beaten, on paper at least, in the uniform department. Northern uniforms were neat. But Southern uniforms were just plain gaudy and gallant!

The prescribed Southern cap, for instance, "of the pattern of the French kepi," was much like the Union forage cap in shape. But it differed in its far bolder use of color. True, general officers, staff and engineers, had just plain dark blue caps. But they were gold-braided, with four gold braids for generals, three for field officers, two for captains and lieutenants. The braids extended vertically from the band on the front, back, and both sides of the cap to the crown, and the center of the crown was embroidered with the same number of bands. That's lots of gold braid for a plain old blue cap!

Note, too, if you will, that the basic color of the Confederate headpiece was blue. Confederate trousers, by regulations, were blue too, dark blue for generals and staff, sky blue for regimental officers and enlisted men. That's something that the artists and movie costumers nowadays often miss.

In the artillery regiments, for officers and enlisted men alike, the caps had a dark blue band, but the sides and crown were scarlet. Infantry replaced the artillery scarlet with light blue, while cavalry had a yellow cap above the blue band. The number of the regiment, when Johnny could get it, was worn on the front, in brass or gilt metal.

In the early days of the war both sides, intrigued by the French African getups, had havelocks for hot weather, white duck or linen cap covers, with a long, dangling, squared flap hanging down in the back to shield the neck. These had been invented by Sir Henry Havelock, of the British Army, for service in India. You were supposed to get sunstroke on the back of your neck, I guess. But maybe there was a difference between the American and the East Indian or African sun, because the Civil War troops on both sides very promptly discarded these dinguses, sneering at them as "nightcaps." Few were left in Indian-fighting days.

Confederate regulations didn't provide for hats, so hats were what practically all the gray soldiers wore, if they could get them; that is, every-body but Stonewall Jackson, who was a law unto himself and wore a shabby little blue cap with a splintered bill. The hats were usually gray, but some-times they were black.

All Confederate officers, from lieutenants to generals, by regulation wore double-breasted cadet-gray frock coats, skirts extending halfway between hip and knee. Usually general officers of all ranks contented them-selves with the simple two-button grouping of a brigadier, eight buttons in

CONFEDERATE OFFICERS' CAPS AND ADORNMENTS

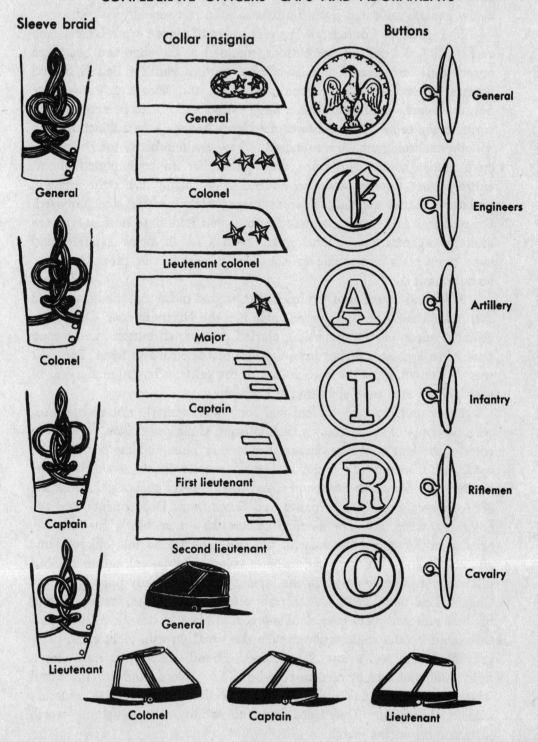

Sleeve braid

General

Colonel

Captain

Lieutenant

Collar insignia

General

Colonel

Lieutenant colonel

Major

Captain

First lieutenant

Second lieutenant

General

Colonel

Captain

Lieutenant

Buttons

General

Engineers

Artillery

Infantry

Riflemen

Cavalry

each row, the rows 4 inches apart at the top and 3 at the bottom. Officers below general rank had seven buttons in each row, equally spaced.

By regulation Confederate general and staff officers wore large 1-inch and small ½-inch gilt convex buttons, rounded at the edge and bearing a raised eagle and stars. Engineer officers' buttons had a raised E in Old German lettering. Artillery, infantry, cavalry, and rifles had ⅞-inch large buttons, ½-inch small ones with a large raised A, I, C, or R, according to corps, in the center. Enlisted men of artillery had an A on a ¾-inch button. All other enlisted men were supposed to have the number of their regiment on a similar button. But since these gauds had to be imported almost entirely from Europe, and the Federal Navy made that right difficult, probably button regulations were more often violated than obeyed. On uniforms in museums and collections, you find state buttons, private military organization buttons, many with CSA in block capitals, and even more plain homemade or nondescript buttons. Or often there are no buttons at all.

The stand-up collar of the frock coat hooked in front at the bottom and then sloped away at a 30-degree angle like the Northern coat. Cuffs were 2½ inches deep on the underside, carried three small buttons, and sloped upward to a point 4 inches from the end of the sleeve in front. The coat was slit behind, a pocket in each fold of the skirts, a button at the end of each pocket, and another button at each hip.

Dress uniform coat for enlisted men was similarly double-breasted, with two rows of seven buttons each in front. Cuffs and collars were in the color of the arm of the service, red, yellow, or blue, and the edges of the coat were trimmed with braid of the same color. Facings—which is just another word for collar, cuffs, and edge trimmings—for generals, the adjutant general's office, the Quartermaster and Commissary Departments, and the engineers, were buff. For medical officers they were black; for infantry, cavalry, and artillery, the color of the arm. This means that officers' cuffs and collars also were supposed to be in colors, like the enlisted men's, but often as not they were not. In the famous Matthew Brady photographs of General Lee, taken in Richmond right after the Surrender, you see Lee in his best uniform, plain gray double-breasted frock coat with collar rolled, three stars on the collar without even the usual wreath, plain cuffs, plain gray pants. He had a low, flat-crowned, bound, rolled-brim hat, with a light band, and a fancy civilian-type bow. No hatcord. And low shoes and white socks, like Uncle Billy Sherman, as that famous Union general's soldiers called him. They considered his white socks something worth watching for on the march.

For fatigue duties there was a gray blouse, so-called in the regulations, double-breasted, with two rows of seven buttons each and a small turnover collar. This one you do see in pictures of Confederate soldiers. You see also single-breasted coats, cut like the Northern infantry or fatigue coat, sometimes plain, sometimes trimmed, with standing collar and cuffs in the color of the arm. You see also a shell jacket on some mounted officers and troopers, much like the Union cavalry jacket, but gray, and with solid-color cuffs and collar, if trimmed at all.

There were no shoulder straps on Southern uniforms. Officers' insignia was worn on the collar and cuffs, following the French influence again. The distinctive sleeve insignia was looped gold braid, knots called galons, extending around the seam of each cuff and clear up to, often beyond, the bend of the elbow. The braid was ⅛ inch wide, and in the elaborate loopings a general had four braids, field officers three, captains two, and lieutenants one. The arrangement of the loops was somewhat like the officers' braiding on Union overcoat sleeves, though more elaborate.

On the coat collar were more devices, for a general officer three gold stars embroidered in a gold wreath on each side of the collar, the front edge of the wreath ¾ inch from the edge of the collar, the center star 1¼ inches in diameter, the other two ¾ inch, the stars set in a horizontal line. Brigadier to full general, this insignia was the same. Full colonels had three stars without the wreath, each star 1¼ inches high, the front star set ¾ inch from the front edge of the collar. Lieutenant colonels wore two stars, majors one, set ¾ inch from the collar edge; a captain had three horizontal gold bars, each ½ inch wide, the top bar 3 inches long. The front ends of these bars were each set ¾ inch back from the backward slanting collar edge, but the back ends were in a vertical line. A first lieutenant had two bars similarly placed, and a second lieutenant one. The bars, of course, were of gold lace or braid.

Officers' sashes, before we abandon the coat trimmings, were of buff silk net for Confederate generals, and here, in the color, is another distinguishing mark of a gray general officer. Staff, engineers, artillery, and infantry officers wore red silk sashes, and cavalry yellow ones; they were supposed to be long enough to go twice around the waist, tie at the left hip, and still leave endings not over 18 inches pendent beneath the sword.

Trousers were sky blue for regimental officers and enlisted men, dark blue for all other officers, which includes generals. The generals also had two stripes of gold lace down the outer seam, ⅛ inch apart and ⅝ inch wide. Staff officers had a 1¼-inch gold stripe with a gold cord on each edge. Regimental officers had a 1¼-inch stripe in the color of their arm. NCO's had a 1¼-inch cotton-webbing stripe in the appropriate color. Privates had plain pants.

Overcoats, cadet gray, were much like the Northern greatcoats, except that both foot soldiers and mounted men were supposed to have the double-breasted, mounted variety, with cape to button with eighteen buttons! The buttons must have been crowded on the infantry cape, which was supposed to reach only to the elbow. Cavalry capes reached the cuff. Confederate regulations add forlornly (Par. 1528): "For the present [the overcoat] to be a talma with sleeves, or waterproof material, black." Well, a man had a chance of swiping that, from some stray Yankee.

There's more, of course. Black stock or cravat for officers, tie not to show—this rule was more often violated than not—black leather stock for enlisted men, which you can bet they never wore! Plain black leather waist-belt for soldiers, sword belt for officers, 1¾ to 2 inches wide, with gilt, rectangular sword-belt plate, 2 inches wide, raised bright rim, silver wreath enclosing "arms of the Confederate States." Plates with CSA were about as far as they usually got on that last. Texas regiments often wore buckles with a single Lone Star, by the bye.

But the South just didn't have manufacturers of stocks of military gauds. Even the supply of gray cloth soon failed. And so perforce, long before the war ended, thousands in the Southern armies had made a change foreshadowing by thirty years or more a similar revision in the U. S. Army. They had shifted from no-longer-attainable gray to "butternut," a shade of brown very similar to much-washed khaki or olive drab. Home-spun, home-tailored garments, the coats, usually cut very much like the Northern infantry coat but often adding slit or inserted pockets on both sides and breast, were dyed with home-brewed walnut dyes (the butternut is one of the walnut family) to a light brown. Typically the cloth was linsey-woolsey, a combination of cotton and wool, the two fibers producing a brownish cast on a whitish background. "Nigger cloth," it was called. It had been much used for slaves' garments before the war. But it was warm and serviceable, and its appearance speedily provided the Southrons, as their more formal expositors called them, with a less formal name, and not as bad as the hated "rebels," either—"Butternuts," meaning the men themselves.

A gray or black hat, usually of wool, rounded of crown and rather small of brim, was what the Confederate typically wore at the war's end. Footgear was whatever he could get. By regulation he was supposed to have Jefferson laced boots, while officers could wear ankle, Jefferson, or regular high-leg boots. Spurs for officers and men were gilt metal or brass, sword knots for officers were plaited leather with tassel. Sergeants also wore a sash of worsted in the color of the arm when they carried sword or saber. The shirts, when any were issued, were of gray flannel. And that about dressed the soldier, North and South, at the close of the great conflict.

Men on both sides wore their uniforms home, and pieces of military garb and gear would continue to show up all over the West for more than a generation to come. Officially the defeated Confederates were not supposed to wear their Confederate Army buttons, though they could continue to wear the gray as civilian garments if they changed the buttons. Some complied with this Yankee ruling; some did not. Officers, by the terms of the surrender, had been allowed to keep their sidearms and the men their horses, since the Southern trooper supplied and owned his mount. When the end came a great many Confederates simply quit and went home without formality, carrying all they had.

For the Federal Army, uniform styles remained about as described until 1872, when the shock of the French defeat at the hands of the Germans in the Franco-Prussian War sent Gallic military prestige plummeting. From then until the end of the frontier period the American Army was under Prussian influence, meaning slashed cuffs and coat skirts, even spiked helmets, just like the Kaiser's best!

This change began in the general orders of 1872, when generals and staff officers were given hats like naval officers'. Artillery and cavalry officers

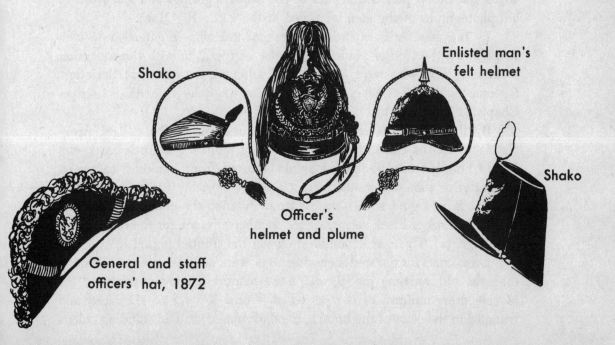

Shako

Enlisted man's
felt helmet

Shako

Officer's
helmet and plume

General and staff
officers' hat, 1872

drew black felt helmets with gold cords and tassels draping the sides, a huge gilt eagle on the front, a flowing horsehair or yak-hair plume atop, scarlet for artillery, yellow for cavalry, and a brass scale chin strap. Enlisted men had similar helmets with mohair cords in place of gold. Infantry, officers and men, drew a shako, a tall stiff cap like the German model. Atop the front of the shako was a pompon, white for the infantry, the beginning of a change of the infantry color from blue to white, which continued until the Spanish-American War. In 1881 the shako was abolished, and helmets were issued, with white plumes for infantry field officers but spikes for company grade officers and enlisted men.

Also in the 1872 changes came a dark blue flannel blouse—the word is in the regulations—for field service, and new dress coats for practically everybody except generals, who clung to the old Civil War model, blue velvet cuffs, collar, and all. The new dress coats for all other officers were the double-breasted type Civil War colonels and majors had worn, nine eagle buttons evenly spaced in each row for field officers, seven for captains and lieutenants, cuffs and collars same material as coat, and a new addition to the insignia, also German in origin—gold stripes on the cuff. These were set vertically, three double stripes of gold running the depth of the cuff, pointed at the upper end, and with a small button below the point for field officers, two stripes and buttons for captains and lieutenants. These cuff ornaments were abolished in 1880. But I am describing the uniform of the 1870s, the Custer period, the peak of the Indian fighting. You will see it in old photographs of the men who died at the Little Big Horn.

By the new series of orders all regimental officers gained a 1½-inch stripe down the trouser seam in the color of the arm, with the exception of infantrymen, who were given a dark blue stripe, welted at the edge. Generals and staff officers wore dark blue pantaloons, with no stripe. Chaplains had plain black pants.

By the way, I haven't described the uniform of the gallant Army chaplains. At the close of the war they had plain black frock coats, one row of nine buttons closing the single-breasted front, standing collar, no epaulettes or shoulder straps, plain black hat or Army forage cap with a silver U. S. in a gold wreath on the front. In 1880 the chaplain was given shoulder straps of black velvet, with a shepherd's crook for the rank device (see page 32). This was his uniform during the frontier period.

Dress coats for enlisted men after 1872 were much shorter in the skirts than the old wartime model, and more modern-looking, resembling the Marine dress uniform of the period of World Wars I to II. Faced and trimmed in the color of the branch, the dark blue coats had standing collars

UNIFORMS, 1872–1888

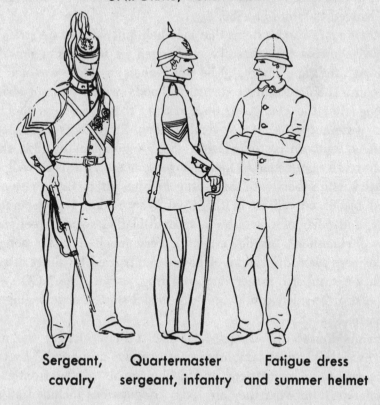

Sergeant,   Quartermaster   Fatigue dress
cavalry   sergeant, infantry and summer helmet

and a 4-inch color patch on each side with the number of the regiment or the corps badge in brass in its center. Coat sleeves had a vertical three-button patch, like German coats, in the arm color, skirts were slashed, faced with color of the branch, and ornamented with four buttons (also Germanic). Shoulder straps in the branch color were set the length of the shoulder, as on modern Army uniforms. The bolsters to hold up the waist-belt were replaced by two cloth straps on each side, buttoned on the waist seam. The coat was single-breasted, with nine brass buttons. Trousers were light blue, waistband 3½ inches wide, "pockets in front opening at the top." Sergeants had a 1-inch stripe down the outer side of each leg and corporals a ½-inch stripe.

Undress for officers became a dark blue sack coat, usually serge, single-breasted, five buttons, with black braid around each button and buttonhole, extending back 6 inches and terminating in herringbone and loops. Knots of black braid were set on each cuff, and the coat was slashed at the hip on each side for sword slings. The sword belt was worn under the coat. Fatigue hats for officers and men were black. And in 1889 suspenders were issued to each enlisted man annually. By the middle eighties white had been firmly established as the infantry color, even the field of the shoulder straps being changed to white in 1886.

Here are a few more items that may help put the picture straight. The old caped overcoat for officers was changed in 1885 for a new "ulster" coat, though the cape could still be worn when an officer was not on duty with troops. The new ulster coat had a "hood," which was not abandoned until long after the change to olive drab. Crossed rifles as the infantry emblem were authorized in November 1875. Straw hats were permitted "in extreme southern latitudes" after 1881. Regulations of 1872 abolished the sash for all save generals, and changed officers' swords as well, leaving the cavalry with sabers with three-branched guards, artillery with one-bow guarded blades curved as in the Civil War model. But generals, staff, infantry, and other officers drew a straight-bladed sword, steel scabbard, one-bow, "clamshell" turndown guard, very much like the noncommissioned officer's sword, but more elaborate and carried by slings attached to rings on the scabbard, rather than to a frog, as with the NCO sword. In 1889 the straight-sided conductor's-cap model started superseding the old fatigue cap.

Having dressed the troops, let's take a short look at the manuals. Usually issued by private publishers and merely "authorized" by the War Department, Army regulations and drill manuals of the frontier period were different from what they are today. *Regulations* included all sorts of things—uniforms, equipment, organization, courts martial, parades, grand guards, camps. The real drill manuals were called *Tactics*, and those for militia and volunteers usually included drill for infantry, cavalry, and light artillery in the same volume. Both Union and Confederate War Departments, of course, authorized *Regulations,* while prominent officers wrote volumes on *Tactics* for the various arms. Since the drill was virtually the same, North and South sometimes used the same manuals, and all the manuals were much alike. At the beginning of the war the North used General Winfield Scott's *Infantry Tactics*; after 1863 Casey's *Infantry Tactics*. Scott's manuals for artillery and cavalry were also used early in the war. William J. Hardee's *Rifle and Light Infantry Tactics* was used by both sides and was especially liked by the South.

General Emory Upton's *Infantry Tactics*, published in 1867, marked a change; it was not French or German in derivation as the others had been, but peculiarly American, breaking the infantry up into squads of eight men and having them wheel by fours. There were no definite infantry "squads" in Civil War days, but Samuel Cooper's *A Concise System of Instructions and Regulations for the Militia and Volunteers of the United States* (1836), in a revised edition of 1849, had introduced the idea of forming soldiers into squads (there was no set number of men to the squad) and of maneuvering horsemen "by fours." The cavalry drill manual of the early frontier fighting after the war was the *Tactics* of General Philip St. George Cooke, published in 1862.

Not until 1891 did the U. S. War Department issue three sets of separate drill regulations for infantry, cavalry, and artillery—service publications as contrasted with the privately written and published manuals that had preceded them.

But even if the Army was dilatory about tactics after the war, at least it did make one improvement. Sutlers, the mitigated curses of the wartime armies, the voracious individuals who followed the troops and operated sutlers' stores, selling corps badges for $2, canned peaches for $1 a can (yes, there were canned goods in Civil War times; a Frenchman trying to win a prize offered by Napoleon I for better ways to preserve food had thought up the idea)—sutlers were sternly abolished. Instead there were post traders, private individuals who ran stores in the frontier posts and camps. But they weren't sutlers; certainly not!

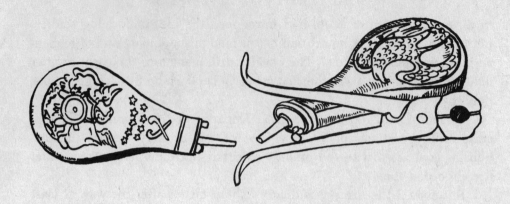

II

FIGHTING GEAR

THE EARS of General Basil W. Duke, late of Morgan's Cavalry, are not burning, I am sure, in that mild Valhalla clime the Good Lord set aside for all us good Confederates. But maybe the General's ears will tingle a little when, ungratefully, I recall his prediction, right after the war, that there wasn't any future for breech-loading firearms, because with one of the durn contraptions a soldier could shoot up all his ammunition too quick!

But there has been an amazing nation-wide revival of interest in muzzle-loader shooting. Cartridges for modern powder-burners cost you fifteen cents each or thereabouts, whereas you can shoot one of those old charcoal-burners all day for the price of a chunk of plumber's lead, fifty cents' worth of caps, and a dollar's worth of powder. And what a world of drama, of blood, sweat, and tears, of triumph and tragedy, those old guns could reveal if they could talk!

Starting with his rifle, let's arm and equip the Civil War–Indian-fighting soldier now, with an eye also to the gear he packed. The Union infantryman's rifle, by the end of the war, was probably a Springfield Model 1863 or 1864, there being very little difference. It had a 40-inch barrel, usually mounted a triangular bayonet, blade 18 inches, though there were some sword bayonets, too; it weighed 8 pounds, 10 ounces, without bayonet, and had on the right side a huge musket hammer that made a "klick-kluck" sound. From this hammer's sound the name Ku Klux for the later secret society of the South is said to have been taken. There were other rifles too, U. S. Model 1855, Special Model 1861, made by many private contractors, including Colt; a brass-mounted Model 1863, made by Remington, and others. But they were all similar—58 caliber, single shot, muzzle-loading.

The lock was percussion, taking a big copper musket cap on the nipple under the hammer. There was a leather sling strap, 45 inches long and with a single brass adjusting hook, reaching from a swivel right in front of the trigger guard to another on the middle band. The government eagle and date were stamped on the lock plate, which is the piece on the side of the rifle, under the hammer. Or, if the piece was a contractor's rifle, as some were, the contractor's name would be on the lock plate.

At the start of the war all sorts of obsolete and hastily imported shooting irons had been brought into use; specimens turned up all over the West for the next fifty years. There were flintlocks, many of them altered to percussion; old Springfields; private contractors' arms; huge German and Austrian muskets bought abroad, some of them as big as .70 caliber. But the principal infantry weapons of the war were, for the North, the Springfield, which takes its name from the great arsenal at Springfield, Massachusetts, and for the South, the very similar Enfield, imported from England.

Springfield carbine

The cartridges for these weapons were cased in paper. The very word "cartridge" comes originally from the Latin *carta*, paper, and for three hundred years before the Civil War soldiers had been wrapping their gun fodder up in individual paper packets, so fast does the military mind leap onward to better things. You could make up these cartridges yourself, if necessary, although they were generally supplied by the arsenals in large cases holding small packages of usually ten cartridges each.

To make cartridges yourself, you did just about what the workers in the arsenal did. You began by rolling stout paper around a "former," a

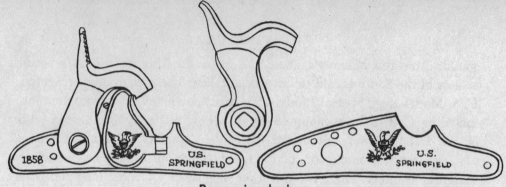

Percussion locks

CIVIL WAR CARTRIDGES

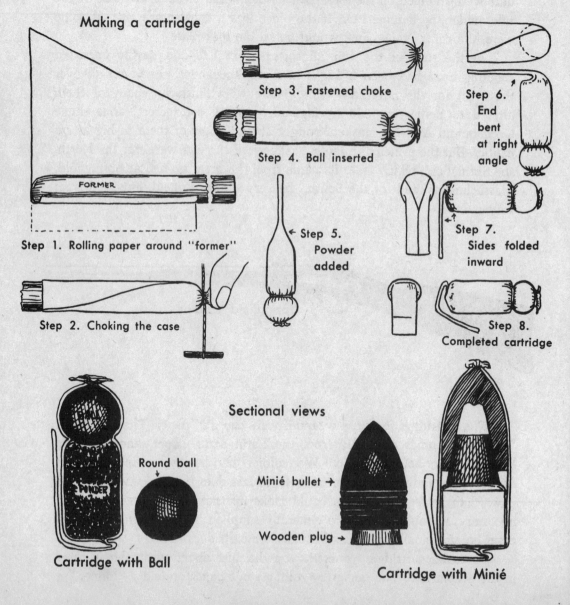

Making a cartridge

Step 1. Rolling paper around "former"

Step 2. Choking the case

Step 3. Fastened choke

Step 4. Ball inserted

Step 5. Powder added

Step 6. End bent at right angle

Step 7. Sides folded inward

Step 8. Completed cartridge

FORMER

Sectional views

Round ball

Minié bullet →

Wooden plug →

POWDER

Cartridge with Ball

Cartridge with Minié

hardwood stick of the diameter of the bore and about 6 or 7 inches long. You closed the end of the paper cylinder thus formed with a stout thread. This was called choking the case. Then, having removed the wooden former, you dropped in the greased lead bullet. This could be a round ball; a conical "Minié" bullet; a "buck and ball," which was one round ball and three buckshot; or twelve buckshot. These round balls you then secured with another half-hitch of the thread. Then you poured in the measured powder charge, sixty grains of musket powder. Finally you folded the open end of the paper into a tail, twisted and folded it back against the cartridge, and you had one round. One round means one shot.

The round musket balls weighed 500 grains; "elongated balls" that had generally replaced the round ones at the end of the war—they looked very much like modern pistol bullets—weighed 480 grains. The Minié bullet, a French idea, weighed 500 grains, and was a conical slug with a cavity in the base, in which a plug of wood or iron was inserted. When the cartridge was fired, this plug drove into and expanded the lead bullet, so that the sides fitted more closely into the grooves in the rifle barrel and less gas escaped. The result was that the rifle shot harder and straighter. But by the time of the war the Army had found out that no plug was needed in a Minié; the force of the exploding gases was enough to expand the bullet, so the plugs were out. Minié bullets made much more vicious wounds than the old round balls, tending to shatter any bone they struck, which the round ball generally didn't. A Minié bullet gave the rifle a range up to 1000 yards, as compared with about 200 for the old round ball. But if you think that means you could hit anything 500 or 600 yards off, guess again!

Up until 1840 most of the U. S. Army long guns had been muskets, smoothbore like a shotgun, though the rifle had been known for a very long time and had done deadly work in the Revolution, the War of 1812, and on the frontiers. This stubborn clinging to the far less accurate and shorter-ranged smoothbore continued simply because it is so devilishly difficult to get a proper-sized bullet down the barrel of a muzzle-loading rifle.

If the ball is small enough to go down easily, the grooves and lands (the lands are the ridges that stick up) of the rifling can't bite in and their effect is lost. A lot of powder gas also leaks past the bullet, up the grooves. But if the bullet is big enough to fill the grooves and thus take full advantage of the powder charge and of the spinning effect that rifling gives a bullet (which helps its accuracy tremendously), then it is one deuce of a job to get the bullet down the barrel.

In Europe some bright ordnance officers had "solved" this problem by providing their soldiers with a steel ramrod and a sturdy mallet, to hammer the bullet down into place! Lots of fun, with an enthusiastic enemy shooting at you, while you hammered away. Some of the German and Austrian muskets imported by both North and South at the beginning of the war had a spike or shoulder sticking up from the breechblock in the powder chamber, upon which the soldier was expected to impale and so expand the bullet. The American frontiersman had partially solved the problem too, by patching the bullet; that is, wrapping it in a little greased patch, usually of linen cloth. But none of these devices worked as well as the Minié, which could be rammed home quite easily, and then fired out with far more accuracy.

A soldier loaded by the numbers, in eight or nine "times," which meant individual operations, such as handling cartridge, withdrawing ramrod, ramming charge home, and so on. He had to bite the tail end off the paper cartridge before loading it into the gun. This quaint requirement just might keep a man out of the Army, which might take the deaf, dumb, stringhalted, and practically blind, but not a man who lacked at least two good side biting teeth that met! The powder had to be poured down the barrel, which meant it was exceedingly difficult for the soldier to load the piece when he was lying down. The bullet, with remains of the paper envelope as patching, was then rammed home with a stout iron ramrod with a cup-shaped end; the rod, when not in use, was carried in a groove in the stock just under the barrel.

But even after he had got the Minié home, he still had plenty to do before he could fire the piece. Under the cup face of the big-eared hammer was a nipple, a hollow tube, screwed into a bolster on the barrel and opening into the powder chamber. On this nipple (after earing that hammer back, of course, klick-kluck) he placed a percussion cap, a tiny piece of copper, looking something like a modern pencil cap or a diminutive silk hat, but containing a fulminate charge in the top. When he pulled the trigger, the cap exploded, setting off the powder and, incidentally, squirting quite a lot of smoke and fire out around the lock and right in his face as it did so. And there is quite a story behind those caps.

For the earliest firearms, the shooter had to carry a lighted, slow-burning fuse around with him, a yard or so of stuff like the wick on a fox-hole lighter, which he jammed against the touch hole of his weapon when he wanted to shoot. This was right inconvenient, so the flintlock was gradually developed in various forms. This was a lock in which the hammer held a small piece of flint rock in a sort of jaw, or vise. When the trigger

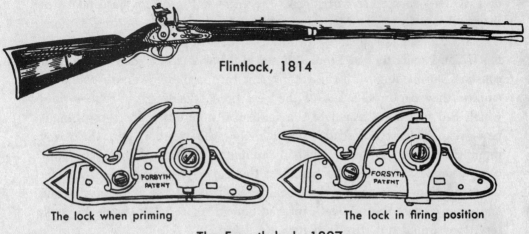

Flintlock, 1814

The lock when priming   The lock in firing position

The Forsyth lock, 1807

was pulled, the flint was snapped down obliquely against the steel surface of another piece of the lock, called the frizzen. This was on a cover which protected the flash-pan or priming-pan. The cover hinged forward, so that, when the flint struck the striking surface, the cover flipped upward, exposing the priming powder and permitting sparks to shower down.

This procedure was not only slow; it was mighty risky. Try shooting a flintlock and you gain respect for our hardy ancestors. At the beginning of the nineteenth century a Scottish clergyman, the Reverend Mr. Alexander John Forsyth, began experimenting with detonating powders. His first successful brew was chlorate of potash, sulfur, and charcoal; his next was fulminate of mercury, niter, and a little frosting of powdered glass. Either of these concoctions would explode when hit with a hammer. Forsyth patented his powder in 1807, along with an ingenious magazine lock which fed a little of the powder into a touch hole, where it could be detonated by the hammer blow and so fired the gun.

He did not invent the percussion cap; that simplification and improvement came from the brain of Joshua Shaw, American artist, who, in 1814, glued some of the touchy powder inside a little cuplike cap, first made of iron, then of pewter, then finally, after 1816, of copper.

The powder was corrosive as the dickens, and much too explosive to use as anything but a toucher-offer. But the cap was fairly weatherproof, fairly sure-fire; and only in the twentieth century have chemists developed a better, noncorrosive primer. That little button-looking thing in the base of a modern center-fire cartridge is the primer, the direct descendant of the percussion cap. The Sioux Indians also had a hand in putting it there.

The Sioux made their contribution to the progress of firearms during the Union-Pacific-Railroad-building era, right after the Civil War. In their constant skirmishing with the troops sent to guard the western course of empire, they captured a few of the new breech-loading, .50-caliber rifles which had just been issued to the soldiers. Ammunition for these brand-new weapons was not readily available on the frontier, and the Army promptly clapped a ban on anybody selling it to the red brethren. They caught nobody violating the ban. Just the same, presently the wily Sioux were shooting their captured breechloaders back at the indignant Army, and when at last the soldiers captured enough material to solve the mystery, they found how the Indians were doing it.

They were picking up empty shells fired by the soldiers, solid-head, non-reloadable stuff. Punching a hole in the head of the shell, they crammed an ordinary percussion cap into it (they had some percussion caps for their old muzzle-loaders), then dropped a little rock into the shell, to serve as a striking surface or anvil. Then they filled up with musket powder, added a bullet, and, presto, they had a perfectly good reloaded cartridge. They had beaten the Army to the outside primer and easily reloadable cartridge.

While we're at it, let's look at gunpowder, too, at least the old black variety used in Civil War and Indian-fighting days. It was a mixture of saltpeter, charcoal, and sulfur, in proportions of about 75 parts saltpeter, 15 charcoal, 10 sulfur, and you could make it yourself, though I'd advise you not to; with practically no effort you can also blow yourself sky high. Black powder was ordinarily corned; that is, caked with a little water and then rolled into grains, fine grains for pistols and light rifles, coarser "musket powder" for the bigger pieces. Civilians bought it from the powder factories in kegs or small tin flasks. But it was also homemade at times, when the pioneers could get the ingredients. Black powder's smoke is *white*, by the way, and there's lots of it.

Scorning paper cartridges, a true old Mountain Man or frontiersman carried his powder in a powder horn, accompanied by a bullet bag, and his idea of a proper charge for Old Betsy was just enough powder to make a little pile covering the ball, on his palm. But for issued cartridges, the Civil War soldier, North and South, had a huge cartridge box in which to carry his forty rounds, plus another smaller pouch for percussion caps.

Getting back to the rifles that these cartridges were fired from, the typical Southern infantry rifle was the Enfield. It differed from the Northern Springfield in having a 39-inch barrel, caliber .577 (close enough to the

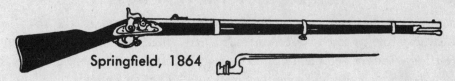

Springfield, 1864

Confederate gun sling

Enfield, 1852

Springfield so that you could interchange ammunition without trouble), and it sported brass mountings. That is, the nose cap, trigger guard, and butt plate, though not the bands, were brass instead of iron, as on the Springfield, and were usually kept well polished. The rifle was sighted to 900 yards, and the British cartridges carried 70 grains of powder and a 530-grain lead bullet. The sling strap on the Southerner's rifle, if it had any, very often was homemade, of folded cotton webbing, with only the loops and tightening part made of leather. There were, of course, many other kinds of Southern rifles, some made in the South. But the Enfield is the type piece.

The Enfield and Springfield bayonets were very similar, with 3-inch sockets to slip over the barrel, using the front sight for a stud, a locking clasp to keep the bayonet in place, and a triangular blade about 18 inches long. A short rounding arm or shank jutted out at right angles from the socket, holding the blade offset about one and a half inches from the barrel, so you could shoot with bayonet attached. It had not always been so. The earliest bayonets had actually plugged right into the bore, quite embarrassing if you felt a sudden urge to shoot, and couldn't get the darn bayonet out.

These better offset bayonets I am describing were called angular bayonets. There were also various saber bayonets: the Enfield sword bayonet, used by some Southern troops, had a slightly curved single-edged blade nearly 23 inches long, while the Kentucky bayonet, used on the so-called Kentucky rifle by some Northern troops, had a blade almost 25 inches long! Northern Zouave regiments often carried Remington rifles, flashily brass-mounted, which also had saber bayonets much like the Enfields.

These sword bayonets usually had steel crossguards and brass hilts, and they were attached to the rifle with a muzzle ring and a spring lock that engaged a stud on the piece, much like a modern bayonet. They were carried in leather scabbards, usually brass-mounted, and slung in a separate sword frog that looped over the man's belt on the left side. The Civil War angular bayonet, however, had a very characteristic scabbard, black leather, brass-tipped, and with an attached frog, a curving loop of heavy leather held together by no less than seven huge copper rivets between scabbard and belt loop. The Civil War bayonet scabbard had no swivel or U. S. plate, as later models did. Rifle and bayonet, these were the infantry arms.

Now the equipment. The Union infantry belt and buckle—Hollywood please note—were different from those used by the other arms. The buckle, particularly, was distinctive, a big, brass oval, 3½ by 1½ inches, with a lead-lined back and 1¼-inch U. S. in block letters inside a raised oval rim on the front. Fastening arrangements were simple. Two spear-headed prongs held the belt on the right side, while on the other side a single smooth prong hooked into center holes in the belt. On the loose ends of the leather, which tucked under to the right when you buckled on your gear, was riveted a wide brass keeper, a bent strip which clipped over the outer leather and thus kept the belt end tidy. The belt was heavy black leather, 2 inches wide.

Sometimes, in addition to the bayonet scabbard on the left side and the small fleece-lined percussion-cap box on the right front, this waistbelt also carried the monster cartridge box, 8½ inches wide, 7 high, and more than 2 inches thick. Of even heavier leather than the cap pouch, this box had double flap covers, the outer one covering the entire front and fastening on the bottom with a brass stud and strap. Under the outer flap in front was a small flat pocket, also with a flap, for cleaning patches and such. Here, or in the cap pouch, where a loop was provided for it, was the nipple pick, a short stout length of wire, with a finger loop on the end. This was used for cleaning out the nipple on the rifle, which, because of the extreme fouling of black powder, had to be done often. There were two separate cartridge boxes on the inside of the leather covers, made of tinned steel, 5½ by 3½ by 1½ inches, slipped side by side in the pouch. Each was weirdly divided into unequal compartments; the upper "tray" was open at the top and separated into two wells, 2 inches and 1½ inches wide; then there was a tin floor in the middle of the box; and the lower half was open on the face. The idea of all this elaboration was to protect the fragile paper cartridges, which tended to

UNION EQUIPMENT

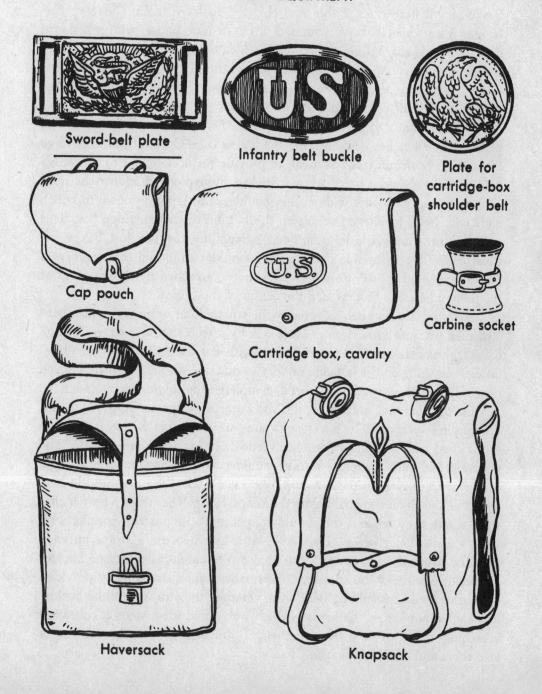

Sword-belt plate

Infantry belt buckle

Plate for cartridge-box shoulder belt

Cap pouch

Cartridge box, cavalry

Carbine socket

Haversack

Knapsack

become deformed, spill their powder charges, or even tear wide open if they were jostled around too much. Particularly it was just too bad if they got wet.

So the immediate supply was kept in the upper part of the tins, the reserve in the lower compartments, and, in the smallest well, probably a few cleanout cartridges if the man chanced to have them. Cleanout cartridges were a special type, wrapped in tan or blue paper, with a little tin disk set on a shank behind the bullet, the idea being that when one of them was fired, the disk might scrape out some of the black powder fouling that clogged the piece after every few shots. Ordinary cartridges were wrapped in whitish or buff colored paper.

On the front flap of the cartridge box, there was usually a brass oval plate, 1¾ by 2¾ inches, also carrying the letters U. S. On the back were large loops, both horizontal and vertical, to provide for attachment to the waistbelt, or to the shoulder belt. This was another huge piece of infantry harness, 56 inches long, 2¼ inches wide at the shoulder, and tapering down to 1-inch ends with holes for large buckles on the bottom of the cartridge box. This belt was worn over the left shoulder, suspending the box just below the waistbelt on the right side or rear. This shoulder sling had for ornament a round brass eagle plate, 2½ inches in diameter, attached by three prongs at the point where the belt crossed the center of the breast.

A round tin canteen covered with worsted, or sometimes just bare japanned tin, was carried on the left side by a web shoulder strap. A large haversack of black waterproofed canvas, with a white detachable "rice bag" inside, was slung on the left side under the canteen. And a big wrinkly black canvas knapsack, carried on the back, completed the soldier's equipment.

On the knapsack and haversack, the waterproofing was black paint—not drab, as in later days. The haversack's sling strap was black canvas, and the sack closed with a shallow flap, one vertical leather strap and buckle. The knapsack had quite elaborate leather shoulder straps V-ing out from a single center point of suspension at its top, like a rucksack; there was a little loop here, too, by which you could hang the knapsack up. The straps were 2 inches wide where they crossed the shoulders, ending at about the armpits with brass and leather rosettes. Here were attached two more straps on each side, the larger 1¼-inch straps going on down to catch-roller tongue buckles on the lower edge of the knapsack, the smaller 1-inch straps being provided with brass hooks resembling bent nails, whereby the straps could be hooked into each other across the breast—which was a bad idea, since it restricted breathing—or down onto the waistbelt, if you happened to be carrying a load there and it needed hoisting.

The blanket went in a tight roll atop the knapsack, secured there by two leather straps. The knapsack cover fastened at the bottom with three leather straps and buckles. There was a large pocket in the cover, but the body of the knapsack itself simply strapped together, and could be opened out flat. Not pretty-looking by any means, this knapsack was nonetheless deemed one of the most comfortable and convenient the Army ever had.

Mess equipment consisted of a tin plate, usually carried under the straps on the back of the knapsack; a large tin cup with a riveted handle, very often slung on the belt or canteen strap; and a knife, fork, and spoon, supposed to be packed in a leather sheath, like a knife scabbard, on the belt. But often the soldier carried these in his sock.

He cooked in the tin plate—which he often made by cutting or blowing apart a canteen—or on the end of his ramrod, and made his black coffee right in the tin cup. Field cooking, making bread by twisting dough around a ramrod or sharpened stick, toasting bacon on the end of a ramrod—and you better not get caught using your bayonet; the heat could draw the temper—baking eggs or whole fowls in mud balls, and so on, had long since become an art on both sides. In addition to individual mess gear, each mess—men ate in small groups, a dozen or so—might have a few kettles, pots, and pans for such hard-to-handle items as beans, roast meats, and the like. There was also a food container issued, a rectangular tin can, 6½ by 5½ inches, with a tight-fitting, detachable cover, an open-ended handle to attach to the belt, and U. S. duly stamped on the side. I have one, with perhaps the rarest relic that has survived the war, one lone white rock-hard bean still sticking inside!

One more detail: squares of oilcloth, for ground cloths, rain covers, etc., were issued to some of the Northern soldiers, and, of course, Johnny Reb soon had some, too, via capture. He used his for mixing dough, among other innovations.

Usually only one blanket was carried, by regulation 7 feet long, 5½ wide, gray woolen, weighing 5 pounds and with the 4-inch letters U. S. in black in the center. In the field the soldier usually had also to pack along with him his part of a "dog" or shelter tent, very much like the pup tent of today's infantry, but white, not drab as it is today. This tent was copied from the French *tente d'abri*, and sometimes given that name.

Along with all this junk, the soldier carried on the march his rations as well, anywhere up to a ten-day supply or more. A ration is one day's allowance of food for one soldier. In the old Army it was pretty simple, a pound of hardtack, three-quarters of a pound of bacon or salt pork, about an ounce of coffee, two ounces of sugar, a little salt, and maybe on the wagons, for the company kettles, some rice, beans, or peas. No K rations, no cigarettes, no chewing gum, no candy.

Hardtack, for the benefit of those fortunate enough never to have encountered the awful stuff, was hard unleavened bread, baked in cakes looking somewhat like a modern soda cracker, but much thicker, about 3 inches square, decorated with what looked like nail punctures and almost as indestructible as a railroad frogplate. "Army Hard Bread" came in huge boxes from the bakeries. It lasted for years, and it stayed with you indomitably and abdominally. One favorite way to get the stuff down was to soak it in boiling coffee; another was to crumble it into stews.

In addition to the dog tent, the Yank also had a larger A tent for camp use, and a still larger conical Sibley tent very much like the Sibley still current in the Army. This tent, by regulations, was supposed to house seventeen mounted or twenty foot soldiers—not that the cavalry kept their horses in the tent too; they just had so much more gear to house. And there were even sheet-iron tent stoves, complete with stovepipe, which typically waited for a howling blizzard night and then burned the tent up, even as now. But the original Sibleys had a smoke vent and flap at the peak, like an Indian teepee.

In the Confederate service, things were much simpler, and Johnny Reb usually carried his gear in a blanket roll, slung over his left shoulder. This convenient and simple arrangement was also adopted by the U. S. Army some twenty years later; they kept the haversack but discarded the knapsack, which was not readopted as part of the field pack until early in this century. A haversack, usually of white or drab canvas with self sling; a canteen of tin or very often of cedar wood, shaped like a little flat barrel; and the usual cap box, cartridge box, belt, bayonet, and scabbard completed the Southern foot private's paraphernalia. If he had a belt plate, it was usually rectangular brass, as noted, with a large C S or C S A. Officers sometimes had gilt plates with a silver wreath encircling the C S. Or they had two-piece buckles, usually imported from England; one piece was a round disk bearing the C S or coat of arms, and it locked into a slot in the center of the encircling wreath; the disk was on one end of the belt, the wreath on the other. Also imported for some of the regiments were two-piece lion-head buckles—the lion of old England, really, challenging the eagles of the North.

In his catch-all haversack Johnny Reb carried his rations, if any, and his mess gear, which seldom consisted of more than a tin plate and cup, maybe a fork and spoon, which, along with his Bowie knife, made up his basic social requirements. No Southern gentleman was considered ade-

Confederate buckles and belt plate

Light cavalry saber

Foot officer's sword and scabbard   NCO's sword and scabbard

quately garbed in the Civil War period unless he had on him somewhere at least one fightin' and, when necessary, eatin' knife, preferably of the pattern made famous by the redoubtable Colonel James Bowie of Alamo fame. We deal with these knives when we get to civilian weapons in Chapter V.

First sergeants, sergeant majors, and musicians of foot troops on both sides had, or were supposed to have, a sword, a straight-bladed, brass-hilted affair, with a blade from 26 to 32 inches long, single-guard bow, and a brass-mounted leather scabbard plus a sword frog to wear it in. At best this was a pretty puny weapon. But it looked real nice on parade, at least, and the NCO sword wearers had also red worsted sashes, as we have noted, and, at least in the Northern service, belt plates with eagle and silver wreath very much like those of commissioned officers. Cavalry NCO's, however, carried sabers instead of the small swords.

Cavalrymen in the Union forces had sabers, generally from some private contractor, say Ames, of Chicopee, Massachusetts. If a man lost his, the kind government charged him about $7.50. Chicopee sabers were real fighting weapons. But to carry a pistol, at least by regulation, one had to be either an officer or a cavalryman; another good reason for adopting Jeb Stuart's tuneful advice about jining the cavalree. Because the revolver was really *the* weapon of the Civil War, the high style, just as, curiously, the knife was again the high fashion of World War II.

Strictly speaking, the word "pistol" refers to a single-shot, single-barreled, or at best double-barreled, hand firearm, or it did until the advent of the semi-automatic pistol in the last days of the nineteenth century. A repeating weapon with its charges in a revolving cylinder was called a "revolver" in Old West days, and a "gun" meant a cannon. The habit of calling just any old firearm—pistol, revolver, rifle, blunderbuss, or whatnot—a "gun" and the user a "gunman" or "gun fighter" crept in only later. Wild West fiction writers, including (with a blush) me, too, have added a whole lot of fancy lingo to the West that the real Old Westerners never even heard of. But let's get the record straight for once, anyhow.

In the early post-Civil-War West you packed a "six-shooter," or a "revolver"—or maybe it was a "five-shooter," or even a "four-shooter," for there were such. There was a wide variety to choose from. Not only was the making of pistols and revolvers a great American fad of the fifties and sixties, but in the war both sides had imported a fantastic assortment of funny and phony hand weapons.

To arm its soldiers, the North had purchased nearly 400,000 revolvers of more than a score of different makes, while the South, scouring Europe and even contriving to manufacture a few of its own (usually copies of Colts), had done almost as well, in variety at least. But the weapon in the soldier's pistol holster as he headed west after the war was in all likelihood either a Colt Army .44, Model of 1860 (Colts were by far the most popular revolvers on both sides), a Remington .44 Army, or a Starr Army .44.

Each of these had about an 8-inch barrel, was about 14 inches long over all, weighed about 3 pounds, and was a single-action, six-shot per-

REVOLVERS

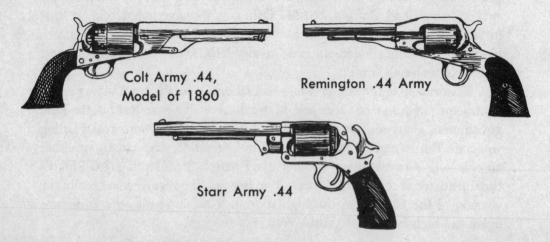

Colt Army .44,
Model of 1860

Remington .44 Army

Starr Army .44

cussion. That meant that the hammer had to be eared back by the thumb for each shot, and the weapon had to be loaded either with bulk powder and separate bullets, or with some of the various paper, foil, or cloth cartridges factory-made for the arms. The charge had to be rammed home, chamber by chamber, by the loading lever. This was a rod latched under the barrel, which swung down to operate a short ramrod plunger in the pistol frame, which plunger in turn forced the charge into the chamber of the cylinder. Finally, a percussion cap had to be placed on each of the six nipples on the back of the cylinder. It was a lengthy and tedious task.

Except that there was no strap, nothing, over the top of the cylinder, the Civil War Colt looked very much like the later Colt Single Action Army, the cowboy gun of the Old West, which is described in Chapter V. The Single Action Army, a cartridge weapon, did not reach the Army until 1874, and Hollywood Civil Warriors armed with it are, well, mighty progressive. The Remington Civil War Army revolver, quite similar in general outline, did have a strap over the cylinder, like a modern revolver, and so did the Starr, the third of the top trio. And only with the Starr could you actually do what careless modern Western writers are eternally having characters do with Colts—"break open" or "break" the pistol for reloading. The Starr had a hinged frame, much like some modern small revolvers. A screw just in front of the hammer could be removed, whereupon the barrel hinged downward and the cylinder could be taken out for cleaning or reloading. But the frames of the Colt and the Remington were solid, though the Colt could be taken apart by knocking out a wedge just in front of the cylinder; and the cylinder could be removed from the Remington by dropping the loading lever and pulling out the pin on which the cylinder rotated. If you "broke" or "broke open" a Colt or Remington revolver you just busted it and needed a gunsmith.

The directions that came with the revolvers warned you sternly not to take loaded cylinders out of the weapons, but, nevertheless, they were sometimes sold with extra cylinders. An old codger, who told me about Quantrill's guerrillas—about whom he seemed to know an amazing lot for such a peaceful old man—said that those enterprising outlaws used to carry extra loaded cylinders for their .44 Dragoon Colts, just as modern troopers carry extra automatic pistol magazines. And they could reload almost as fast.

All three of these weapons, in good condition and expert hands, were remarkably accurate, with an extreme range up to 300 yards. But never forget that a pistol is a close-range fighting tool, usually sighted for 25 to 50 yards, so it is well to discount most tales about the marvelous long-range shooting of pioneer pistoleers.

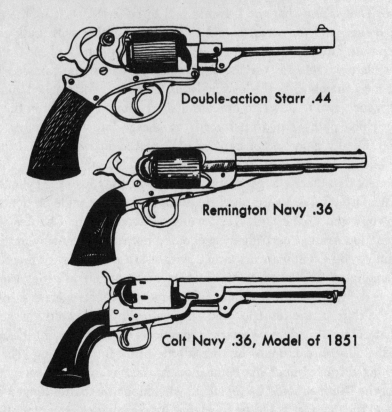

Double-action Starr .44

Remington Navy .36

Colt Navy .36, Model of 1851

There was also a double-action Starr, with a shorter, 6-inch barrel and an ingenious "selector" on the back of the trigger, whereby you could make the gun either single- or double-action. In double-action weapons you simply pull the trigger and the hammer rises, trips, and falls, all in the one operation, faster than single-action, but requiring a longer trigger pull and so more likely to throw you off your aim.

All three makes had so-called Navy models, in .36 caliber, this being the official Navy bore. Since these Navy models were both lighter and smaller than the Army guns, many Army officers and men, as well as civilians and Navy personnel, preferred them to the heavier Army model. They were especially popular with Southern troops. The Colt Navy revolver, Model of 1851 (there was also a Colt Navy Model 1861, with a round barrel, caliber .36, looking much like the Army model), usually had a 7½-inch octagonal barrel, with a naval battle scene engraved on the smooth round cylinder, weighed 2 pounds, 10 ounces, and had a wooden stock, usually walnut. The principal difference between the service and the civilian models was that the service gun usually had an iron trigger guard, the civilians getting a brass one.

These Navy Colts were favorite dueling pistols. After the war, as cartridge guns came in, quite a few were converted to use metallic cartridges, by proper alteration of the cylinder and hammer and, usually, installation of a side ejector rod to punch out the empty shells. There were Navy and Army Colts, converted or otherwise, in the Old West clear up to the nineties. The Navy .36, by the way, was converted to take .38 cartridges, and the Army percussion .44 usually to .44 cartridges, but sometimes to .45. The loose tolerance in the barrels of the wartime models made this not too difficult.

The Colt Army Model 1860 was a round-barreled revolver and came in two barrel lengths, 7 and 8½ inches. Revolvers made for the service usually were cut for a shoulder stock, two slots being provided in the bottom of the recoil shield (the fat rounded part of the frame between hammer and cylinder) for the prongs of a detachable, wooden butt stock, which converted the pistol into a carbine, and which was practically never used. Sometimes, however, this detachable stock was also a canteen, which was at least of some value. There was also a Colt Belt Model, .36 caliber, lighter and smaller than the Navy gun, and a Colt five-shot, .31-caliber Model 1848, often called the Wells Fargo Colt, since the famed express company used it to arm its messengers. This gun, in the original form, had no loading lever, and was much favored by gamblers and such gentry.

Confederate revolvers were bought or captured Yankee weapons, European importations, and pretty crude Southern-made ones, usually patterned after the Colt Dragoon, Army, or Navy models. Leech & Rigdon, and Rigdon, Ansley & Co., Georgia firms, made Colt Navy imitations, as did Griswold & Grier, these latter pistols being brass-framed and very showy. J. H. Dance & Bros., of Columbia, Texas, made Dragoon-pattern .44s and .36s, with a peculiar flat frame, no recoil shield behind the cylinder. Geronimo, the Apache, and also Bill Longley, rated Texas's No. 1 gunman in Eugene Cunningham's classic *Triggernometry*, used Dance revolvers. Tucker & Sherrod—or maybe it was Sherrard, Taylor & Co.; the records are pretty confused—made several hundred Dragoon imitations at Lancaster, near Dallas, Texas. Kerr, Deane, and Adams revolvers, excellent five-shot, .44-caliber, double-action weapons, and six-shot, .36 and .44 double-action Tranter revolvers were imported from England.

From France came LeFaucheaux .12-mm. (this is about .46 caliber) pinfire six-shooters; and a strange weapon, the "grapeshot pistol," was invented by Doctor Colonel Jean Alexander François LeMat, of New Orleans. This one was a dilly, a ten-shooter, no less! The huge cylinder held nine cartridges, while below the pistol barrel was a .60-caliber shotgun barrel, which could be fired by flipping down the adjustable nose on the

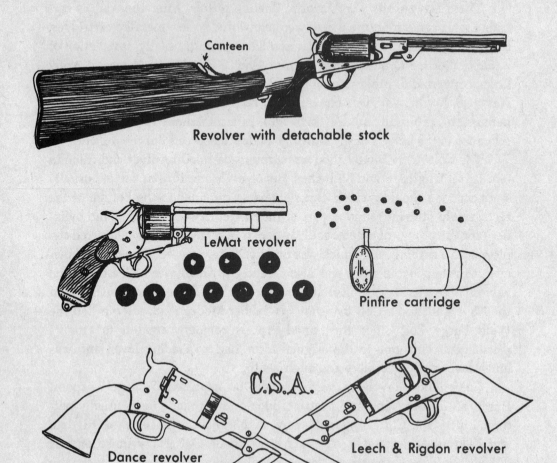

Revolver with detachable stock

LeMat revolver

Pinfire cartridge

C.S.A.

Dance revolver

Leech & Rigdon revolver

hammer. The LeMats were about .44 caliber and evidently only percussion during the war. But later they were made for pinfire cartridges, and some pinfire weapons (the LeFaucheaux, for one) were used in the conflict. Pinfire cartridges, incidentally, were the first form of completely metal-cased ammunition. A small pin projected at right angles to the base of the shell. The primer was inside in a little pill, and when you pulled the trigger the pin crushed into the shell and so fired the charge. The pin had to be slipped into a tiny slot in the cylinder wall, so loading was difficult. Pinfire shells were scarce, too, so the system was never popular in America, though used to some extent by both sides in the war.

Smith & Wesson, just before the war, had brought out the first of their revolvers, which were destined to be world famous. These were funny little pistols with a hinge in the top of the frame just in front of the cylinder and the catch below, so that the barrel tipped upward when you "broke" the pistol to reload. They were single-action, had a stud trigger (no trigger guard), and came in .22 and .32 rim-fire, which seems remarkably puny for military weapons. But they were metallic-cartridge guns, the first really satisfactory American hand guns to use such fodder. In both the six-shot, .32-caliber, and seven-shot, .22 sizes, they were purchased and carried by many officers. The little .22 with its 3-inch barrel weighed only 8 ounces, and the .32, with 5- or 6-inch barrel, not much more. Even the redoubtable Wild Bill Hickok did not scorn to carry one.

These various revolvers the wearers packed in heavy black leather holsters with wide rounded flaps, secured by a strap under the flap which buttoned to a stud on the holster. With typical military predilection for the awkward, the holsters were carried on the right-hand side of the belt, waist high, the pistol butt forward, seemingly as awkward a way to tote a gun as even an arsenal could devise. This backward idea persisted in Army holsters clear up to World War I. But the reasoning was not as stupid as it might appear. The primary weapon of the cavalryman was supposed to be the saber, wielded in the right hand and worn attached to the left-hand side of the trooper's belt by two long leather slings. The pistol was an auxiliary weapon. It had to be on the right-hand side and it had better be in a holster from which the left hand could draw it if necessary. Hence the left-handed holsters.

It was not unreasonable that the conservative military mind preferred the saber. Short-ranged though it may be, the blade is perhaps the hardest of all weapons to face, because you can see it coming. The Northern saber had a curved 36-inch blade, a three-branched brass guard with leather wire-wrapped grip, and a steel scabbard with two rings. The Confederate saber, if any, was either a crude copy of the Northern one, or, more likely, a weapon imported from England or Austria, with a curved blade and iron cup guard, or from Prussia, when it had a long, straight blade and probably a basket guard. But very many of the Confederate cavalry carried no sabers at all, preferring two revolvers.

Dismounted, the trooper carried his saber hooked up, guard to the rear. There was also, for the enlisted man, a heavy black saber knot, a 1-by-18-inch doubled leather strap ending in a leather tassel, looped to the guard. The wearer was supposed to thrust his wrist through this when using his saber, and thus keep from losing his weapon entirely if it were knocked from his hand in combat. Officers, of course, had fancier sword knots, usually plaited leather in the field, but, for dress wear, gold cord with acorn end for generals, black and gold lace with tassel for other officers.

Cavalry officers of the 1860-70 period were supposed, at least, to carry a saber much like that of the troopers, save that the officer's model had a more decorated hilt and blade. Dismounted officers below field grade had a sword with brass basket hilt, usually decorated with cut-out leaf designs and the letters U S; the 30- to 32-inch blade was etched and decorated with more military designs, and the leather scabbard had two rings and brass bands and tip. Field and staff officers had a similar sword, but browned or bronzed steel replaced the leather in the scabbard. Generals had a steel-scabbarded, straight-bladed sword with a single bow and a clamshell guard, one side of which turned down for comfort in wearing. Save that it was much more ornate, and carried by rings and slings rather than by a frog, it was very like the NCO sword. In the seventies, when so many changes were made, this, slightly altered, became the infantry officer's sword. Medical staff and Pay Department officers had a similar straight sword with an ornate crossguard hilt, no bow, and the letters M S or P D.

Both the belts and the buckles of the mounted troopers differed considerably from those of the foot soldiers. The mounted belt plate, as noted, was rectangular, cast brass, with the spread eagle encircled by a silver wreath. The belt, of heavy black buff leather ("buff" means a kind of leather, buffalo or oxhide, not a color), adjusted to size by folding back through a slot in the belt plate to the right, with a single sharp brass hook fitting into one of the holes in the belt. A separate brass catch on the left end of the belt engaged a flat blunt hook on the back of the plate as the regular means for buckling on the hardware. The two saber slings were attached separately to the belt by brass rings and stitched-on straps, the short sling in front, at about the point of the hip, the long sling some 7 or 8 inches farther to the rear. And joining the brass rings of the belt, just above these slings, was something else surprising, a shoulder strap or sling. A Civil War Sam Browne!

The Sam Browne belt, credited to General Sir Samuel James Browne in the Afghan Campaign in the late seventies, was officially adopted by the British Army in 1900, and used in the American Army from the First World War until the beginning of the Second. But Civil War troopers, faced with the impossible task of carrying a 5-pound saber on one side, and as much more weight in pistol and cartridges on the other, without having the darn belt slide right down to their ankles, had the idea first. The American Civil War shoulder sling, not quite as fancy as the Sam Browne, adjusted in back with a single hook, was worn over the right shoulder, diagonally down to the belt on the left, and hooked with a heavy brass hook into a large brass ring in front.

This only begins the Civil War trooper's harness, remember. In addition to saber and revolver, he also had a carbine--after they gave up the fool notion of making the revolver do double duty. So, on his belt, he had a somewhat smaller version of the infantry cartridge box, flatter, and with a single tin inside, for carbine ammunition; a cap pouch like that of the infantry; then perhaps another pouch for pistol ammunition, and still another for pistol caps. That is, unless he carried his caps mixed and his cartridges mixed, or had combination pouches, which some were. It was quite a load, regardless.

Nor was this all. In addition to saber, pistol, ammunition, and what-have-you, the trooper also carried his carbine slung on his person—because the horse couldn't shoot, no doubt. Seriously, of course, it was done to keep the weapon in the possession of the trooper, no matter where or what. A carbine, by the bye, is a light short-barreled musket or rifle, intended primarily to be carried and used by a horseman.

The carbine sling was a black leather shoulder belt 3 inches wide, about 60 inches long, with a brass belt tip on one end and a brass two-pronged bar buckle on the other. Usually this buckle was worn in back. Slung over the left shoulder, the carbine sling came diagonally down on the right side. Sliding loosely on the sling was a loop and a polished-steel snap hook, to attach to a carrying ring that was ordinarily set on the left side of the carbine, at the small of the stock.

This idea of a carbine sling on the man persisted in our cavalry service clear up to the Spanish-American War, although later the broad strap was narrowed to 2 inches and sometimes was made of blue webbing rather than leather. But the broad, loose, flopping carbine sling crossing the breast, carrying the carbine slung muzzle down, was a distinguishing feature of our cavalrymen all through the Indian-fighting days, long after the saber had been relegated to the saddle, or even left home entirely.

When you got on your horse, with your saber unhooked and flopping at the ends of its long slings on one side, and your carbine similarly dangling on the other, even at a half trot you were all set to beat yourself and your horse to death unless you did something about all that flying hardware. So, for the carbine at least, regulations provided a carbine socket, a cylinder of black leather looking rather like a napkin ring, 2½ inches high, 2¾ inches in diameter, with a buckle and strap to attach to the quarter strap on the off (right) side of your saddle. When you mounted you poked the muzzle of your carbine through this socket and so tied it down.

The socket, notice, was not a scabbard or even a boot. It was not supposed to support the entire weapon. You did not leave your carbine on the saddle when you dismounted, but wore it right with you; if not, you might not live long to regret the oversight. The brass-mounted carbine "short boot," about 14 inches long, open at both ends, but covering the carbine from trigger guard to fore end, and the carbine scabbard, or "long boot," covering the entire piece except for the butt stock, were developments of the more peaceful eighties and nineties. With these two, of course, you could leave your carbine on the saddle, if you cared to risk it. But you still wore your sling, regardless.

Like the revolvers, the carbines used in the war and seen in the West for years afterward came in an amazing variety. At first there were muzzle-loaders on both sides, all sorts of American and European makes. Some of these were as large as .70 caliber, practically shotguns. But muzzle-loaders were so clumsy for men in the saddle to handle that they were soon discarded, except for direst emergencies. The principal cavalry carbines of the war and in the immediate postwar period were the Sharps, of which more than 80,000 carbines were purchased; the Spencer, a magazine arm, which topped even the Sharps in purchases, but got into the war too late to see full use, except in the last year; and then, in rapidly descending order, the Burnside, Starr, Smith, Gallagher, Maynard, Ballard, Cosmopolitan, Remington Joslyn, Sharps & Hankins, Henry (this was a forerunner of the famous Winchester, another magazine arm), and perhaps a score more.

Inventing carbines was one of the principal sports of the times, it would seem. Most of these were single-shot percussion arms, using paper- or linen-cased cartridges. But some had metallic cartridges; the Burnside carbine's cartridge, for example, had one with a little paper-covered hole through which the percussion cap was expected to burn. Some were rim-fire, some were even magazine arms, repeaters! Standard barrel length for a carbine was 22 inches, and the weapons averaged around 7 pounds weight. With their shorter barrels, carbines were, of course, considerably shorter-ranged than the infantry Long Toms with their 40-inch barrels.

Striving to extend the scope of their famed equalizers, the Colt company also had offered carbines and rifles made on the revolving-cylinder principle, in calibers ranging from .36 to .58. These were not too popular with the troops, since, with their much heavier charge, they had the bad habit of letting go with all five or six chambers when you were merely trying to fire one. If you survived, it was still disconcerting. These are now very rare military arms.

Let's start, then, with the Sharps, the favorite cavalry weapon of the early West, the buffalo hunter's special, and perhaps the best known of all American guns no longer with us. The Sharps breech-loading mechanism

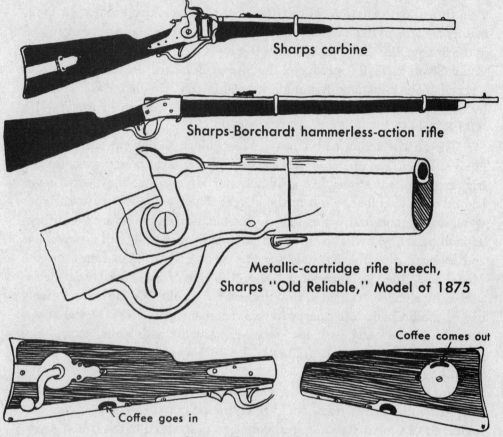

Sharps carbine

Sharps-Borchardt hammerless-action rifle

Metallic-cartridge rifle breech,
Sharps "Old Reliable," Model of 1875

Coffee comes out

Coffee goes in

Sharps Coffee Mill carbine

was invented in 1848 by Christian Sharps. The Sharps Rifle Manufacturing
Company was organized in 1851. Their rifles and carbines proved popular,
both in the Army and with civilians. Sharps parted with the company in
1853 and went his own way, operating as C. Sharps & Co., and, for a time
during the war, as Sharps & Hankins, making rifles and carbines for the
services, among them a peculiar carbine with a leather-covered barrel for the
Navy. Around 1866, dissolving the Sharps and Hankins partnership, Sharps
resumed as C. Sharps & Co., specializing as before under this name in pistol
making. It was during this period that he produced the little derringer-
type four-barrel pistols, in .22, .30, and .32 caliber, the Sharps "stingy guns"
so beloved by gamblers, peace officers, and others in the West. Sharps
died in 1874.

Meantime, plagued by a storm of lawsuits, the Sharps Rifle Manufacturing Company was making more than 100,000 weapons for the Civil War.

Its carbines were especial favorites on both sides, and the Confederates even turned out imitations of the Sharps at the Richmond armory. In 1874, mainly because of the lawsuits, the old company failed and was reorganized as the Sharps Rifle Company; in 1875 it moved from Hartford to Bridgeport, Connecticut; in 1876 it produced the Sharps-Borchardt hammerless action, a very famous target and hunting arm, and in 1881 it failed, done in at last by the repeaters. But it had produced one terrific weapon in its day—the "Old Reliable."

The Sharps action had a heavy breechblock sliding up and down in grooves behind the chamber, worked by a finger lever which was also the trigger guard, something like a Winchester, except that the Sharps lever had no extra loop for the rest of the fingers. The Civil War Sharps carbines were, for the most part, .52 caliber percussion, using a linen-cased cartridge, 22-inch barrel, 38 inches over all, 7¼ pounds weight, and with a swivel bar and loose ring on the left side for the carbine sling. Sometimes, on the Model 1859, the big brass patch box on the side of the stock would be replaced by a coffee grinder, with a detachable crank! The idea was to issue one of these Coffee Mill Sharps to each company. The "New Model 1859," and the Model 1863 carbines, however, usually had plain stocks. The weapons had a leaf sight, graduated up to 800 yards, which was pretty much hogwash.

But under 500 yards a carbine could deliver plenty trouble, while the long guns, the Sharps rifles, could really reach out there. There were two regiments of United States Sharpshooters, so designated in the Union Army, and these fellows were good enough to pick off snipers at 800 yards! Ten years later, in 1874, the famous frontiersman and buffalo hunter, Billy Dixon, collected himself one Indian in the Battle of Adobe Walls at a good seven-eighths of a mile, using a Sharps .50 buffalo gun. That's good shooting in anybody's league. Incidentally, the word "sharpshooter" does not come from the name of this rifle. It was in use long before the Sharps was invented. But sharpshooters and Sharps inevitably were closely associated.

After the war, the Sharps was not only adapted to the new .50-caliber Army metallic cartridge, but also to a whole series of other metal-cased loads, .40-50, .40-70, .44-75, .45-100, and .45-120-550 (a very famous long-range target and hunting cartridge), on up to .50-170-700, a tremendous shell big enough to kill anything, including the shooter on the butt end. These figures indicate, first, the caliber of the gun (which is the diameter of the bore measured in hundredths of an inch—.50 caliber indicates a bore ½ inch in diameter); then the powder charge in grains; then the weight of the bullet, also in grains. The old black powder loads are referred to, remember, *not* modern smokeless powder, which is much more powerful. Cartridge nomenclature was just developing in Old West days, and varied from maker to maker. But usually the two or three figures were as given. Thus the government cartridge used by the Army from 1866 (when the Model 1866 Springfield replaced the old muzzle-loaders) until 1873 was usually called the .50-70 Government, the weight of the bullet, 450 grains, not being given. But for the new Model 1873 Springfield, the cartridge cartons for the infantry Long Toms said .45-70-405, and, for the carbines, .45-55-405. This was the carbine load used by Custer at the Little Big Horn. In the early eighties these loads were stepped up to .45-70-500 for the rifle and .45-70-405 for the carbine, and since the shells were the same, the arsenals started stamping the base of the shell with R for rifle and C for carbine, and also with the year of manufacture.

The Spencer, called by General Grant the best rifle in the hands of the troops at the close of the war, was also ace high in the early West, a real frontier gun. It had been invented by Christopher M. Spencer, then still in his teens, just before the war. More than 90,000 Spencers were manufactured for the great conflict. This was the gun which the envious Confederates said the Yankees "loaded on Sunday and shot all week." Actually, the Spencer was just eight-shot, carrying seven of its fat, rim-fire, tapered, copper-cased cartridges in a tubular magazine in the butt stock, while another could be inserted in the chamber.

But notice, please, that its cartridge figures are different! Most of the Spencer shells were tapered, or bottleneck, fatter at the base than at the mouth. But the .56-56 Spencer cartridge, the cartridge that did most of the actual Spencer fighting in the war, was a straight-sided shell, .56 in diameter at the base of the copper case and .56 at the mouth also—which is what those two sets of figures mean for this rifle and cartridge. Other Spencers used a .56-52 shell and still others after the war a .56-50. These, as the figures indicate, had tapered shells, smaller at the mouth of the case than at the rim. But the Spencers we're particularly interested in, the Western Indian-fighting gun, were .56-50's, firing a .50-caliber bullet. So many of these were used in cavalry-Indian scraps that they were called the Indian Model, and the West is strewn with their old slugs and corroded cases. Custer's famous Seventh Cavalry used these in the Battle of the Washita with Black Kettle's Cheyennes in 1868, and so did the Fourth Cavalry under Mackenzie in its campaign against the Quahada Comanches. They were fine guns. Incidentally, the .50-caliber Spencer Model 1867 sporting rifle would shoot both the .56-52 and .56-50 cartridges. There was also a .44-caliber Spencer, using a No. 46 cartridge, actually a .46 bullet.

The Spencer Model 1865, .56-50 Indian Model carbine, looked quite a bit like the Sharps, with a similar trigger-guard loading lever that opened the breech and ejected the empty, and a similar huge musket hammer to be eared back for each shot. But this gun, as noted, had also a seven-shot magazine, a tube that slid in through a hole in the butt plate. And there was a "quick-loading" cartridge box to go with it, the Blakeslee, a leather-covered wood affair containing six or seven tin tubes of cartridges, seven in each tube, which could be inserted into the gun in one operation—it said there! This small trunk was worn on a shoulder strap.

Just in front of the trigger guard was a magazine cut-off, invented by Edwin Stabler, making it possible to shut off the magazine and use the gun as a single shot—"So you wouldn't shoot up all your ammunition," honest! But at that, if you didn't know exactly how to work that lever, the darn magazine could jam the gun. In 1871 old Se-tank, Kiowa Indian chief, was being hauled back to Texas by a detail of U. S. cavalry to face charges of having murdered assorted Texans on one of his raids. Watching his chance, the chief suddenly pulled a knife, stabbed a corporal, grabbed a Spencer, started to lever in a shell—and the gun jammed. The chief then got very fatally shot.

The Winchester company bought out Spencer in 1868, but Spencers were popular in the West for many years more; and the cavalry mourned when the repeaters were turned in for single-shots. Writing about them sixty years later in his fascinating *On the Border with Mackenzie*, Captain Robert G. Carter, Congressional Medal wearer, thanked God for the Spencers and testified that they would kill at ranges up to 500 or 600 yards.

But the real Civil War "Western" gun, one destined to become as famous as the Colt, was the ancestor of the Winchester rifle, another lever-action gun called the Henry. This rifle, produced by a mechanical genius named B. Tyler Henry, resulted from the marriage of a still earlier weapon, the Jennings rifle, with a funny little pistol, the Volcanic.

The Volcanic resembled a miniature Winchester, with a tubular magazine under the barrel and a lever to work the breech mechanism. But it had one unique feature. Its bullet was also its own cartridge case!

This looks like a darn good idea, unless you happen to know that the real purpose of a cartridge case is to keep powder flame and gas from squirting back in your face. Only secondarily is the case a neat package for powder, bullet, and primer. But this fact wasn't very well understood back in the fifties. So the Jennings rifle had a hollow bullet, with the powder charge inside, and Messrs. Smith and Wesson went this one better, by sticking a

OTHER ARMY CARBINES

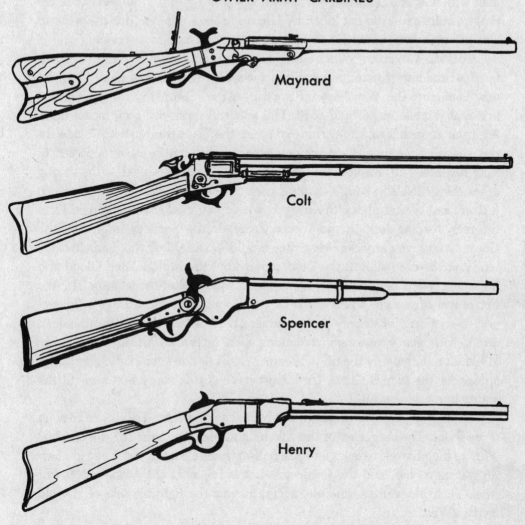

Maynard

Colt

Spencer

Henry

big cap, fulminate of mercury, inside the slug, making it do as percussion cap and propellant too. It wasn't a great success.

One of the financial backers, Oliver F. Winchester, took over the Volcanic assets, hired Henry to rework the product, and came up in time for the war with the .44-caliber Henry rifle, brass frame, lever action, fifteen-shot, rim-fire, loading through a tubular magazine under the barrel; you poked the cartridges in at the muzzle end of the magazine. It was clumsy to load and not too high-powered, and the "authorities" considered it horribly complicated, to boot. But with one shot already in the chamber, you had a sixteen-shot rifle, quite something against maybe a single-shot muzzle-loader. And its partisans were cheerfully willing to "shoot against any living man with it at one thousand yards with any other gun."[1] Doubtless at lesser ranges, quite a few did get killed by Henrys in the Civil War, for the weapon was privately purchased by several organizations, and saw service.

In 1866 Governor Winchester (he was Lieutenant Governor of Connecticut and a shirt manufacturer in private life) reorganized again, and the new company, the Winchester Repeating Arms Company, turned out the first real Winchester, Model 1866. This was still a rim-fire gun, barrel ranging from 20 inches on the carbine to 27 on the "Turkish musket" (made for the Turkish government); magazine capacity thirteen in carbine, fifteen in rifle, seventeen in musket. But the gun was much improved with, among other things, Nelson King's loading port on the right side of the receiver, just in front of and above the trigger, where you could stuff shells in from the rear, loading fast, to shoot even faster. If the Spencer impressed the Confederates, you wonder what they would have said of this gun. It came too late to be used against the Confederacy, but the Indians, Red Cloud and his Sioux, were beginning to learn about Winchester-made guns. In the Fetterman Massacre—when the Injuns won a scrap it was always a "massacre"—near Fort Phil Kearny on December 21, 1866, two civilian frontiersmen armed with Henry repeaters were along with the troops. All the whites were killed. But, judging by the piles of empty shells beside each body, about fifty apiece for the two civilians, they must have got as many Sioux as all the eighty-one soldiers did.

In 1873 Winchester brought out Model 1873, center-fire, .44 caliber, in three styles. The magazine of the rifle held fifteen shots; that of the carbine, with 20-inch barrel, twelve; and the half-magazine model, six. The rifle barrel was 24 inches, and the frame was not brass, as in the Model 1866, but steel. This rifle, sturdy, reliable, accurate, was the fighting rifle of the old civilian West.

In 1879 a .38-40 Model 73 was put out, and then a .32 and even a center-fire .22! In 1875, trying to beat the slump, Winchester offered its "One of One Thousand" rifles, a premium-grade arm, specially selected and finished and with "1 of 1,000"—or later the same spelled out—engraved on the barrel. This cost $100. Or you could have a second choice, "1 of 100," so marked, costing $60. It was only a moderately successful promotion, and was given up after two or three years.

The 1873 was made until 1898, and Winchester also made many other models over the years. In 1876 the company produced a Centennial Model

---

1. *The Crack Shot, or, Young Rifleman's Complete Guide*, by Edward C. Barber. New York, 1871.

76, handling a .45-75-305 cartridge. The Royal Northwest Canadian Mounted Police adopted this one in carbine style. In 1894 came the famous Model 94, and the next year nickel-steel barrels, making possible use of smokeless powder. With them came the new .30-30 caliber. More than a million and a half Model 94's have been sold. But, note, the .30-30 first appeared in the mid-nineties. It's a Western but hardly an Old Western firearm.

III

HORSE TRAPPINGS
AND BATTLE FLAGS

IF YOU think the idea of wild American Indians running around in Hungarian hats with feathers stuck in them is funny, what do you suppose was on the other end of the chase, beneath the U. S. cavalry? Hungarian saddles, no less, by courtesy of George B. McClellan, onetime commanding general of the Union Army. Back in the 1850s McClellan, then a captain and a seasoned soldier and frontiersman, was serving a tour of duty as military attaché and general U. S. public eye in Europe, right over where Kossuth and his hats had been causing all the trouble. The fine Hungarian cavalry was a sight to behold, and young Captain McClellan looked rather thoroughly into their outfits and underpinnings. Especially the latter, their characteristic saddles.

These Hungarian saddles were almost like hammocks, with the heavy leather seat stretched between pommel (front) and cantle (back) and an air space over the horse's spine. McClellan improved on this, really marrying the Hungarian and the old Army Ringgold tree. The model he offered the War Department when he returned home had an open slot down the middle, over the horse's backbone; and the two side bars (pieces that fit flat against the horse) were joined by a fairly high wishbone pommel and rounded

Saddle trees

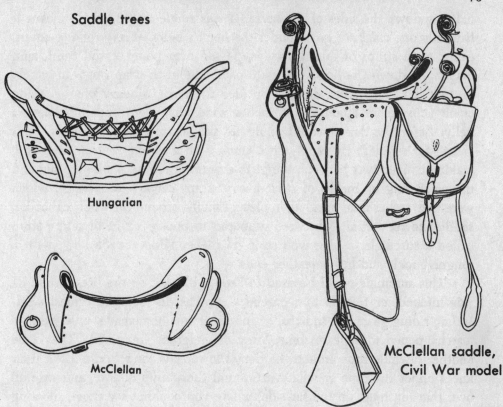

Hungarian

McClellan

McClellan saddle,
Civil War model

cantle, the whole covered with shrunk-on rawhide. It was a good tough piece of hoss harness, a war saddle that, with minor variations, would continue to be the Army saddle until they canned the last cavalrymen in tanks in World War II—ninety years later. Quite a service record.

In the Civil War model, the wooden foundation, the side bars ironed to pommel and cantle pieces, called the McClellan tree, was covered only with rawhide sewed on while wet. Drying, it shrunk, making the saddle iron-hard and almost indestructible.

But the poor trooper who rode it was, of course, destructible or, I guess, expected to be self-reparable. True, the sewed seams were along the edges of the side bars, where they were not supposed to chafe horse or rider; but the rawhide had a nasty habit of cracking and erupting a line of hard edges most anywhere, edges that could cut like saw teeth. Later, the rawhide trees were covered with smooth black leather, which eliminated this little irritation. But the improvement came some years after the war.

The Civil War McClellan had saddle skirts, two squarish aprons of harness leather fastened to the side bars by brass screws, and hanging about halfway down the sides of the horse. It was single-rigged, which means it had only one cinch, or girth, under the horse's belly. Heavy rigging straps, called girth straps or quarter straps, passed over pommel and cantle and diagonally down the horse's sides to catch the girth-strap rings—to which, in the Civil War model, directly buckled the girth, a heavy blue webbing cinch (*cincha*, in Spanish), 4½ inches wide, that went under the horse's belly. Later the Army would equip its saddles more like civilians' hulls (slang for saddles) by supplying a cinch with a simple ring on each end, making connections between the girth-strap ring on the saddle rigging and the cinch ring by means of stout heavy straps called cinch straps, which were tied, rather than buckled, in place. Finally, around the whole caboodle, saddle, horse, and all, you were supposed to buckle a sort of safety strap called a surcingle, a blue web strap 3¼ inches wide and 60 long, with a tongue buckle and heavy leather ends.

This surcingle could be used to keep a blanket on the horse when he was hitched, or to ride him bareback. It was, in fact, the typical wild-Indian riding gear. For Indians, of course, it was homemade, unless they'd just happened to capture some Army or emigrant equipment. They'd tie another rawhide rope around the pony's lower jaw for a bridle, hook their knees under the rope or whatever around the pony's middle, and ride all over that mustang, on the far side, where you couldn't see them, shooting under the pony's neck, even under his belly! No Cossack was ever a better equestrian than a Plains Indian.

Another thing, while we're off after Injuns. It was their usual custom to mount and dismount from the right, the "off" side of the horse. The "near" side is the left side. Unless you're an Indian you get neither on nor off, voluntarily at least, on the off side. Instead, you put your left foot in

the stirrup and swing your right leg over, because that puts your right hand and right leg where they'll be most useful if the horse acts up.

Horses are very much creatures of habit. If one has been taught that a rider will always mount from the left side, he'll raise a ruckus if somebody tries it the other way, and Indians trying to steal white men's mounts and white men after Indian-raised cayuses used to run into trouble that way now and then. For that matter, the pony could smell the difference between white men and red men too. Many a pony gave his owner, white or red, the alarm.

To finish with the McClellan saddle, it had two stirrup straps, coming down from stirrup loops attached to the edges of the side bars just behind the pommel. These were under the saddle skirts, came out of them through slits, then picked up separate sweat leathers or fenders, wide triangular pieces of leather which protected the rider's legs from the saddle skirts on down to the wooden leather-hooded stirrups. A buckle and a series of holes made the stirrup strap adjustable. When a man first forked a saddle he adjusted these stirrup leathers to the length of his leg. In the Army, of course, he used the military seat, which was pretty close to, but not quite like, the cowboy seat.

There's a lot of real technique, and even more foolishness, in this how-to-ride-a-horse business, but, briefly, there are two principal styles of riding and assorted in-betweens. The first main style is the way medieval armored knights rode their war horses, with long stirrups and legs hanging straight down, the style called in Spain and Mexico *a la brida*. The second, called *a la jineta*, is the way the Moors taught the Spaniards to ride in order to come out alive from a lightning-fast cavalry fight—with very short stirrups, the rider almost kneeling in the saddle. The in-between styles use moderately long stirrups with the knees more or less bent. Of these last, if you sit on your behind in the saddle, stirrups slightly shortened so your foot rests almost level in the stirrup, you have the military seat. If you lengthen the leathers about a hand's breadth so you can comfortably stand in the stirrups and ride on your crotch (which is called the crotch seat), or sit on your buttocks, if you prefer, that's the cowboy seat. The other kinds don't apply here.

The heavy stirrups, made of oak or hickory, had a 3- to 4-inch tread, and were of one piece of bent wood, with the upper ends separated by a wooden bar called a transom, around which the stirrup leathers looped. The front of the stirrup was covered with a heavy leather hood, riveted to the wooden frame, covering the whole front and sides of the stirrup and extending about 2½ inches in front of the tread to accommodate the toe.

This bottom space, between tread and hood, was open. Usually on the front of the hood was a stamped oval with the block capitals U. S. Stirrup hoods were called *tapaderos* by the cowboys, and theirs were often very fancy. But not in the Army!

Stapled loosely to the front and back ends of the two side bars of the saddle were four brass rings, to which were strapped the saber, or canteen, or carbine boot, as cruppers, breastplates, martingales, and such fancy tack got discarded on the tough frontier. The crupper, which was issued and used during the war, consisted of a dock, a padded ring which fitted around the horse's tail, plus attached straps to fasten to the crupper rings on the rear of the saddle. It was supposed to help keep the saddle in place, but did more to keep the poor cayuse's tail sore than anything else. A breast-plate was a similar arrangement up front, a strap around the horse's neck, its ends fastening to the front rings on the saddle—to keep the saddle from sliding back. It often had brass insignia—the U. S. eagle or such—attached. A martingale, usually combined with the breastplate, was a strap-and-ring rig attaching to bridle, or reins, and thence to the cinch under the horse; this was to make the horse keep his head down. The breastplate and martingale were ordinarily officers' dress trappings, seldom seen on the frontier.

Under the saddle you put a blue wool blanket, 67 by 75 inches, with an orange border stripe and orange letters U. S. in the center. Ordinarily you folded this blanket into a rectangle of six thicknesses, folding it first the long way, then twice more to make the pad. Then, particularly if you were an officer, you might have a saddle cloth, either an underhousing that went over the blanket or pad but under the saddle, or, as the saddle

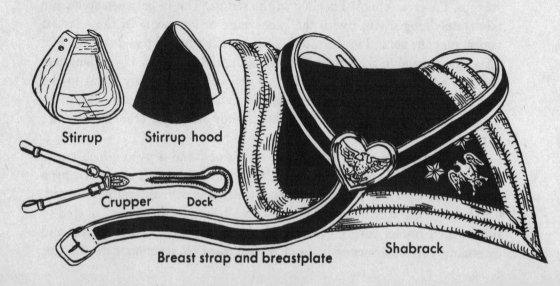

Stirrup   Stirrup hood

Crupper   Dock

Breast strap and breastplate   Shabrack

cloth was originally intended to be used, as a covering for the whole works, protecting you almost completely from horse sweat and leather stains.

Underhousings were usually dark blue, with an edging of 1-inch gold lace for officers. Overhousings were officers' stuff, and another notion borrowed from the European armies, particularly the German service, which called them *"schabraken"*; Americans speedily naturalized this to "shabrack" and then "chevrac." You'd see shabracks on colonels', staff officers', and particularly generals' mounts, covering virtually the entire saddle, and very gorgeous, with much gold lace, spread eagles, and stars of the riders' rank embroidered on the rear corners. These, too, soon disappeared on the frontier. Even the blankets were soon changed to gray, with a red stripe in the border for artillery, a yellow stripe for cavalry.

Now the stuff on the saddle. The trooper's overcoat or talma for wet weather (later it would be a slicker) was usually carried strapped on the pommel in front of him, held there by three long coat straps rove through slits in the saddle. On the cantle behind were his blanket and tarpaulin (then usually called a "paulin" and not as now a "tarp"), similarly rolled and strapped. Under that, hooked to the saddlebag stud on the back of the cantle, was a set of saddlebags.

The saddlebags were two leather pouches, about 14 by 15 inches, joined by a leather flap called the seat. They hung down on each side of the horse, and here the trooper carried a currycomb and brush. The brush had a heavy leather back with a strap that fitted over the hand, and the currycomb was of iron, had three double rows of teeth and a wooden handle, "Carpenter's No. 333 Pattern." Sometimes these went in a smaller set of bags called pommel bags, slung up front. But usually they were in the saddlebags, along with a 14-inch iron picket pin for staking the horse out to graze, a spare horseshoe, a few nails, the trooper's rations, extra ammunition, and so on.

There was also a 30-foot lariat to lug along, but this the trooper usually rolled into a coil like a hangman's knot and carried from one of the saddle rings or dangling from the halter. The canteen in post-Civil-War days also snapped to the saddle ring with a short sling.

Finally, there was a feedbag or nosebag, for feeding oats or whatever to the horse. This was a cylinder-shaped canvas bag, with straps to go over the horse's nose and fasten around his neck. On the march you carried this nosebag tucked over one end of your blanket roll, on the cantle. If you were an officer, or the farrier, or somebody else having to carry extra tools or gear, you might also have a valise bag, a cylindrical bag, usually of leather, about 16 inches long and 5 or 6 in diameter, ordinarily with a

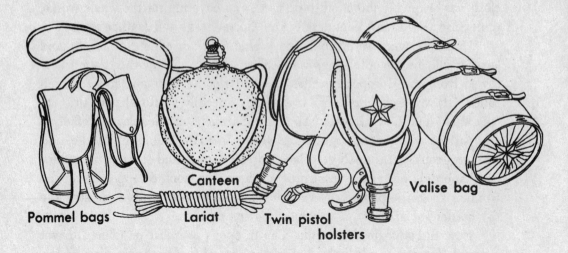

Pommel bags   Canteen   Lariat   Twin pistol   Valise bag
                                                   holsters

shoulder strap. You could carry this like a blanket roll, strapped to your saddle. Or, if you were in the artillery, you strapped it across the saddle of the off horse in your team, the one you didn't ride.

Generals and the like sometimes had this valise in very fancy form, with pleated ends, sometimes displaying insignia, strapped behind their saddles for additional dress gaud. Generals and such also had another fancy trapping at times, twin pistol holsters hung over the pommel, gilt-trimmed, and very gorgeous indeed. This had been the way all horsemen had carried their huge flint or percussion horse pistols, and the idea of saddle holsters, carrying the pistol on the horse, not on the rider, lasted in the civilian West long after the war.

The artillery, by the bye, usually had a saddle entirely different from the cavalry's—a "Jennifer," much more of a pad saddle than the McClellan, with a stitched padded seat and a high, curving, wishbone, brass-rimmed pommel and cantle. Both North and South made saddles with this tree, and imitation McClellans were also made in the South. The Jennifer, and the similar but somewhat more elaborate "Grimsley," ridden by many officers, U. S. Grant among them, were harder on the horses' backs than the McClellan was. But General Jeb Stuart liked Jennifers, nevertheless, and horse artillery drivers rode 'em on the gun and caisson teams.

Army saddles came in three sizes, 11-inch, 11½-inch, and 12-inch seats, the size number on a plate riveted to the pommel. Half the riders would take No. 2, 11½-inch size, and about 35 per cent the No. 3. The cavalry horse averaged 1000 pounds; the trooper was supposed to weigh under 165, and the saddle and gear—it was hoped—under 100 pounds.

Now the bridles. First came a halter, with cheek pieces, noseband, and

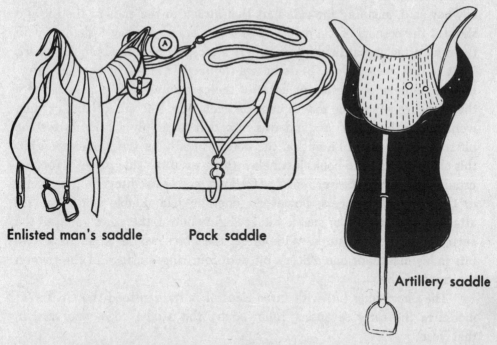

Enlisted man's saddle   Pack saddle

Artillery saddle

a large hitching-strap ring to use in tying the horse. A halter has no bit. To take the animal to water, there was a watering bridle, a simple snaffle bit and reins which could be attached to the halter. Usually you just left the halter on the horse. But when you rode, over the halter went the bridle proper, this carrying a steel curb bit and curb chain, to go underneath the horse's jaw.

A bridle is composed of a headstall, which, in turn, is made up of a crownpiece, going over the horse's head behind his ears; throatlatch billets or straps, which go down around his neck; a browband, which passes across his forehead above his eyes; and cheek straps, which go down the sides of his head to catch the eyes, or rings, of the bit, at each corner of his mouth. Sometimes, just above the bit, there is also a noseband, passing horizontally from cheek strap to cheek strap over the face.

The military curb bit is one with a hump, like a U, in the middle of the bar that goes in the horse's mouth, the idea being to exert more controlling pressure when you pull on the reins. Civil War Army bits came in four sizes: No. 1, the "Spanish bit," so called because it was the most severe, having a hump or port 2¼ inches high, and also a curb ring instead of curb strap or chain (this bit was intended for horsebreaking and handling real wild ones); No. 2, with a 2-inch port; No. 3, with a 1½-inch port, and No. 4, mildest of them all, with ½-inch port. The bits were all

4½ inches between branches, as the Army called them, or cheeks, as the
cowboy said, meaning the side bars that attach to the ends of the bit and
show at the corners of the mouth. The lower branches were S-shaped, with
the reins attaching at the bottom, where a crossbar held the branches apart.
That is, they were levers. Brass bosses stamped U. S.—or sometimes carrying the regimental number or letter of the company—were attached where
the branches joined the mouthpiece on each side. The curb chain, or ring,
went under the lower jaw and was intended to supply a fulcrum for the
bit so leverage could be put on the horse's mouth. In the Model 1863 bit,
this chain attached to hooks just below the eyes of the side pieces. Troopers
usually had just one set of reins, 5 feet long, ends sewed together, attached
to the curb bit. Officers, however, generally had double reins, one set
attached to a bridoon or snaffle bit, for light control, the other going to the
curb, for sterner measures. With these, the horse would either have two
bits in his mouth, or one officer's bit with four rings, instead of the two on
the trooper's bit.

The Shoemaker bit, with three sizes of ports, replaced the Civil War
model in the early seventies, followed by the Model 1892, one size, in
that year.

Where the browband joined the cheek straps, above and behind each
eye, there were usually brass rosettes, 2½ inches in diameter, lead-backed,

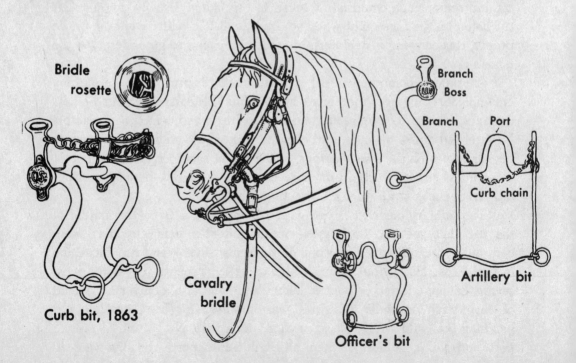

Bridle
rosette

Branch
Boss

Branch   Port

Curb chain

Curb bit, 1863

Cavalry
bridle

Officer's bit

Artillery bit

and with U. S. or U. S. A. entwined. Officers sometimes had the eagle on these, and generals their stars. Finally, for linking horses together when one man must handle several, as when a troop dismounted to fight on foot and every fourth man was horseholder, there was a link strap, a 15-inch thong buckled to the left rein ring of the bit, with the snap on the other end hooked into the throatlatch buckle. This was unsnapped and hooked to the bit of the next horse, and his, in turn, to the next, thus tying the horses' heads close together. In bivouac or camp, troop gear included a picket line—a long rope to which the mounts were hitched. And there might be a pair of hobbles for the horse, horse handcuffs to hold him.

Now that we have the soldiers mounted, let's look at the flags and guidons. In the Civil War period and for some years thereafter the matter of regimental colors, standards, and such was not as rigidly regulated as it was later. State organizations might have their own flags; patriotic women on both sides used to make the flags and present them proudly to their favorite outfits, who received them with a great deal of chivalrous show.

There were crude sewing machines during the Civil War, so some of

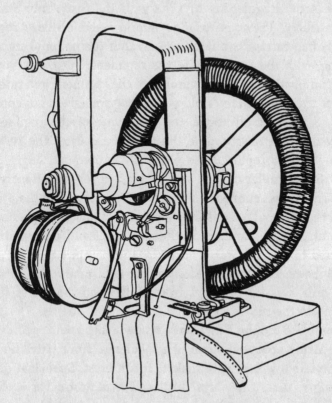

Howe's first sewing machine, 1845

the flags were machine-sewed. Elias Howe, 26-year-old apprentice to a Boston watchmaker, had invented a hand-cranked sewing machine in 1845 which could do 250 stitches a minute, about five or six times as many as an expert hand seamstress. During the war, Howe supported a Union regiment with his sewing-machine royalties—and served in its ranks as a private! But battle flags, dress uniforms, and such were still, for the most part, lovingly, almost religiously, handmade. And they varied accordingly, as did usage.

It is a curious and now little-known fact that the Army as a whole did not carry the Stars and Stripes until almost the twentieth century. Old Glory was designed originally as a naval flag, not an Army ensign. The last Army units received it only in 1895. Unofficially it doubtless was often otherwise, but from the time the Army was reorganized after the adoption of the Constitution, until 1834, the national flag carried by Army units in the field was the arms of the United States, a spread eagle on a blue field. This is practically what we would recognize today as a regimental standard, or color.

The Army Regulations of 1834 gave the first Army Stars and Stripes to the artillery. Previous to 1834 infantry and artillery regiments pretty generally had carried two flags, as now, but the national standard, or color, was blue, with the eagle, while the regimental flag was white or yellow, bearing simply the name and number of the regiment in a rather ornamental scroll. In 1834 the artillery's old yellow flag was given gold crossed cannons, with U. S. on a scroll above and the name of the regiment on another scroll below, and this became the regimental flag. The newly authorized Stars and Stripes replaced the eagle as the national flag.

In 1841 a similar change was authorized for the infantry; the blue flag with its eagle was retained as the regimental color, and the Stars and Stripes became the national color. But the cavalry outfits, flying a similar but much smaller blue eagle standard as their national and only emblem, were not authorized to use the Stars and Stripes until April 13, 1887, and for some obscure reason the change was not actually made until 1895. Reality, in other words, was far different from Hollywood movies of frontier cavalry streaming to the rescue beneath the Stars and Stripes.

From 1818 on, the Navy made its own flags and so achieved uniformity. But the Army accepted some of its banners from patriotic private hands and contracted with private makers for the rest. Specifications were vague. Accordingly, the Army flags displayed a fantastic variety of differences, especially in the stars, which were sometimes six- and even seven-pointed, and might be silver, or even, as in the Civil War period, gold instead of

Variety in stars

white. They were grouped on the blue field pretty much according to the fancy of the maker. Really hard and fast regulations for making Old Glory, prescribing all details, were not laid down until 1896.

So we're going to find quite a flock of apparent discrepancies. But, for the Civil War and immediate postwar period, infantry and artillery, officially, at least, had two flags, the Stars and Stripes as a national color and an additional regimental flag. And the cavalry had only one.

The infantry and artillery flags were 6 feet, 6 inches, on the fly, 6 feet on the pike, had yellow fringe on all except the pike side, and were carried on a pike 9 feet, 10 inches, long, including the spear tip. The flags were adorned also with a long cord and tassels, of blue and white mixed silk for the infantry, red and white for the artillery. The name and number of the regiment were in gold on the center stripe of the national colors. Yes, an inscription on Old Glory—strictly forbidden now.

The colors were usually carried by sergeant color-bearers who, dismounted of course, used a simple black leather shoulder belt, over one shoulder only, to support the socket for the butt of the pike.

The cavalry, as we have noted, had a single standard, not yellow, the cavalry color, but blue, carrying the spread eagle, like the infantry regimental color, and with the name and number of the regiment similarly inscribed on a scroll below the eagle. Cavalry flags, by the way, are always called standards; colors is the infantry designation for flags. This cavalry standard was much smaller than the infantry flag, only 2 feet, 5 inches, on the fly and 2 feet, 3 inches, on the lance; that is, it was practically square. It was fringed with yellow, and its lance was 9 feet long.

Cavalry companies were provided with a swallow-tailed guidon, 3 feet, 5 inches, from lance to end of swallow-tail, 15 inches from lance to tip of the fork in the middle, and 2 feet, 3 inches, on the lance. This by 1861 regulations was half red, half white, dividing at the fork, the red above. On the red was U. S. in white, and on the white the letter of the

Arms of the United States, to 1834

National colors of the U.S. Army,
1834–1861

U. S. Artillery flag, regimental

U. S. Artillery flag, national

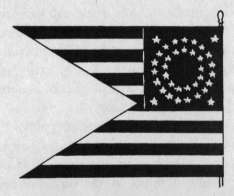

U. S. Cavalry and Light Artillery guidon

U. S. Cavalry standard

company in red. In 1863 this was changed and new regulations gave both cavalry and horse artillery a guidon that was the Stars and Stripes in swallow-tailed guidon form. This provision was withdrawn in 1865, but the Stars and Stripes guidon must have remained in use in some of the cavalry, regulations or no regulations, because Custer's famed Seventh carried at least one of these striped guidons into the fatal fight on the Little Big Horn, Sunday, June 25, 1876. Such a Stars and Stripes guidon was recaptured from the Indians in the Slim Buttes fight, some two and a half months later, and in the National Archives there is a contemporary photograph of it, taken in the captured Indian camp.

Cavalry standard and guidon lances, 9 feet long, were nearly a foot shorter than the 9-foot, 10-inch, infantry pikes. Cavalry flag-bearers had a special right stirrup, with a socket attached, to hold the butt of the lance. All troopers, of course, handled the reins in the left hand.

At the outbreak of the Civil War there were thirty-three stars in the flag. Kansas had come into the Union as star number 34 on January 29, 1861, but in accordance with law its star was not added to the flag until July 4, when the war had been going a good three months. At the end of the war there were thirty-six stars, West Virginia and Nevada having come in meanwhile. Logically enough, considering the North's contention that the Union could not be dissolved, the stars of the seceding states were retained on the national flag, and the South also kept two stars for states it did not really have—Missouri and Kentucky, which were expected to secede but didn't.

There were various arrangements of these stars on the blue union (the union is the blue field in the upper left-hand corner): sometimes the stars were grouped in the form of a large star; sometimes in a cluster; sometimes one large star was in the center with other smaller stars set in a circle or oval about it. As we have noted, very often in the Civil War these stars were gold, and now and then silver, rather than white. At the close of the war, however, some sort of order was emerging, and the stars were usually set in alternate rows of seven and eight, and the regulation color, white, was winning out.

On Army posts, the garrison flag, flown from the post flagstaff, was 36-foot fly by 20-foot hoist, and the storm flag, used in bad weather, was 20 by 10. The flag was flown only in the daytime, from morning to evening gun. Ordinarily the post flagstaff was on the parade ground in front of headquarters, and here the trumpeters would gather to sound calls, and here there would be an ancient cannon to fire the requisite guns.

All this, of course, does not even begin to exhaust the flag lore of the old Army. There were flocks of other flags. The great conflict, in fact, had developed a whole rainbow rash of them, many of which persisted into the Indian-fighting days. Brigades, divisions, army corps, and armies all had their distinctive flags, as did some special units. Hospitals, for example, flew a yellow rectangular flag with a big green H in the center, and smaller similar flags were used to mark the routes to field hospitals and first-aid stations.

Our Red Cross did not exist during the Civil War—either the organization or the emblem. The woman destined to be the founder of the American Red Cross, Miss Clara Barton, was a Civil War relief worker, deeply interested in the welfare of the soldiers. She worked with the International Committee of the Red Cross, then a new and mainly a European organization, in the Franco-Prussian War, and in 1873 she brought the Red Cross idea to the United States. In 1881 the American Red Cross was formally organized, with Miss Barton as its first president, and in 1905 it was chartered by Congress. The Red Cross as an emblem of mercy became Army Medical Department insignia only in 1887. Frontier Army medical personnel had a green maltese cross edged with white as their emblem. Hospital stewards had the familiar caduceus.

Headquarters of larger units were marked by special flags, and generals, then as now, also had their personal flags. Thus Sheridan's famous battle flag was a red and white guidon with two big stars.

There were far too many more flags to catalogue here. A really fancy one was the flag of the Cavalry Corps of the Army of the Potomac, a swallow-tail guidon with a blue triangle on top, a red one on the bottom, a white triangle with its base against the lance completing the field, and on this white field large gold crossed sabers. That, now, was high color!

Sheridan's battle flag

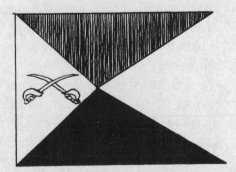

Guidon of the Cavalry Corps
of the Army of the Potomac

CONFEDERATE FLAGS

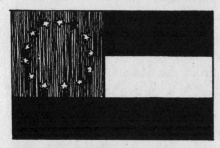
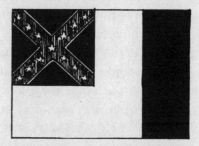

The Stars and Bars, March 4, 1861 Confederate National Flag, March 8, 1865

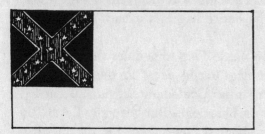
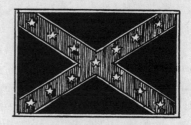

Confederate National Flag, May 1, 1863   Battle Flag, 1861

Confederate colors and standards, like Confederate equipment generally, varied almost from A to Izzard, and the South as a whole was not
nearly so much given to flags as were the Northern people. Even though
they were seceding, a great deal of love and respect for the Stars and
Stripes still remained in the breasts of many Southerners.

The Stars and Bars, the first Confederate flag adopted by the Confederate Congress March 5, 1861, retained so many characteristics of the Stars
and Stripes that you couldn't tell at a distance which flag it was. This detail
distressed Confederate General P. G. T. Beauregard no end at First
Manassas—or First Bull Run, as the Yankees preferred to call it. As the
battle hung in the balance, Beauregard spied a heavy column of troops
coming. He could see their slanting color but in the breathless heat he
couldn't tell which flag it was, Union or Confederate. Doubtless he died
several deaths before at last a vagrant puff of breeze fanned out the flag
sufficiently for him to recognize the Stars and Bars, signaling gray rein-
forcements coming to guarantee the South a smashing victory. But, not
caring for any more of that sort of suspense, Beauregard immediately
started a campaign to get a more distinctive flag. At length he, General
Joseph E. Johnston, and Congressman William P. Miles, who had been
chairman of the Confederate committee that had chosen the Stars and Bars
design but who didn't like it either, came up with the Battle Flag.

But let's begin by describing the Stars and Bars. Like the Stars and Stripes, it was red, white, and blue. It too had horizontal stripes of red and white, and a blue canton, or union, carrying white stars, in the upper left-hand corner; in this case thirteen stars, set in a circle. You can see that at a distance this would be hard to distinguish from the Stars and Stripes. So after Manassas the Stars and Bars was not often seen in the field. It was used as a garrison flag, on ships, and over government buildings.

The Battle Flag, as Beauregard, Miles, and Johnston conceived it, had a red square field. On this red field was imposed a Saint Andrew's Cross, its arms extending from corner to corner. The cross was blue, edged with white, and carried thirteen white stars. The entire flag had a narrow border of white.

Unhampered by regulations, the Battle Flag sometimes showed fewer than thirteen stars, particularly on flags made early in the war. Some examples had no stars at all. Some Arkansas Confederate regiments carried Battle Flags with plain white crosses on blue fields. But generally the Battle Flags were as described: big ones, about 6 feet square for the infantry outfits; and smaller ones, sometimes made guidon-style, and about the size of the Union cavalry standards, for the mounted units.

Strangely, yet perhaps appropriately, the real fighting flag of the South, the Battle Flag, never had any official recognition at all, save by happenstance! Conceived on the battlefield, and carried on every major field after Manassas up to Appomattox, it was not the banner of the Confederacy, but instead the personal flag of the gray fighting man. And as you can see at football games and such, in both South and North, it is not forgotten even yet.

The official emblem that replaced the Stars and Bars was the so-called National Flag, authorized by the Confederate Congress May 1, 1863. Its difference from the Stars and Stripes was, in a way, ominously prophetic, because it was mainly white, a white field twice as long as it was deep, with the Battle Flag set as the union in the upper left-hand corner, in a square two-thirds the depth of the flag itself. This National Flag caused immediate criticism because it was flapping and ungainly and, what was worse, showed so much white that it could be, and sometimes was, mistaken for a flag of surrender. Finally, on March 4, 1865, only a few days before the end, the Confederate Congress adopted a suggestion by Major Arthur L. Rogers of the artillery, changing the dimensions of the flag and adding a vertical red bar that covered half the outer end of the fly, measuring from the union. This flag flew briefly over Richmond and was hauled down by Grant's incoming men. There is no record that it ever reached any field of battle.

Another Confederate color worth mentioning was the Lone Star Flag of Texas, with two broad horizontal stripes, the upper white, the lower red, and a vertical blue stripe set against the pole and carrying on it a large single white star. This was also made in swallow-tailed-guidon form for cavalry. This flag, often carried by Texas regiments in the war, had been the official emblem of the Republic of Texas, 1836-45, is still the state flag of Texas, and can still be seen south of Red River just about as often as the Stars and Stripes.

Confederate regiments usually had regimental names and numbers inscribed on the middle white bar of the Stars and Bars, or under the cross of the Battle Flag. Battle honors, the names of the battles and campaigns in which the outfit had been engaged, were often inscribed on the flag.

Confederate regiments ordinarily carried but one flag. But plenty of Union regiments had but the one flag also, usually the Stars and Stripes. Which flag, when there were two, took precedence on the right had not yet been firmly established, and sometimes you would see the national emblem there, sometimes not.

The color-bearers on both sides were usually noncommissioned officers. Confederate color-bearers often had small crossed flags in colors on both sleeves above the elbows. The company guidon bearers were ordinarily privates. Dismounted, they carried the cavalry guidon like a pike or lance, in the bend of the right arm, vertical, the ferrule about a foot from the ground. The guidon bearer usually followed the unit commander unless otherwise ordered.

Guidons, infantry colors, cavalry standards, and the like were actually in the fighting line in Civil War days, not left in the rear as now. Their purpose was not only to identify the troops beneath them, but to serve as rallying and leading points in movements. "Following the flag," or "rallying around the flag," had real meaning in those days, because just that was done in battle.

For issuing commands where the voice would not suffice, cavalry companies had trumpeters. But infantry companies had drummers, equipped with large wooden-shelled snare drums, which the drummer boys, often mere youngsters enlisted at sixteen or even earlier, carried snapped to a white web shoulder sling, or more often, especially in the field, a black leather one. The drum had the eagle coat of arms of the United States painted on the shell, on a blue field for infantry, red for artillery, with the company letter and number of the regiment usually on the scroll under the eagle. The use of drums as field music for infantry persisted for years after the war; and thus, in case of sudden attack on a mixed command, the infantry drummers would beat the "Long Roll," their alarm signal, while the cavalry trumpets would sound "To Horse."

I have, in my plunder, one bit of drummers' gear with which I have taken great delight in baffling visitors, both civilian and military. It is a 3- by 3½-inch, once highly polished brass plate, bearing two hollow brass cylinders that look like fieldglasses or model cannons. Practically no one ever guesses what it is. Actually, it is a drumstick carriage, so called, a drumstick holder which the drummer wore hooked into the front of his drum sling.

IV

CIVILIANS OUT WEST

WHEN a researcher starts rooting back into the sixties and seventies, trying to find out how people dressed, how they fared, what they carried in their pockets when they went West, how Cousin Fritz the cowboy looked when they met him, he runs into some of the darnedest things. Here are a few samples I'll bet will throw anybody who isn't ninety-seven years old or hasn't painfully looked 'em up.

Suppose, as a gay young blade riding the stage into Fort Watcha Gotcha, Western Territory, in 1871, you have spilled grease on your nice new nankeen trousers. You're going out to ask Major Shurtz of the Eleventh Cavalry for his daughter's hand. (There were only ten cavalry regiments then, so all fictional exploits were performed by the Eleventh.) You know the major doesn't think too much of you, a mere civilian, anyway. So you duck into the stage station with your carpetbag and break out your fine new broadcloth pantaloons, and they've come through spotless, even with a razor-edge crease down the exact front of each leg. What do you do? Put 'em on? No, you effete modern, back in 1871 you would jolly well have kept on the greasy pair! A neatly pressed pair of trousers with the crease down each leg would have marked you instanter as a cheap John. They would have ruined you with Papa.

Neatly creased pantaloons, to our forefathers, were a sure sign they'd been just bought, ready-made, from the stack in the shop. To wear such was practically as horrible a faux pas as asking to borrow somebody's toothbrush would be today. If you were anybody at all, back in the sixties and seventies, you had your Sunday go-to-meeting garments made for you by a tailor. If you didn't, you rushed home, preferably by a dark back street, and carefully pressed all the creases out of your store-bought garments so that the legs looked like old elephants' trunks and the sleeves like sausage covers. It was not until the nineties that creases in trousers were accepted in polite society as evidence of cleaning and pressing rather than of bargain hunting. Now you know why Abraham Lincoln was always pictured in those awful baggy pants.

As for the grease spot on your pantaloons, well, the modern cleaning industry, as we know it, didn't really get its start until the nineties. But there might be a post tailor at the fort. There certainly would be laundresses, on the post or in town. Or, finally, if Mamma had brought you up right, you'd have some home remedies to try.

Nankeen being a yellowish-brown cloth, the spot would probably show horribly. But since nankeen is also very durable—it was originally brought to America in the clipper ships as the pride of Nanking, China; hence the name—you probably could wash the darn pants without too serious results. Yes, there'd be soap available out here on the frontier, probably homemade, from saved kitchen fats and wood ashes. It would be thick yellow stuff that maybe would remove your hide too, along with the spot. But you could buy soap in stores, and the Army also issued soap to its soldiers.

Maybe you'd decide to try sponging the spot, and the post surgeon or town druggist might help. You'd want benzine—yes, they had it in 1871. They'd had petroleum products since 1859 when "Colonel" Edwin L. Drake (actually he was a retired railroad conductor) had drilled the first successful wildcat oil well, a mile and a half south of Titusville, Pennsylvania, finishing it for a twenty-barrel pumper at the staggering depth of 69 feet. There were some rip-roaring oil booms in Pennsylvania and West Virginia during the Civil War, and oil activities had even started out West, in Texas and Kansas. It is little known or appreciated, but the oil game was Old West drama too, as fabulous in its way as the cattle drives. Confederate cavalrymen, the old Ashby Brigade under General W. E. Jones, had even raided and burned a whole Yankee oil field at Oiltown, West Virginia, in the spring of 1863, sending flaming oil boats floating down the Little Kanawha River in a spectacular holocaust. They knew something about refining in the sixties, too, having had lots of experience with whisky and such. True, sometimes the "coal oil" they made had a little too much gasoline in it and blew up in the lamp, with distressing results.

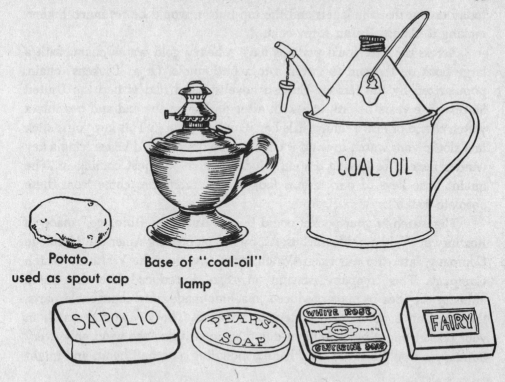

Potato,
used as spout cap

Base of "coal-oil"
lamp

But to get back to you and your pants, if there wasn't any benzine, then maybe the medico or druggist could supply you with some spirits of hartshorn, which we know as ammonia today, or with some alcohol. I'll bet you could get the alcohol! You'd mix this with hot water and scrub with a brush, being careful to brush with the nap of the cloth. Then you'd iron on the wrong side. It might work.

If not, you'd try turpentine, which was nearly always available, being ships'-stores stuff known even to our great-great-grandfathers, or a decoction of soapwort roots, or warm water into which Irish potatoes had been very finely scraped. Or you could try rubbing chalk on the wrong side, or using salt and alcohol, one part salt to four of alcohol. And that's enough ancient and dubious cleaning recipes!

But, assuming you have finally got the pants situation in hand, what else would you be wearing? This being a trip out to the extreme Western frontier, you'd doubtless be garbed a bit more roughly than at home. But, since you're dressing up to impress your future papa-in-law, you'd probably have a black broadcloth frock coat and vest to match, to go with those broadcloth trousers in your carpetbag. Or you might prefer a coat of some brown stuff to complement the nankeen pants. This most likely would be a sack coat not much different from our single-breasted business suits of today except that the lapels and the top button would be set much higher, making it almost like an Army coat.

Across the vest you'd perhaps have a heavy gold watch chain, with a large hook on the end to fasten into a buttonhole. Or a "Dickens" chain, popularized by the famous English novelist, who had visited the United States some years before—one with a toggle bar on the end and possibly a watch charm or else a funny little key dangling from it. This key you'd stick in a slot in your watch to wind it up, since no doubt you'd be carrying a key winder instead of having a stem winder, which was just coming in. The quaint little keys of our various lodges and fraternities come from these obsolete watch keys.

The watch in your pocket could be an "American Horologe," made in Roxbury or Waltham, Massachusetts, by the pioneering American Horologe Company, later the American Watch Company, now the Waltham Watch Company. This company, starting in 1850, introduced into the watch industry the idea of mass-produced, machine-made, interchangeable parts, thus starting another great American business. The key-wound watch in your pocket might have an eight-day movement you need wind only every Sunday; it would have spidery hands, including a second hand, and might

WATCHES, WATCH CHAIN, AND WATCH FOBS

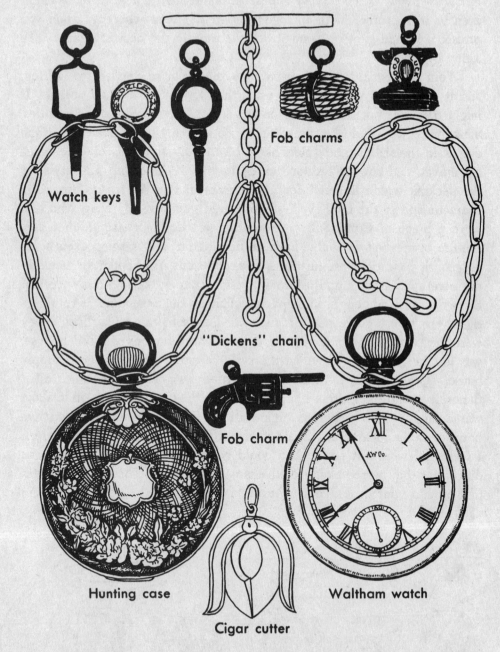

Watch keys

Fob charms

"Dickens" chain

Fob charm

Hunting case

Cigar cutter

Waltham watch

have the old-fashioned IIII instead of IV on the dial; it would probably be in a hunting case, which means that a hinged metal lid protected the glass. Or it might be a B. W. Raymond, the famous railroad watch made by the National Watch Company, later the Elgin National Watch Company, of Elgin, Illinois. This watch was first produced in 1867. Or, again, it might be Swiss—Swiss watches were almost as numerous then as now. It might even be a "repeater," with an ingenious arrangement whereby, when you pressed a button, a mechanism struck the time to the nearest quarter, like a tiny Big Ben.

Your shirt would doubtless be linen, since you're dressed for visiting, and it pulled over your head, as usual, had lots of tail but no pockets. It might or might not have ruffles on the front. But by now, the seventies, your shirt collar would be turned down, not sticking up to poke you in the eye as in the sixties, and you'd likely be tucking the ends of your black silk cravat, tied bow-tie fashion, under the tips of the collar. This style for the necktie, which lingered for many years in the West, was especially characteristic of the chill-eyed, slim-fingered gambler, the chap who also wore a brace of Colts, Starrs, or Southerner derringers, single-shot, .41, rim-fire, or maybe two double-barreled Remington .41's, in the pockets of his gorgeously brocaded vest, just for special occasions. Your collar, particularly out here away from laundries, might just be paper, to be worn once and thrown away. You bought these paper collars by the dozen and, if your eyesight wasn't very good, perhaps they did look something like linen. They were cheap too. Montgomery Ward, the now world-famous mail-order house, was just beginning its career in the early seventies as a Grangers' supply house. (Grangers were what the embattled farmers of the time called themselves, and the Patrons of Husbandry, or the Grange, founded in 1867, was a mighty and vociferous organization.) Ward's would sell you five boxes of paper collars, plus a pair of suspenders, all for $1. The suspenders, I feel sure, were not paper. You could get five real linen shirt fronts, or dickeys as they were called, for the same small price. These monstrosities tied around your neck like a baby's bib, and buttoned to the shirt at the

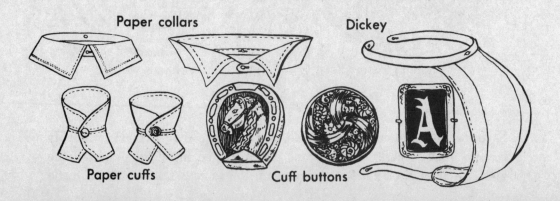

Paper collars

Dickey

Paper cuffs

Cuff buttons

bottom. Well starched, they had the horrid habit of flopping up in your face when a button let go. If you didn't like paper collars and cuffs to wear with them, you could, so help me, get steel, flexible, enameled collars, which I suppose you put on with a monkey wrench.

The celluloid collar, of flamboyant memory, was just around the corner. (Celluloid is a trade name, by the bye, like Kodak.) John Wesley Hyatt, American inventor and father of the Hyatt roller bearing, still rolling merrily along, perfected celluloid in 1869 and began to put it on the market in 1872. Celluloid collars could be conveniently cleaned with a damp rag. Inconveniently, they also could, and sometimes did, go up in a flash of fire, should one drop, say, a hot cigar ash or a burning match head in the wrong place.

Dress-shirt cuffs were hard-starched and sometimes detachable. They were worn with cuff links of infinite variety. Typically, the cuffs of the seventies were much wider than today's, making possible the occasional gambler's sleeve holdout device for extra cards, or various arrangements of concealed weapons, usually a derringer or knife. No really smart gambler ever used a mechanical holdout, since merely to be caught with one on would have been damning. But holdout weapons were common enough, varying from a simple sheathed knife strapped to the forearm, to more elaborate spring or elastic suspensions for small pistols—"stingy guns"—which the wearer could produce, maybe, by merely throwing his arm out briskly, snapping the weapon down into his hand.

The sleeve or vest-pocket pistol was ordinarily a derringer. The name comes from Henry Deringer (one "r"), famous early inventor and arms maker of Philadelphia who made such pistols before the war, as well as excellent rifles. Imitators sought to avoid his ire by rolling that extra "r" into the name of their product. Incidentally, it was a squat-barreled percussion Deringer that John Wilkes Booth used to assassinate Abraham Lincoln. But by 1870 the derringer—two r's—would probably be a rim-fire cartridge weapon, .41 caliber, stud trigger (that is, no trigger guard; the trigger popped out of a notch when you cocked the single action), the barrel sliding forward, tipping, or sometimes rotating, to load one or two shots. Sharps, as we have noted, and Starr were offering four-barreled pistols of the same order. But Colt, Remington, National Arms Company, and Southerner derringers were even more popular, all these except some models of Remington being single-shot, usually .41. The "knucks" derringer was a queer little piece, with an all-metal frame and a hook handle that made the weapon look like some kind of wrench: it was meant to be used as a brass knuckle as well as a pistol.

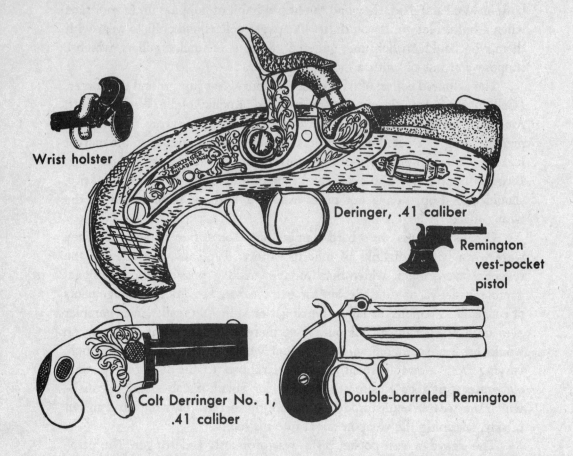

Wrist holster

Deringer, .41 caliber

Remington vest-pocket pistol

Colt Derringer No. 1, .41 caliber

Double-barreled Remington

But the derringer destined to be most famous of all was the double-barreled Remington. It had started its career during the Civil War and went on well into the twentieth century before manufacture ceased. Its two 3-inch barrels were one atop the other. Full length it measured 4⅛ inches, weighed 11 ounces; single-action, stud trigger, .41 rim-fire, it cost you in the seventies around $8. For about $10 more you could have it fancy, with ivory or pearl stocks and engraving. Probably its effective range was something on the order of 15 or 20 feet, but it was a tremendously popular hideout weapon for men of violence on both sides of the law, for more than fifty years. What its .41 slug could do to an outlaw who had just lifted your Colt Peacemaker, or to some ornery polecat across a poker table, was plenty sufficient.

The hook handle was the real mark of the derringer, of whatever make. You could also buy a vest-pocket pistol, if you preferred; maybe one of Remington's single-shot sawhandle types, .22 or .41 caliber. It would cost you from $3.75 to $5.

Coming from the East, you probably wouldn't be worried about such Western professional touches as hideout pistols as yet. You might have a percussion or a converted holster revolver, but you'd have to wait a couple of years, until the Smith & Wesson, Rollin White patents were good and dead before you could buy a Colt Peacemaker, or, for that matter, Smith & Wesson's own new Schofield .44. But by 1872 you would be able to buy a Remington "Improved Army Revolver," single-action, five-shot, rod ejector, 8-inch barrel, for around $15. And in .46 caliber, no less. A he-gun!

We look at these civilian charcoal burners in Chapter V. Meanwhile, having somehow solved or dissolved the spot on your pantaloons, you'd now be hitching up your suspenders, or "galluses," as the West preferred to call them, and looking finally to your boots.

This being a Western trip, very likely you would be wearing boots, rather than ankle or Jefferson shoes. They might or might not, most probably would not, have cowboy high heels. (By the bye, in 1870 the word "cowboy" was still loosely defined in the language, and in the effete East might still mean a Tory, since some of the pro-British renegades of the Revolution had called themselves cowboys.) You could buy all sorts of boots, from jack boots to Wellingtons, a flat-heeled half-length boot made popular by the Duke of Wellington and incidentally still with us. And

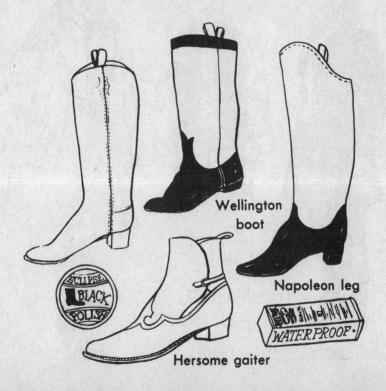

Wellington boot

Napoleon leg

Hersome gaiter

boots, while we're getting them on, are in descending order: the most expensive kind, handmade and hand-lasted to your personal measurements; bench-made, which had some hand work in them but were made up ahead, only partially to your individual requirements, if at all; and finally, ready-mades, the store-bought variety that you might get for as little as three or four dollars—which, of course, were duly despised by any proper old-time cowboy.

There were various blacking preparations available. But in the West boots and shoes were often greased, or treated with tallow. Bear's grease, if you could get it, was a prime favorite, for either your hair or boots; and there were bears all over the Old West.

And now that we've got to your hair, you'd be wearing it pretty long, since the barber trimmed it with shears only. Mountain Men, the old trappers who had first explored the West, Army scouts, buffalo hunters, and the like often affected really long hair, down to their shoulders.

OLD WEST FASHIONS

1870s   1890s   1880s

On your head, in 1871, you'd probably have a soft felt slouch hat, most likely black. Light-colored hats, much like cowboys' hats, had been a Southern style for years, and were known as planters' hats. These were very wide-brimmed, usually light gray, light tan, or even white, though not as white as some of the really white hats one sees today. They had a comparatively low flat-topped crown, something like the *poblano* hat you see California vaqueros wearing in parades and rodeos even today— or like a pillbox cap, if you don't know any California vaqueros. But, coming from town and riding the stage, you'd probably be wearing something that looked very much like a smaller version of the Army Kossuth hat, with bound edge and a chimney-pot crown, worn undented. Or you might have a bowler—that was a derby with the sides of the brim rolled higher than we remember the hard hat—or a homburg, not too much different from today's, or even a high hat, still popular, still considered *the* dress hat, though it would most likely be silk rather than beaver fur as before the war. Even Westerners wore these when they dolled up—gamblers particularly, and even gun fighters. One downy cowboy got himself into a right smart of trouble one night down Texas way when Ben Thompson, the redoubtable pistoleer and onetime marshal of Austin, decided to sport a frock coat and plug hat downtown; the cowboy mistook him for a tenderfoot and decided to make him dance. It was the sort of social error one doesn't make twice.

To wear a hard hat on the range was also a grievous mistake, but curiously, in the early West, some hardy souls did so, while in town even cowboys, on occasion, would dress up fit to kill, complete with derby hats. Butch Cassidy and his famous Wild Bunch outlaw gang actually had their

Planter's hat

Slouch hat

Wool hat

High hat

Bowler

THE WILD BUNCH

Left to right: Harry Longabaugh, Bill Carver, Ben Kilpatrick, Harvey Logan, George Parker (alias Butch Cassidy)

photographs taken in just such getups in Fort Worth once. They lived just long enough to regret it, because the law also got hold of that picture and recognized the boys.

The inevitable distinction between aristocrats and commoners was indicated by the material of which the hat was made, fur or wool. The headgear of the poor man was typically made of wool felt; it marked the wearer as one of the "wool hats" or "wool-hat bunch," always a term of derision. There were of course various styles of wool hats, and Western farmers, the Grange in particular, had a regulation top piece with narrow curled bound brim and a tall, chimney-pot crown, worn undented. It cost about $1.50 or less. But, as a general thing, the wool hat had a rounded crown, very nearly the shape of the head and not very far above it, while the brim was shapeless, drooping, and often pinned back, since wool felt does not hold its shape well. So you wouldn't be likely to arrive wearing one of those.

Nor would you be likely to be sporting a headpiece similar to those on many of the riders swarming out there in the dusty street. Those wild horsemen were mostly Texans, roaring up the cattle trails clear from down on the Bravo (which is a nickname for the Rio Grande). The hats many of them wore were Mexican sombreros, with high curved edges to the very wide brim, a regular mountain peak of a sugar-loaf crown, dented into a blunt point at the very top, and a *barbiquejo* (chin strap) dangling long and loose under the wearer's jaw. Curiously, that sombrero pointed peak would spread all the way up to the northern ranges with the longhorn herds and then, in a modified version, wash clear back to Texas again as the "Montana peak," the style of hat-creasing that eventually, about the turn of the century, would supplant the fore and aft crease of the campaign hat, even in the conservative Army.

But, by Joe, you could be wearing a John B. Stetson, even in 1871. Stetson, a hatmaker by trade, launched his world-famous firm in Philadelphia in 1865. Previously he had been in the West, in Illinois and Missouri, and then in the Colorado gold-rush camps during the war years. So he knew first hand what Westerners wanted in the way of a hat. Determined to make quality his selling point, he did just that, and didn't once manage to sell a dozen hats at a time during his first half-year in business. But then things got better, the term "John B." took its place with Colt and Winchester among the great names of the West, and by the time Stetson died in 1906,

Sombrero

Stetsons

the John B. Stetson Company was selling two million hats a year, all over the world. The first Western model was the Boss, and after it came the Carlsbad, destined to become *the* cowboy style, and the Buckeye, extra wide and high. A John B. cowboy hat cost you $10 to $20 or more, a considerable investment in those days, when a top hand's pay was $30 a month or so. But it was practically a life investment, since a Stetson would last almost forever. A true Westerner's hat and boots were his most expensive pieces of clothing, handmade boots, cowboy style, costing $10 to $25 at least. Shirts could be had from $1 up, suits from $10—which would buy a pretty darn good suit in the Eastern cities—and overcoats were about the same as suits.

You'd probably arrive from the East with a greatcoat, one with a waist-length cape like the Army overcoat, but in any shade except Army blue. Back home in the closet you might have a Chesterfield with a velvet collar, but this you wouldn't be wearing out West. Possibly you would also have a traveling blanket or shawl with you. Men used them in the sixties and seventies, and with reason. It got cold in those open stagecoaches, and all you had for warmth was perhaps a flask, and a hot brick slipped in at your feet at the start—well, hot for a little while, anyhow. There'd be a case to carry your blanket or shawl in—it might be a Scotch shawl, with a tartan plaid—and in addition you'd have a carpetbag or two, similar to our own traveling luggage but made of heavy carpeting, hence the name. The vultures who went South after the war to batten on the defeated were said to have carried their all in just such bags, and the term "carpetbagger" in the mouths of Southerners was one of loathing. (A native Southerner who had turned coat to prey on his fellows, and there were a number such, was called a "scalawag.") Your bags, carpet or leather, plus a small calfskin-covered traveling trunk too, if you insisted on such luxury, would be in the "boot" of the stage—a hinged platform at the rear that folded up flat when not in use.

Now let's go through your pockets. You might have a lead pencil. Wooden pencils, with graphite "leads," were common and had been for a long time, having first been made in the beginning of the eighteenth century. You would not have a fountain pen. They'd been trying to make a practical fountain pen for a hundred years and more, but the first really workable ones didn't appear until the 1880s. But you might have a pen case containing a penholder and some steel pen points, which they had been making for fifty years, or a gold point. You might have a vial of liquid ink, or some ink powder to make it when needed. With the pen case might be a penknife with which you could make a pen out of a goose quill. That

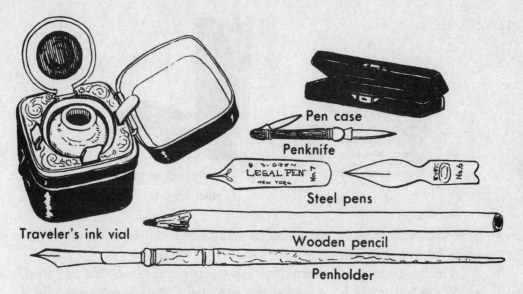

Traveler's ink vial

Pen case

Penknife

Steel pens

Wooden pencil

Penholder

was what the small, sharp-bladed pocketknife was for and how it got its name.

Probably you'd also have a match case and some matches. What could be done with phosphorus had been known for a long time, but the stuff was so expensive that the match was not invented until 1827, by John Walker, an English druggist. His inventions sold under the name of Lucifers, smelled appropriately, and were hard as the devil to light, for that matter. You had to draw them smartly through folded sandpaper to ignite the things. Phosphorus "strike-anywhere" matches came next, made in the United States from 1836 on. The heads had yellow or white phosphorus, sulfur, and other stuff in them; they also smelled when you struck them; and they were poisonous. In fact, you could commit suicide by eating match heads, and some fools did. There were even safety matches, a Swedish invention, put on the market in 1855. But naturally there weren't many of these in the West. There were no paper book matches anywhere; they were not invented until 1892.

Old-time matches came in boxes, or sometimes in blocks; that is, the sticks were sawed out, all but the ends, which were left attached to one another. You just broke one off, like a tooth from a comb, to use it. Since you could set the whole block on fire too if you wished, or sometimes when you didn't wish, here was a gadget that might come in right handy when you were being chased by Indians or outlaws. It's next to impossible to throw a single lighted match from the back of a running horse and have it stay lighted long enough to catch even thick dry grass. But it could be

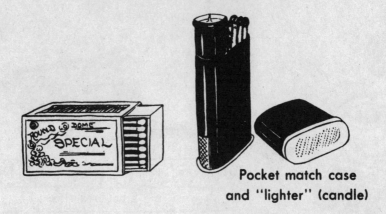

Pocket match case
and "lighter" (candle)

done with a block of matches, and several times frontiersmen saved themselves by just that stratagem.

Finally, there was the primitive fire-making apparatus, flint and steel, which you just might have had on this trip to the Wild West, especially if you were going where stores were few and far between. This apparatus, as you bought it in the sixties or seventies, was a D-shaped piece of steel which you held over your knuckles, to strike sparks from a chunk of flint into prepared charred linen, all provided in a little kit. The prepared tinder would catch the glow readily, and you could make your own tinder after the store-bought supply ran out. You blew carefully on the glowing coal, feeding it with wisps of grass, shavings, paper, or whatever, until you had a flame. Or you could use store-bought splints tipped with sulfur, called "punks," which burst into flame when touched to the glowing tinder. Any way you did it, it was quite a business.

Sometimes you'd find a household equipped with a real old-time fire-lighter, a little metal box for the tinder with a flintlock attached. You just pulled the trigger as on a rifle. Or you could make fire the way the Indians did, which was not exactly by rubbing two pieces of wood together, but a better version of that idea—a fire drill. This was a crude, easily improvised bow, whose loose string rotated a wooden drill in a notch on a flat piece of wood until friction created tiny, glowing coals. After which you proceeded as with flint-and-steel coals.

Fire was very important to frontiersmen. In our day we can scarcely realize to what lengths they would go just to start one, or to keep it going once they got a blaze started. At night you banked the fire most carefully on your rancho hearth, or else you might have to ride clear to the next house and "borrow a chunk of fire," which you carried home, most carefully, in a bucket of ashes.

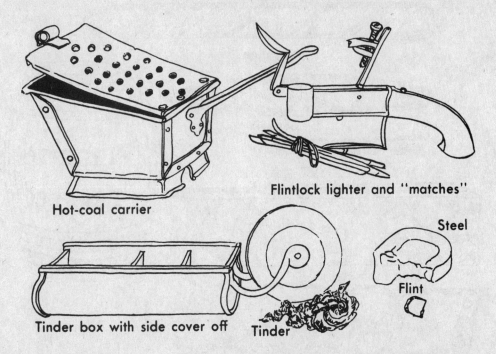

Hot-coal carrier

Flintlock lighter and "matches"

Steel

Flint

Tinder box with side cover off   Tinder

So even an Easterner would probably have matches in some kind of waterproof match safe, and maybe a burning glass, and maybe even flint and steel as well.

Along with the matches you'd perhaps have some cigars. There were innumerable brands in the seventies, just as now. Americans had been making and smoking cigars for a long time. Even some of the Indians had smoked their tobacco in cigar-like rolls. Before the Civil War cigars ranked next to chewing as the most popular means of taking tobacco, and the Connecticut Valley area of New England in particular had rolled out cigars by the barrel—literally, millions of them packed in barrels, several thousand to the barrel. They were known as "long nines," a thin panatella type; "supers," more like modern cigars except that they were made with a twist or pigtail on the end to hold them together; and "short sixes," which even across the generations still smell perfectly gosh-awful and undoubtedly were. Saloons often gave you short sixes for free, or sold them two for a cent, so you can imagine. The Conestoga-wagon freighters often smoked these or worse, and so gave the name "stogie," a contraction of Conestoga, to that sort of cigar.

And there were varieties even worse than the short sixes, some made of European-grown tobacco. But you could get Cuban cigars too, fine ones, clear Havana, wholesaling for $15 to $17 a thousand as compared with $4

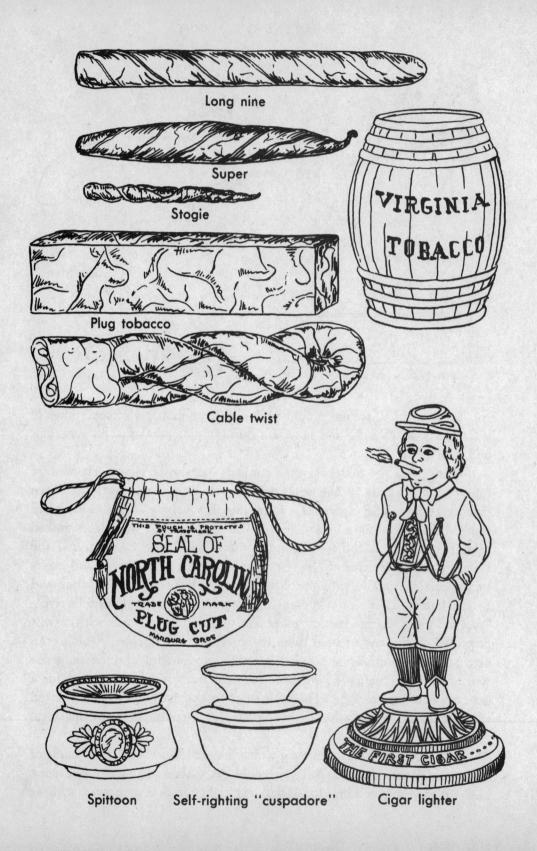

Long nine

Super

Stogie

Plug tobacco

Cable twist

VIRGINIA TOBACCO

THIS POUCH IS PROTECTED BY TRADEMARK
SEAL OF
NORTH CAROLINA
TRADE MARK
PLUG CUT
MARBURG BROS

THE FIRST CIGAR

Spittoon   Self-righting "cuspadore"   Cigar lighter

a thousand or less for domestic brands. This, remember, was before the Civil War.

During the great conflict the federal government really piled on the internal-revenue taxation, so in the seventies prices were higher, and a good cigar cost you at least a nickel. Oh yes, there were many evaders of aforesaid taxes, both on tobacco and on whisky. Illicit liquor or tobacco vendors were called "blockaders," in reference to the wartime blockade of the Southern states.

There were scores of different brands of chewing tobacco, too. Plug and twist were the forms in which chewin' was sold, and some of the brands, mostly long since vanished with the cuspidor, were Wedding Cake, Winesap, Star of Virginia, Rock Candy, Henry Clay, and Daniel Webster. Chewing tobacco, if you're unacquainted with the frontier art and article, is tobacco more heavily cased, as a general thing, than smoking tobacco, the "casing" being the sauce used to improve the taste. Usually it was a secret formula, made of licorice, molasses, sugar, fruit juices, syrups, or whatnot. Smoking tobacco is ordinarily cased too, but nowhere nearly as heavily as chewing tobacco.

In smoking materials, aside from cigars, the taste of the Old West was also quite different from that of today. Pipe tobacco was sold in plug form, or "plew," as the Mountain Men called it. A plew was originally the whole skin of the beaver, sold by the skin, not the pound, so when you bought the whole plug of tobacco you bought the plew. There were tobacco cutters, knives to hew off smaller purchases. You bought tobacco in quantity very much as you might buy bacon, or cloth, often under no brand name at all. But, even before the war, several very famous brands had developed wide markets, and some of these persisted into the Indian-fighting days.

Thus Lone Jack, a granulated pipe tobacco made by John W. Carroll of Lynchburg, Virginia, was a highly popular brand in the 1850s, was much liked by both Southern and Northern soldiers during the conflict (the Northern soldiers got theirs by trading on the picket lines Yankee coffee, newspapers, and so on for rebel tobacco), and continued in wide demand for years after the war.

Another Lynchburg brand, Maurice Moore's Killikinnick—not to be confused with the Indians' smoking mixture, kinnikinnick, which was usually shredded red willow inner bark—faded out of the picture after the war. But so well remembered and so popular was it that there were numerous imitations, and at last the name grew to mean a certain sort of granulated smoking tobacco.

But the real boom in smoking, and the most famed of all the Western

Bull Durham labels

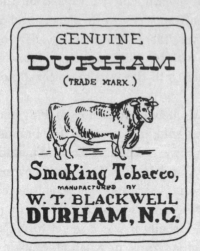

First trademark, 1866   The famous Durham bull

brands of tobacco, came only after the war. As did more recent conflicts, the Civil War produced a tremendous increase in the use of tobacco. During the struggle, often right in the tobacco-producing areas, the soldiers had only to pick up what they wanted from the fields and barns they passed. But manufactured tobaccos, with their secret processes and sauces, tasted much better. So the troops of both sides preferred the manufactured brands, which were supplied to them by sutlers, all too often at outrageous prices. Among the brands that came along after the Surrender, by far the most popular was Bull Durham, destined speedily to become the great cowboy smoke.

Bull Durham was started by ex-Confederate John Ruffin Green, near Durham's Station, North Carolina, in 1865. For a trademark, Green took the bull picture from the label on jars of Colman's mustard, which was made in Durham, England. (Yes, you could get prepared mustard in the sixties and seventies, and Lea & Perrins Sauce, in bottles, much as now.) Before he died, in 1869, Green took William Blackwell into partnership, and Blackwell bought Green's interest from the estate, reputedly paying only $500 for the bull trademark! The little muslin sack with its label, "Blackwell's Genuine Durham," and the full-view picture of the bull, would soon become as much a part of the cowboy West as the Colt or the Stetson.

All over the Western country you soon could, and still can, buy Bull Durham, with its little packet of cigarette papers and its round tag dangling on the end of the sack's drawstring. Spending millions for advertising as the business grew, putting up everywhere huge signs showing the triumphant bull (and incidentally shocking the good ladies of the times no end with some of them), the Bull Durham people saw to it that you knew about their product. In the 1880s, just for one quaint item, they had a bull's-bellow steam whistle on their Durham factory—a well-nigh perfect imitation, so people said. You could hear it for thirteen miles, and just to blow it once cost $5, even in those economical times.

There were, of course, many competitors and imitators—Sitting Bull (after the famous Sioux), Pride of Durham, Duke of Durham, Ridgewood, a pipe tobacco that had gone to the Civil War in soldiers' haversacks, Duke's Mixture, put out by W. Duke and Sons, and many others. In the fifties, Robert Mayo of Richmond, Virginia, had contracted with the Navy to supply tobacco, and his brands, Navy Tobacco and Navy Plug, were popular and likewise had their competitors. Dime Durham was another of the muslin-sack brigade. We might note that it had long been a custom of frontiersmen, going far and wide from sources of supply, to carry their smoking tobacco also in plug form, whittling off a pipeful when they craved one. A plug has much less tendency to reduce itself to dust than does granulated loose tobacco, jolted, perhaps, for endless miles on the back of a mule or in a springless freight wagon.

Notice that I am not including any tailor-made cigarettes in these listings. Cigarettes were known, even before the Civil War. But they were considered "wicked," sissified, unmanly, unhealthy, or what have you. You snuffed, chawed, smoked a pipe or see-gars; you even "rolled your own" without too much criticism. But "ready-mades" or "tailor-mades," no sir!

As a matter of fact cigarettes, at least in the homemade style, are about as ancient as any other form of taking tobacco, the idea of rolling the makings in a cornshuck "paper" having occurred to the Indians. Texans and other border wayfarers had long since adopted the Mexican custom of rolling 'em in cornshucks. By the bye, you *cannot* ordinarily lick a cornshuck wrapper and make it stick; you have to hold the darn cigarette in shape while you smoke it. But to buy cigarettes already rolled was to most Americans in the sixties and seventies still a dubious foreign fad. The Philadelphia Centennial Exposition of 1876 was the first place where ready-made cigarettes, extravagantly displayed and promoted, got a real start in America. Out West, right up to World War I, you practically never saw a cowman smoking ready-mades. He rolled his own, yes, and sometimes with one hand, too—it can be done, although it is just a stunt. The cowboy's hand-built smoke was, as he called it, a "quirly."

Certainly no old Injun fighter took time out to smoke a Camel cigarette, because they didn't hit the market until 1913, or to try a Chesterfield (1912) or a Lucky Strike (1916). Oddly enough, Lucky Strike was also the name of an old-time ex-Confederate's brand. It was applied by Dr. Richard A. Patterson, late surgeon in the Confederate Army, right after the war to some "flat goods" he was putting out, that being the trade name for smoking or chewing plug tobacco.

If you weren't any good at rolling your own, even in the seventies you could buy a little metal pocket cigarette roller, very much like the one your tobacco dealer tries to sell you when you decide to "save" on cigarettes, if not the identical article.

Now let's look at the money in your pockets. In the early seventies the nation was still on a paper-money basis, as it had been since early in the war. Small metallic change had practically disappeared by 1862, along with big metal also, gold and much of the silver. Congress had made "greenbacks" (paper bills so called because of their color) legal tender, and had likewise provided for fractional notes, "shin plasters," in denominations of 3, 5, 10, 25, and 50 cents. These latter were about the size of modern cigar coupons and remained the much-disliked small change of the nation until 1875, when both greenbacks and shin plasters were ordered redeemed in coin.

But out West, where people had been plagued by wildcat banks and the worthless paper money issued by them even before the war, you'd better

CURRENCY

Greenback

Shin plaster

First
U. S. Coin

Spanish
milled dollar

carry metal if you craved to buy anything. Coming from the East, you might have some very small change in Civil War cents, which were private tokens of well-nigh infinite variety, issued by merchants, manufacturers, and businessmen as small change vanished. They were the size of a modern cent, of bronze, and passed current for one cent. The old copper cents, coinage of which had ceased only in the mid-1850s, were still the government cent you'd usually find, and were nearly as large as a half-dollar.

Actually, out West, you'd have scant use for anything much smaller than a quarter—"two bits," in 1871 as it is still today. The term is Western and frontier. The old Spanish and Spanish-colonial milled dollars, which were called "pieces of eight," instead of dividing into halves and quarters like our dollar, broke down into eight *reales*, or eight "bits," as the American frontiersman who didn't go much for Spanish pronunciation called them. The *real* (pronounced ree-ahl), a small silver coin, was the unit of the old Spanish monetary system. There was lots of Spanish-colonial and Mexican money in the American Old West, though you wouldn't be very likely to find any real reales floating around. Pesos, big Mexican "'dobe dollars," would be what you'd see. But, especially in the mining camps, you might find "bit houses," where everything cost one bit, 12½ cents; or "two-bit houses," where everything was a quarter. In a bit house, of course, you were expected to spend even money, two bits, four bits, or on up, because they generally couldn't or wouldn't make odd change, or, if they did, they would make it with a "short bit," an American dime, and throw you out if you squawked. But just try making a short bit, a 10-cent piece, do service as 12½ cents, if the boot was on the other foot!

As to what you could get for your money in an inn or bar, well, meals—full meals—were anywhere from a short bit, a dime, up. In the big cities along the eastern edge of the frontier—Chicago, Saint Louis, Kansas City, New Orleans—you could get a "lunch," a lamb chop with bread, butter, and drink, or a bowl of stew, or corned beef hash, for 5 cents; steak with onion for from 10 to 20 cents; a full "dinner" for no more—roast beef or pork, potatoes, two vegetables, bread, butter, tea, coffee, or milk, and a piece of pie for a dime! Large tin cup of bourbon or rye whisky—rotgut, of course, but potent—one nickel. Full quart bottle of excellent malt whisky, rye or bourbon, for $1. Cheaper varieties as low as $1.50 a gallon. The farther west you went the higher prices got, of course. But even out on the southern plains where the buffalo hunters were just now destroying the great herds, two bits would usually get you a snort from the whisky peddler's wagon—rotgut, of course, raw red-eye, but souped up with pepper, tabasco, tobacco juice, even, so help me, rattlesnake heads on occasion, to increase the bite.

The sometimes fair but usually fried-hog-and-hominy horrible meals at the stage stations would cost you maybe four bits or even a dollar—they were high! And at the "hog ranches". . .

Hog ranches weren't a feature of the Western landscape in 1871, but they would be shortly, in the Hayes administration. Leaning toward temperance and teetotalism, the Hayes administration tried to stop drinking and the sale of liquor in Army posts. The result, of course, was that around the far-flung Western Army forts there promptly sprang up a crop of blind tigers, frontier speakeasies, "ranches" ostensibly devoted to raising hogs, but actually producing more pie-eyed and pickled ones than anything else. The term "hog ranch" referred to just such a dissolute hangout.

Even clear out in the cattle-trail and mining towns you could usually get more than just bourbon or rye at two bits a pony. Any proper barkeep prided himself on being able to shake up a couple of hundred different drinks. There'd be gin, brandy, rum, maybe some Irish or Scotch whisky if this was a really fancy place. Cobblers, favorite mixed drinks of the times, were usually some kind of fruit juice or syrup mixed with wine or whisky. There were punches, juleps, smashes, slings, toddies, hot drinks, and cold ones. They had cocktails, too, although it was taking your life in your hands to order one in a Western saloon.

The ice problem was solved in most frontier camps simply by cutting ice in winter from convenient lakes, ponds, or creeks, and storing it in ice houses, which were thick double-walled structures, usually made of logs, with the space between the walls filled with sawdust or earth. Down on the Rio Grande, where you generally didn't get winter ice, a bottle of warm beer might cost you one buck or even more, as it sometimes did unwary visitors to old Judge Roy Bean's saloon in Langtry, Texas, a bit later.

Speaking of bottles, they still hadn't satisfactorily solved the problem of how to cap a bottle, back in the 1870s. They had soda water, yes, and other sparkling beverages as well, champagne, sparkling burgundies, and the like. But for capping bottles, they still mostly used corks, wired on, glued on, wrapped on, a weird and wonderful assortment of not-too-good methods. Nobody popped a cap in the sixties, seventies, or eighties, unless it was a percussion cap. The crimped bottle cap, as we know it, didn't arrive until 1892.

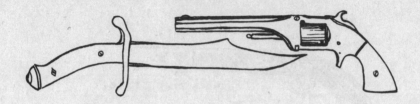

V

COLD STEEL AND HOT LEAD

IN MORE respects than the troubles of Scarlett O'Hara an age had fled with the wind after the American Civil War. There was the little matter of settling one's personal differences, for example. Before the war you would doubtless have taken care of the situation with a sword cane, a tomahawk, or at least a Bowie knife. But after the war, thanks to the untiring efforts of such benefactors as the Messrs. Colt, Remington, Smith, Wesson, *et al.*, you could also, if you preferred, choose action at a distance. You could fast-draw and shoot the scoundrel, suh, in practically no time at all and from clear across the street!

From the time the first ancient forged a sword, and found it superior to rock and club, clear up to the great American fraternal conflict, the blade had been king of battles. True, short-ranged as it was, it was no very good answer to the problem of how to mix in a fight and yet stay bodily out of it at the same time. But it was dependable. The blade, spear, sword, dagger, or knife in your hand never missed fire, never was empty, never blew up, never—well, very seldom, if you knew anything at all about handling cold steel—directed its vengeance a blind country mile to one side of your foe, missing him whole hog and leaving you helpless.

But until the Civil War the pistol harbored all of these unhappy possibilities. If your pistol was a flintlock, it was hideously unhandy to get out of a pocket or holster fast, and it was also mulishly akin to modern cigarette lighters, which operate on much the same principle. Bet your life on it, you could be sure it wouldn't go off at the first pull. If it was percussion, a "cap-lock" gun, the chances were some better but not much. So it was not until the sixties and seventies, when the first fairly reliable metal-cased pistol

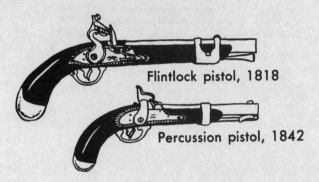

Flintlock pistol, 1818

Percussion pistol, 1842

cartridges appeared, fodder for the first fairly reliable repeating hand fire-arms, that the day of the gun fighter really dawned.

In our standard Western legends, only villains prefer knives. But before the Civil War, in real life at least, it was just the opposite. Cold steel had been the personal standby, the last resort, of the American frontiersman from the very beginnings of our land. In the period from 1800 to 1860 no Westerner, and for that matter no Southerner either, even in the polite and civilized cities, was considered fully clothed unless he had on him some-where at least one knife. And after the 1830s it was almost certain to be a shining example of the most famous fighting blade of all, the Bowie knife.

The true history of this remarkable American weapon has been so obscured by the tall tales of liars and romancers that it is now almost im-possible to arrive at indisputable facts. But the most reliable accounts seem to agree that it was first fashioned by an Arkansas blacksmith, James Black, at Washington Settlement, Hempstead County, Arkansas, in or around 1830.

Washington Settlement was a stopping place on the old Southwest Road to Texas, and Black was a highly skilled metalsmith. Somewhere in his years of routine frontier smithing, shoeing horses, forging wagon irons, and the like, he had developed and perfected some remarkable secret processes for hardening and tempering steel. His knives were known all over the South-west, and he found a ready sale for them among the throngs of frontiersmen moving down the road toward what was then the Mexican State of Coahuila and Texas, but was soon to be the Republic of Texas, and in due time a state in the American Union. It was said that you could shave comfortably with one of Black's knives even after whittling hardwood an hour or so. His prices ranged from $5 for the plainest blade up to $50 or more for gold- and silver-ornamented specimens, in which decorative art Black was also a master. But, $5 or $50, both tremendous sums in those days, the basic quality of the blade was still the same. Plain or fancy, you got an unequaled fighting weapon.

Meanwhile another remarkable figure in his own right, James Bowie of Kentucky, had been acquiring note as a knife fighter, largely because of a bloody mass duel in which he had participated, a fight on a lonely Mississippi River sandspit opposite Natchez in 1827. Impaled on a sword-cane blade, Bowie had still contrived to disembowel his opponent and put the dead man's companions to flight. In this gory struggle Bowie must have used an ordinary hunting knife, or dirk, since the real Bowie knife was still some three years in the future. But at any rate his feat drew wide notice; word of mouth soon blew the duel up to fantastic proportions—a half-dozen killed, a regiment or so just practically sliced to ribbons—and the mild-mannered Bowie found himself famous.

But more was to come. Three years later, returning from Texas, where he had decided to become a Texian and had taken out Mexican citizenship papers (as was necessary then to hold Texas land), James Bowie ordered a knife from Black. He left Black a pattern, as was customary. Black made one knife to the great frontiersman's specifications. But also, knowing his man, Black made another, to his own peculiar ideas. And this one Bowie preferred immediately. He paid, it is said, $50 for the weapon.

It was the original Bowie knife. Six years later, sick, with a badly wrenched back, Jim Bowie waited grimly on his cot in the stricken Alamo until the screaming enemy came in; and then the great blade swung. It took a whoop and a passel of them—nine, anyhow—along, when its owner cashed. The knife vanished then, either cremated with Bowie on the funeral pyre where the Texians' bodies were burned, or, much more likely, swiped by some admiring brown soldado. So we don't know too much about this original.

Not that there aren't descriptions enough! The famous blade drew all sorts of admiring commentary and—according to the claims, anyway—the doughty colonel had gravely presented somebody, usually the storyteller, with "the original Bowie knife." If one-tenth of these yarns are true, Bowie must have been the original walking cutlery store. But undoubtedly Bowie did possess and use a number of knives; probably he did give some of them away; and assuredly, as Raymond W. Thorp, the American fighting-knife authority points out in his book, *Bowie Knife*,[1] these other blades, which may or may not have shown the so-called Bowie pattern, were nevertheless and quite honestly "Bowie's knives." There is no reason at all to doubt the statement of Rezin P. Bowie, the knife fighter's brother, that he, Rezin, made the knife James used in the sandspit duel, a straight single-edged blade as

1. This is the best history of the knife I know and I follow Thorp's account pretty closely here.—*Author's note.*

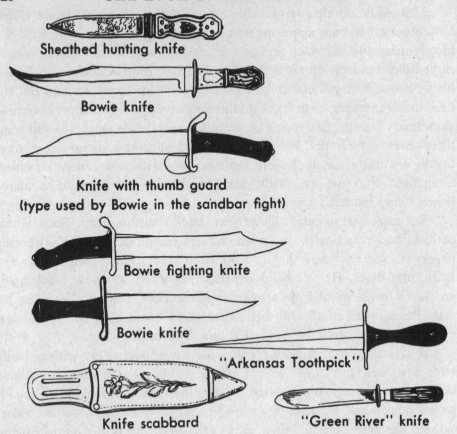

Sheathed hunting knife

Bowie knife

Knife with thumb guard
(type used by Bowie in the sandbar fight)

Bowie fighting knife

Bowie knife

"Arkansas Toothpick"

Knife scabbard

"Green River" knife

Rezin Bowie describes it, and so not what we know as a Bowie-knife blade at all.

As for the first genuine Bowie knife, on the way back to Texas Jim Bowie fell into an ambush—either of three robbers or three hired assassins, the stories vary. This being a perfect opportunity to try some whittling with his new knife, the colonel thoughtfully beheaded one of his assailants, split the skull of the second, and gutted the third. Unfortunately, there was no fourth villain to lose a few legs. But the trial was sufficient, the news ballooned again, and after that everybody and his boy craved a toad-stabber like that'n. The knife was on its way to immortality.

Since you don't lop off heads or split skulls with a penknife, we feel sure that the great original must have had at least a 10- or 12-inch blade, maybe 14-inch, as did hundreds of its close copies soon to come. The blade was about 1¾ inches wide at the guard, straight, or very nearly so, until it neared the curving saber-type point which is the distinguishing mark of the Bowie blade. About 2½ inches from the tip, the blade curved back, ending in a very sharp point.

The front of the blade was ground to a razor edge and the back of the point section, curved concavely, was also sharpened, so that the weapon had a 2½-inch ripping edge on the back, as well as 10 to 14 cutting inches on the front. From the lower edge of this "gullet tickler," as the reverse edge was sometimes called, to the guard, the back of the blade was a rib about ¼ inch thick. Quite often this rib would be sheathed in brass, softer than steel, to catch and hold the opponent's knife and keep it from sliding down to cut

Texas Ranger with knife scabbard

the owner's hand. The crossguard may very well have been taken from Rezin P. Bowie's design. It was a straight two-pronged steel plate, the grip of buckhorn or black walnut, one piece; and the tang or shank of the blade went clear through the grip, ending in a knob on the bottom end.

As the knives became popular, blade lengths varied widely. They ranged from as little as 6 or 7 inches to monsters 20 inches long, sabers or scimitars in anybody else's catalogues! In the Civil War, Bowies were as popular as pistols for personal weapons, perhaps even more so, and several Western Confederate regiments had huge Bowie knives fitted to their rifles as bayonets.

The knife was usually carried in a leather scabbard worn on the belt, the sheath tip of brass or at least generously riveted, since this blade has a bad habit of slashing right through ordinary protection and, in a fall, say, seriously wounding or even killing its own wearer. It was also sometimes carried in a scabbard at the back of the neck, or under the armpit like a shoulder-holster pistol, or in the breast of the shirt, or even strapped to the left forearm, where a flick of a wrist could bring it into action. Or it might be carried in the top of the boot, another favorite place to stash all sorts of weapons.

Typically, the Bowie was not a throwing knife, since it was highly tempered, intended primarily for cutting and ripping. The real throwing knife is shaped much like a dart or spear, and is best made with the fine tempering only at and near the point so that the knife will penetrate but will not snap in two from vibration when it strikes.

A knife carried for both throwing and handwork would, in all likelihood, have been of the straight-bladed poignard or dagger type—or an

"Arkansas Toothpick," as the second most popular knife of the frontier was called. This had a straight pointed blade, sometimes with a single, but usually a double, edge. Guard and grip varied just about as did those on the Bowie, but ordinarily it would have a flat, not-too-wide crossguard with knobbed ends, a walnut, horn, or other smooth-material handle, and the usual thick sheath. The Toothpick, under various other names as well, of course, long antedated the Bowie. Both these knives, incidentally, are fighting blades, and neither is anything but a very poor substitute for a good hunting or butcher knife. The blades are too thick, as well as ill-shaped, for peaceful purposes. But that they were pacifiers the whole history of the West can testify, cold steel being just about the blood-chillingest of all weapons to face.

And what an expert knife fighter could do with one of these blades was a bloody pity, no fooling. He wasn't too likely to throw the thing at you, unless you were running away, or maybe standing off and unlimbering to shoot at him and he had to reach out and get you fast. Knife throwing, by and large, was more of a stunt, like the later gun fanning and rolling, rather than a common fighting technique. But an expert could and might throw, and if he did, he might either grasp the blade by the tip or by the butt of the grip, depending on the style of knife and his own personal fashion. In either case, the knife did not fly like an arrow, but instead spun, rotated in air. The trick, of course, was to make the weapon arrive point first at the target. An expert could drive the blade an inch or more into pine, and could kill a man with lightning speed.

But he couldn't be dead certain of doing so, no matter what the tall tales say. So, ordinarily, the knife was kept in hand and used much more like a fencing sword. The wild backhanding, the whoop, cut, and stab you see in the magazine illustrations and movies, is usually as phony as the "sword fencing" you see in these great historical dramas. Actually, knife fighting is pretty much of a science; you could, and still can, take lessons from professionals, just as in fencing. And, as with the various schools of fencing, the styles in the Old West varied. But, as a general thing, the experienced knife fighter, with his Bowie or Toothpick or the like, stood in a sort of *en garde* position, feet well apart and right foot slightly advanced, body and head held well back, knife pointing out and upward, the thumb against the guard on the side of the blade, as you might hold a sword. Sometimes a thumb stall, or thimble, would be added to the guard so that the thumb could be carried beyond the crosspiece, the better to direct the blade. The idea was to fence, to catch your enemy's strokes on the back of your own blade, fending them outward and away from yourself, at the same time keeping your point straight in line for your foe's body, all set for a deep driving stroke or an upward, flicking, "whittling" one, with no waste motion.

Your prime target was your opponent's body, his torso, from hips to throat. You wasted no time going for his head, and you bore in mind that the soft parts of the human body are mainly downward from the breastbone. A wide, low, sweeping stroke may disembowel your man without much chance of anything happening to your knife, but upward there's lots of bone. Right embarrassing, if nothing worse, to get your knife stuck.

So, upward you ripped and whittled, never forgetting that you had nearly three inches of razor on the back of your Bowie too, more than enough to kill a man. Downward you thrust. But also you never forgot that knife fighting is strictly *épée* style—a hit anywhere counts! If you could whittle off a thumb, slash the tendons of a knife wrist, lay open a too-advanced thigh, that could conceivably do the business just as effectively as a thrust to the heart. So knife fighting was the bloodiest kind of personal combat, with a fatality record probably well in excess of that of firearms duels. It was all the more blood-chilling in its chesslike precision. A couple of real knife experts could, and sometimes did, have at it for hours without doing more than nicking minor portions of each other's anatomies, clipping off a finger, say, or a thumb. The joker was that the man who lost the finger first often got killed next for his slight carelessness. They were right hard customers, our early Western forebears.

Sometimes knife fighters would tie their left wrists together with a bandanna or thong as a guarantee of a fight to the death. There were duels in which the combatants held corners of a handkerchief in their teeth. Sometimes a knife fighter in a rough-and-tumble melee would wrap a coat, blanket, or poncho around his left forearm, using it as a sort of shield, hoping to catch and entangle his enemy's blade while he drove home his own. I recall hearing of one oil-field knifeman who deliberately used his own left forearm, bare, in just this fashion, taking his foe's blade between the bones, twisting his arm to hold it there while he drove his own steel home to the heart. And there were all sorts of novelty variations and importations, for knife fighting is very, very old, and all over the world men have their special tricks.

There were men in the early West who carried and fought with two knives, much as the duelists in Europe had done long before. These were a principal blade, and a "gauche," or left-hand weapon, used mainly for guarding and reserve; sometimes this auxiliary even had teeth, or an upward curved guard to catch and break the enemy's blade, which was the purpose of the point-breaker daggers carried by medieval knights. Sometimes the two knives were carried in the same scabbard, the weapons flattened on one side so that they fitted closely together; and perhaps a man who had thought he was facing one knife would be surprised—it just might be fatally—to find that he was up against two.

There were even double-bladed knives, with the handle in the middle, the blades thrusting out right and left like horns. Just how a man went about packing such a *toro* terror I can't imagine. But on the border I once saw such a knife and they told me it was called a *toro*. And there were then, as now, clasp knives, folding blades that flicked out; skinning knives (these were butcher knives); scalping knives (which were just any old knife an Indian might use to collect hair). But the usual blade of the Old West was either the Bowie or the straight-bladed Arkansas Toothpick, or "frog-stabber," another slang term for this straight blade.

One other knife detail is probably worth noting. The Mountain Men— the hardy trappers, wayfarers, and Indian traders who first explored and exploited the West from around 1800 up to the Civil War—had a famous and I think legendary source for knives called the Green River Works, which the trappers took to be the name indicated by the initials G. R. etched on many of the blades they bought.

I have been able to find no trace of any such cutlery maker. But it was common practice for British blade manufacturers to stamp the royal cipher G. R., meaning George Rex, on their products, and this, I suspect, was the origin of the letters which the trappers took to mean Green River. After 1830, when William IV succeeded George IV and the letters changed, the "factory" seems to have faded, leaving only the expression, "Give it to him up to Green River!" meaning up to the hilt.

But if an alleged knife works was receding into legend about this time, a real pistol maker destined to become an even greater legend was just starting business. His name was Samuel Colt (later, by courtesy, Colonel Colt, though he was never a real Army officer). The revolver he invented was to symbolize an era.

Tradition says that Colt got his idea for a repeating pistol on a sea voyage and whittled the first model out of wood. He did not invent the revolver idea, by the bye. There had even been flintlock revolvers, and Elisha H. Collier of Boston, for one, had produced a beautiful flintlock five-shooter a generation earlier, in 1810. But Colt's was the first practical revolver, percussion, not flintlock, with metal firewalls between the nipples to prevent the flame from one cap from setting off the rest, an efficient way to make each chamber "line up," and other improvements. It too, incidentally, was a five-shooter.

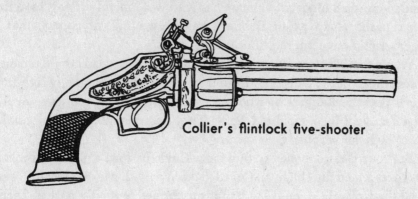

Collier's flintlock five-shooter

Obtaining his first patent in 1836, Colt began manufacture of his revolvers in Paterson, New Jersey. But, as usually happens when you first make a better mousetrap—and don't let them tell you otherwise—both the mice and the public were suspicious. What had been good enough for grandpa was good enough for them. They knew what a pistol should be. So Colt went very painfully broke.

His first pistols, funny little guns with no trigger guards but "sheathed" triggers that popped out only when you cocked the hammer, calibers .28, .31, .36, and perhaps others as well—Paterson Colts, as collectors call them now—pretty nearly joined the Green River knives. But then, movie stuff, here come the Texas Rangers to the rescue! They'd got hold of some of Colt's products down Texas way and had used them against Mexicans and Indians. If Texas then had only had the large-size spending money Texas has now, Colonel Colt would have got rich years sooner. But as it was, Texas was broke. Sensing the market possibilities down there, Colt had even made a trip to the area in 1839. He got as far as Galveston before deciding sadly (or at least so we can surmise) that, first, he needn't take out any patents down there, which had been his original idea, since these guys obviously weren't going to be manufacturing anything but cattle, corpses, and cotton for years and years, and, second, alas, they couldn't pay for anything anybody else might manufacture for them.

So Colt went home, not without leaving a few choice samples of his wares in strategic hands, samples which presently reached Captain Jack Hayes of the Rangers. Enchanted, the Ranger leader succeeded in getting about a hundred of the revolvers for his company, two for each man. What he used for money I can't imagine. The value of the Texian dollar was then descending rapidly and reached an ultimate low of around 2 cents, U. S. But he got the pistols, nevertheless. About a year later, he and his outfit unloaded on some innocent Comanches who were merely trying to ambush and scalp the company in Bandera Pass, expecting, of course, that the Rangers would have but one shot in their guns.

When the fight was over, the Indian chief was dead, the Comanches had scrammed out of range, and the only reason there were any live Injuns left was that the Rangers had not yet realized just how one uses revolvers most effectively in a mounted fight. They'd dismounted, Mountain Man style. Which, for revolvers, was wrong.

But they had no money to buy more Colts. In 1842 Colt went broke. In 1845 Texas joined the Union and in 1846 the War with Mexico began. Texans, and all the Colts they could lay hands on, formed a goodly part of Zachary Taylor's American Army. With some misgivings Taylor sent Captain Samuel H. Walker of the Texas Rangers for more Colts, and between them Colt and Walker cooked up a new one, a real dilly!

The Walker Colts, so called, were he-man size, 15½ inches long, 9-inch barrel, weight 4 pounds, 9 ounces, unloaded, with a trigger guard, a loading lever under the barrel, six chambers in the cylinder, and caliber .44. They could throw their half-ounce slugs way out there. It was no longer necessary to ride right up and powder-brand your man, so he'd know you were trying to shoot him. But they were also ungodly heavy and clumsy, much easier to carry in saddle holsters on the horse than in the belt; and you can be fairly sure nobody ever did any fast gun-slinging with Walkers.

Sam Walker probably never saw the new revolver he had godfathered, since he was killed in the war in the early fall of 1847, and the big Colts did not reach the Army until near the end, which came in February 1848. But Samuel Colt was famous and on his way by now. The next Colt, the Model 1848 Dragoon, was shorter and lighter than the Walker, usually with a 7½-inch barrel. The principal fault of the earlier six-gun, a fragile hook spring to hold up the loading lever, had been corrected and now there was a sturdy latch. In succeeding models, the back of the trigger guard was sometimes straight and sometimes curved, and the stops (the little notches in the cylinder into which the stop bolt falls to lock the chamber in line with the barrel) were sometimes round or oval, sometimes rectangular. These Dragoons are also collectors' items, though much more common than Patersons or Walkers.

The Dragoon Colts were intended primarily to arm the U. S. Dragoons, mounted soldiers who were nevertheless expected to dismount whenever they fought, so they were generally provided with a detachable shoulder stock, and cuts made in the bottom of the recoil shield for the forward prongs of the stock, as in the Civil War Model 1860 Army Colt we have already

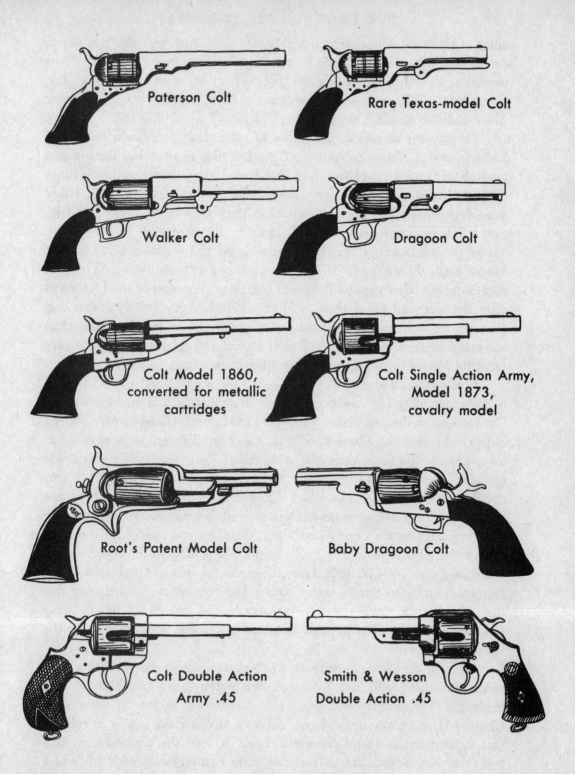

Paterson Colt

Rare Texas-model Colt

Walker Colt

Dragoon Colt

Colt Model 1860, converted for metallic cartridges

Colt Single Action Army, Model 1873, cavalry model

Root's Patent Model Colt

Baby Dragoon Colt

Colt Double Action Army .45

Smith & Wesson Double Action .45

noted. Colt eventually designed a shoulder stock that was also a canteen, a neat idea, though a little late, because by that time even the soldiery was beginning to realize that a revolver just isn't a rifle, or even a carbine. But the Dragoon Colts were widely used in the Civil War, along with the later Army and Navy models described in Chapter II.

There were, of course, a number of other Colt percussion models in addition to the military weapons: a Baby Dragoon in 1848, like the big gun in miniature except .31-caliber, five-shot, barrel 3 to 6 inches, and sometimes made without the loading lever; a very similar Pocket Model in 1849, either five- or six-shot; a Root's Patent Model in 1855, with the old sheathed trigger, a side hammer like a musket hammer, five-shot, .28- or .31-caliber, 3½- or 4½-inch barrel; a five-shot Police Model and a Pocket Navy or Belt Model, made during the Civil War, both .36, and with 4½- to 6½-inch barrels; and doubtless other variations as well. All these pistols were used for years after the war, and all of them, save possibly the very first Patersons and Walkers, were altered after the conflict to use metallic cartridges. More than 200,000 Colt revolvers were used in the great struggle, so they were very plentiful for conversion experiments after Appomattox.

Colonel Colt had died in 1862, and his factory at Hartford had burned in February 1863 but had been rebuilt immediately and was flourishing. Conversions of the percussion guns were made both at the factory and by individual gunsmiths. There were at least a dozen different ways of doing it, all essentially the same, consisting of cutting off the rear of the percussion cylinder (or sometimes supplying a new cylinder bored all through) to permit loading from the rear; somehow filling in the gap left; altering the hammer to rim-fire or center-fire cartridges instead of caps; and supplying some means of ejecting the empty cartridges, usually a rod ejector on the right side of the gun. Sometimes a loading gate was added to the recoil shield, sometimes not. The Colt 1860 Army, thus altered, was the real papa of the famous Model 1873 Single Action Army. The conversion, immediately distinguishable from the Single Action Army by the fact that it has no strap over the top of the cylinder, was in actual use in the West clear up to the turn of the century.

Many of the early conversions, by the bye, were to rim-fire rather than central-fire cartridges, both Colt and Remington being among those who made this intermediate change. While rim-fire cartridges, as we saw in Chapter II, especially in the larger calibers, are nowhere nearly as reliable and satisfactory as center-fire shells, back in 1866 the center-fire system wasn't so hot, either. But as early as 1866 Remington would sell you a cartridge cylinder to replace the old percussion job on your Remington Belt,

Police, or Pocket revolver, while clear up to 1888 you could get the weapons with either percussion or cartridge cylinder, or both. In 1872 Remington offered their cap-and-ball Army revolver converted to .46-caliber rim-fire, the Improved Army, five-shot, 8-inch barrel, rod ejector, all for $15.50 blued, cartridges $3 a hundred. Colt also put out a Model 1872 rim-fire six-shooter, the old percussion Model 1860 Army made over, with a new long cylinder bored all through, a rod ejector and brass trigger guard and back strap. This was, of course, the old frame with no strap over the cylinder.

But the great gun that was to bring Colt the highest glory already was in the works, with patents dated September 18, 1871; July 2, 1872; and the third and final one, January 19, 1875. The first specimens of the Single Action Army reached the hands of the troops in 1874. By 1876 the Army had some 10,000 of the new revolvers. Custer's Seventh Cavalry carried them into their last fight on the Little Big Horn. Colt made these guns until 1940, then stopped, but resumed production in 1955.

Now let's take a good look at this king of all revolvers, for no other hand weapon has ever come anywhere near equaling its fame. You can recognize it instantly; even in a flickering flash in a movie, its shape is distinctive from the plow handle to the big front sight. It has a strap over the top of the cylinder, something no previous Colt except the Root models had had—certainly the Civil War percussions didn't. It has an ejector housing and rod set against the lower right-hand side of the barrel. It has a solid frame. You flicked open the loading gate in the right-hand side of the recoil shield (it simply swung out and down) and then punched the empties, one by one, out of the cylinder, with the ejector rod, which has a coil spring inside its tube housing to carry it back out into place. (Remember, you could *not* "break" or "break open" a Single Action Army to load or unload it.)

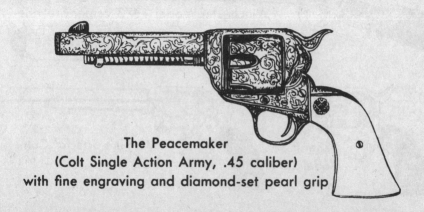

The Peacemaker
(Colt Single Action Army, .45 caliber)
with fine engraving and diamond-set pearl grip

Officially it was called Colt's Single Action Army, sometimes New Model Army (very little used), and eventually, in the manuals, Colt's Army Revolver, Caliber .45. The "given" popular names were the Peacemaker, for the .45-caliber; the Frontier, for the civilian version .44-caliber; and at last Colt's Frontier Sixshooter, for practically any version offered to the public. The original form as it reached the Army in 1874 came in two barrel lengths, the 7½-inch or Cavalry Model, and the 5½-inch or Artillery style. Except for the barrel lengths, there was no difference between the two styles.

Just about the time this revolver appeared, the Winchester people, you may remember, were offering their new Model 1873, the first truly practical repeating center-fire rifle. Colt promptly chambered its new revolver to handle the same .44-40 cartridge, so that the frontiersman need buy and carry only one kind of shell for both rifle and revolver. The combination of the civilian .44-40 Colt Single Action called the Frontier and the .44-40 Winchester proved tremendously popular. Later the Frontier was made and sold throughout the West in .32, .38, and .41 calibers as well. The only difference was in the size of the holes bored in barrels and cylinders, so that the smaller-caliber pistols, with more metal in the gun, actually weighed more than those of larger caliber. Barrel lengths ranged from a minimum of 3 inches in the so-called Sheriff's or Store Keeper's Model (usually made without any ejector) to as much as 16 inches—these extremes, of course, on special order.

Ned Buntline (Edward Zane Carroll Judson was his real name), famed Western blood-and-thunder romancer of the day, who probably contributed as much as anybody to mixing up the facts with fancy, is said to have pre-

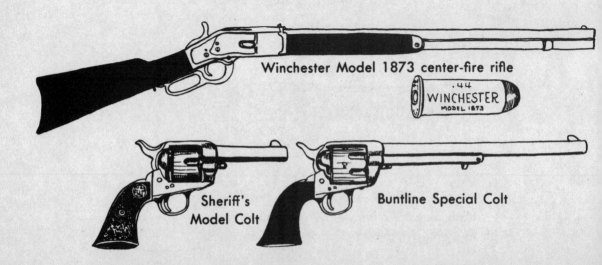

Winchester Model 1873 center-fire rifle

.44
WINCHESTER
MODEL 1873

Sheriff's
Model Colt

Buntline Special Colt

sented five Dodge City lawmen—Bill Tilghman, Bat Masterson, Wyatt Earp, Charlie Bassett, and Neal Brown—with Single Actions boasting 12-inch barrels and detachable walnut stocks, though these monsters seem to have vanished. Some specimens with 10- and 16-inch barrels, plus skeleton stocks and adjustable leaf sights like a rifle's, do exist. These extra-long-barreled revolvers are called Buntline Specials by collectors today, although of course, in the Old West, they had no particular name save perhaps a personal one given by the owner. They were not typically the sort of thing you'd find on a gun fighter bent on business.

What you would find on him, in all likelihood, would be the Colt Civilian Model Single Action .44 or .45, and with a 4¾-inch barrel. It probably would have black rubber grips, rather than the walnut stock of the military versions. And if the user was any kind of a gun slick at all, the action, and maybe other details as well, would have been very carefully worked over, smoothed up, and honed down.

The truth is that the old Single Action Colt was never intended for superprecision work, any more than the Bowie knife was, and most of these stories you hear about its amazing accuracy are hogwash. Its maximum effective range was about 75 yards; it did pretty well to group its shots in a 6-inch circle at 50 yards; and even to hope to hit anybody, say, 200 yards away you had to aim 8 feet above his head!

The sights were primitive, just a groove in the strap over the cylinder, nearly a quarter of an inch wide, and a knife-blade front sight on the end of the barrel. Often as not, tough lawmen or barroom fighters sharpened this front sight to a razor edge, so that when they "pistol whipped" a man— which consisted of holding the hand around stock and frame and slugging with the barrel, *not* holding onto the barrel and getting yourself shot by trying to hammer with the butt—they could also slice the blood from their victim with every blow. But the sharpening didn't improve sighting accuracy. Nor did the fact that, since the rifling twisted to the left, the bullet would drift to the left, a good 30 inches in 300 yards, no matter how carefully you held. Nor did the additional fact that right from the very start there were two kinds of cartridges for the gun, shells that didn't shoot the same at all.

The fixed sights on the Single Action Army were set for 50 yards, sighted in with the kind of .45 ammunition the Army was using at the time the Colt Army came in. This stuff was made for the Smith & Wesson Schofield revolver, which we look at presently. It was .45-28-230, which means a 230-grain bullet, with only 28 grains of black powder behind it. However, along with their new six-gun, the Colt people had produced a new cartridge, with a 255-grain bullet and 38 or 40 grains of black powder, much more powerful. You could shoot the Smith & Wesson ammunition in the Colt, though the Colt shells were too long for the Smith & Wesson Schofield cylinder. But when you put Colt ammo in the Army gun sighted for Schofield fodder you not only got lots more kick, you also shot 2 or 3 inches high even at 20 yards.

Nor was this all the trouble you might get. The miserable cartridges might not explode. The early annals of the West are full of baffled citizens vainly snapping pistols at each other. As an example, with just one more turn of the cylinder maybe even Wild Bill Hickok, pistoleer de luxe, might have lived to die differently another day. The pistol with which Jack McCall killed Hickok in Deadwood on August 2, 1876, missed fire on every cartridge in the cylinder except—luckily for McCall—the first one to feel the hammer.

Besides—and this, no doubt, will be the hardest of all for the modern reader to swallow—the old Single Action Army, the cowboy gun, is terribly delicate in its innards! It looks tough, but it isn't. It busts a part inside with dismaying ease and frequency—usually the cylinder stop spring, or the pawl spring, or the pawl, or sometimes even the mainspring itself. Or the notches on the hammer go wrong, though that usually wasn't much loss. But now we're about done with the defects of the old Peacemaker.

Its one sufficient advantage was that it would shoot, despite and regardless. If the hammer notches broke, you could still thumb home shots. If the hand or pawl, which rotates the cylinder, or the cylinder stop bolt or any of the springs broke, you could still turn the cylinder by hand. Even if the mainspring busted, you could still pop caps by hammering the hammer with a rock, and if a cartridge was no good—well, you had four more chances, anyhow.

Generally the wearer carried five loaded cartridges in the gun and kept the hammer down on an empty. If he was a real gun fighter, as we have noted, he would have the action smoothed and honed to a whisper. He might have the trigger tied back, or even removed from the gun, firing the weapon by earing back the big hammer and letting it slide from under the web of his thumb—ordinarily you cock a revolver with the second joint of your thumb, not the ball. This was called "thumbing the hammer," and in time gave the big gun another name, the Thumb Buster. It seems slow and clumsy when you first try it, and you are likely to flick the muzzle away off the target. But with practice it becomes a very fast and deadly technique. It gets the shot off with one motion, of the thumb, rather than with two, of thumb and trigger finger. And as an idea of just how fast it can be, some gun fighters in the old West could, and some modern gun experts still can, draw from the belt holster, shoot, and hit what they are shooting at within 10 or 12 yards, in around one-quarter of a second.

This is exhibition shooting, please realize, against time, at a target which is not enthusiastically preparing to shoot back. Which makes a tremendous difference. Notice also that this is close-range work, shooting at something man-size and not more than 30 feet away. For most shooters, the range would probably have to be within 18 to 21 feet, 6 or 7 yards, which is the minimum normal range of the relaxed human eye. For distances shorter than 18 to 21 feet, the eye has to accommodate, and that seems a dividing line.

But let's see what happened when the gun fighter drew. Shooting against time and at an inanimate target, we know he could spill five shots from his gun in somewhere around one second. With a double-action gun he could do better than that, five hits in around four-fifths of a second. But what kind of time he would make shooting at somebody who was shooting back we don't know! So far as I have been able to discover, nobody has ever timed a real gun fight, and all that even the gun fighters themselves can tell you is that when you go for your hardware meaning serious business, then and there you change from peacetime to wartime. And they're not the same at all. Literally, it is like what Von Clausewitz said of war: of a sudden you find yourself operating against a terrific resistance, like a swimmer in molasses, a man trying to run through deep mud. And as Old West gun fights abundantly demonstrated, the barroom flash who was gee whiz and lightning at exhibition shooting all too often was the lad who got himself bopped off by some slow clodhopper who didn't know any better than to take his gun out of his pants and shoot the feller fatally.

The impression one gets from an over-all survey of Western gun fights is that they were a curious and unresolved mixture of two things, perhaps two entirely different kinds of fights, which the eye and the intellect have not yet disentangled. They seem to divide into the close-range fight, with one set of customs, mannerisms, and results, and the long-range contest, with, on the whole, very different mores.

In the short-range fight the battlers mixed it at anywhere from pistol muzzles right against each other, up to a magic 6 or 7 yards—across a card table, or a bar, for example. The prime requisite obviously was speed, and at that distance you didn't need to aim. If you were acquainted with your pistol at all, you pointed instinctively, and the Single Action Army has just about the best grip ever devised for swift straight pointing, even from the hip. You could save a vital split second by firing the instant the gun leveled out of the holster, and you could depend on instinct's doing your aiming for you. You could, that is, within that limiting distance!

Beyond the magic circle, however, an entirely different set of factors began to operate; and here, I think, is where we get our confusion about gun fighters and gun fights. Inside the 7-yard circle time was of the essence; outside, direction and location became more important. I mean specifically that at 10 yards and more you had to be able to aim. And good aiming is an intellectual process, involving, first, locating your target exactly and, second, directing your weapon at it, with due accord for all necessary adjustments and corrections.

Even a casual study of Old Western gun fights reveals an amazing number of flat misses, even by the most expert gun fighters, whenever the fight opened to ranges beyond the 20-foot circle. It seems evident that most of these can be attributed to the gun fighter's vain attempt to substitute speed for accuracy. But in a distance fight it is not the first shot fired that matters, but instead the first bullet that goes home. Again I am trying to say succinctly something I think was implied in the Old West's distinction between gunmen and gun fighters and in its unwritten code requiring the peace officer ordinarily not to shoot first.

If you look at the records you will find that the gunman, which was what the West named the criminal hand with a weapon—the outlaw—was a barroom brawler, a man who preferred to get close and unload, relying on speed. Whereas the gun fighter, which was Western for the legitimate pistoleer, was typically the aloof peace officer, the "lone" Ranger, the "Mysterious Dave" marshal, who did not shoot first, but who would shoot back, and with deadly accuracy.

Thus, and strictly in character, it would be the gunman who sawed inches from the barrel of his weapon, tied back the trigger, altered the grip, lowered the hammer spur, experimented constantly with different holsters— always in search of speed. The gun fighter might, and sometimes did, carry a Buntline Special, a pistol with an extra-long barrel, deliberately sacrificing speed for range and accuracy. The outlaws went in gangs—for each Black Bart, operating solo, there were scores of "gangs" or "bunches"—while against them was one Ranger, one marshal, one sheriff. It is a significant point, and, to me at least, it explains something that puzzled me for a long time: why so many gun fighters seemed to be phlegmatic, even stolid, men, heavy-set, at times almost fat, the very antithesis of what I had instinctively expected. They were not the fast type, and again the lingo of the Old West said exactly that by indirection when it placed the gunman in "fast" or "too fast" company. Confronted by such a ball of fire, the gun fighter simply ignored the relatively harmless fireworks, took his gun out of his pants, and shot the feller. But there were bound to be times when the gunman got the gun fighter "by the short hair"—notice the recognition of relative position in that Old West phrase—and then anything could happen. A hideout pistol overlooked in a hasty search cost Marshal Bill Tilghman his life in Oklahoma, and a wildly fired bullet, clipping a gun-hand thumb by the sheerest of accidents, spelled finis for "Long-haired" Jim Courtright, ex-marshal of Fort Worth. Both close-range affairs, you notice.

There are two good reasons for longer barrels, incidentally, both relating to greater accuracy. First, the longer, heavier barrel does not "jump"— that is, kick back—as much as does the shorter, and, second, it provides for better aim. The short radius between the sights is the real bane of pistol shooting. A .44 or .45 bullet can go as far as 1000 yards, but you must aim high in the air, and for hundreds of yards of trajectory the bullet will be high above any enemy's head. If you were shooting at a horseman you figured to be 300 yards away, while actually he was only about 250, you'd miss him! There'd be only about 100 yards where the bullet would be low enough to get him.

Competing with the Colt Single Action for the Army business in the seventies was Smith & Wesson, originally with a single-action, top-break, .44-caliber revolver first called the .44 Smith & Wesson Army and later (since it didn't last very long as an Army gun) S. & W. American. The Army bought 1000 of these in 1871, and William Cody, the famed Buffalo Bill, liked and carried this model for a time. While he was packing it, he guided the Grand Duke Alexis of Russia on a buffalo-hunting trip, and the Duke was so impressed, so it is said, that presently Russia also ordered a large number of the pistols. The Russian Model S. & W. .44, however, was slightly different from the American .44. It had a sort of hump or knuckle on the top of the grip and a spur below the trigger guard for the second finger. It fired a cartridge with considerably more lead and a little less powder: 23 grains of powder, 246 grains of lead, compared to 25 grains of powder, 205 grains of lead, in the American. Both pistols were popular in the West clear up into the nineties.

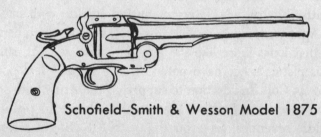

Schofield—Smith & Wesson Model 1875

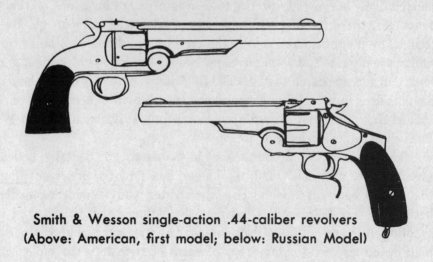

Smith & Wesson single-action .44-caliber revolvers
(Above: American, first model; below: Russian Model)

Not long after the Army had started with the .44's, it switched to .45-caliber Smith & Wessons, adopting what came to be called the Schofield– Smith & Wesson Army Revolver, and continuing to use it, along with the Colt Single Action Army, up to about 1893 or 1894. In the opinion of most shooters it was not as good a revolver as the Colt, and it was never anywhere near as popular. But it was a good weapon nevertheless. Like the Starr Army .44 described in Chapter II, this was a revolver which you could and did "break" or "break open" to reload. The frame about the cylinder was hinged at the lower front corner, and a latch was provided at the upper rear corner. When the hammer was down it locked the frame shut and the revolver could not be opened, in which detail the Schofield was similar to the .45-70 Springfield rifle. But by half-cocking the gun and pulling back on the barrel catch, you could drop the barrel and swing up the cylinder, "breaking open" the pistol, whereupon the ejector, lifting from the middle of the cylinder, would obligingly kick out all the empties, leaving the loaded cartridges just hanging by their noses in their chambers. At least this was the general idea of what ought to happen, and sometimes did.

The barrel latch had been invented by Major George W. Schofield of the Tenth Cavalry, who later committed suicide with one of these pistols at Fort Apache, Arizona, in 1882. Six-shot, with a 7-inch barrel and a clumsy handle that looks more like the grip on a saw or a fat cane than that of a gun, this pistol, as we have noted, fired a slightly less powerful cartridge than the .45 Colt. In addition to supplying the Army with some eight or ten thousand specimens, Smith & Wesson also offered the pistol to the public in the middle seventies, for around $15 to $18. But it never gave any real competition to the Single Action Colt, which you could get then for $15 to $20.

There were also a number of other so-called Army revolvers, not adopted by the services but of the military type and more or less popular in the West. Remington's Improved Army Revolver, Model 1875, put out in .44-40 and .45 calibers, 6-shot, single-action, 7½-inch barrel, walnut grips, and with or without a lanyard ring in the butt, was probably the Single Action's nearest competitor. Remington offered this one in various styles from plain blued steel at around $18 up to pearl handles and fancy gilt engraving, so help me, for about $45! These are catalogue figures; prices were correspondingly higher over the counter in the West. It cost money to bring freight in by wagons, never forget! But even the Remington 1875, with a remnant of the old percussion loading lever still under the barrel, a side ejector rod, and a clumsier handle, was never any real menace to Colt's Single Action. Remington discontinued it in 1889. An improved Model 1890, without the old loading-lever remnant, was made until 1894.

There were still other makes, some of them pretty fair shooting irons. Forehand & Wadsworth, Hopkins & Allen, Marlin, Moore, Merwin & Hulbert, which made a fine five-shot .38 single-action in the mid-seventies, and Whitneyville Armory were some of the makers. Mostly they offered small pistols, .32- and .38-caliber, and so their products did not figure too largely in the West, where large calibers were king, except perhaps for hideout or stingy guns. But they were there.

Then there were the double-action models—"self-cockers," as they were called. "Double action" means that the hammer is cocked, eared back, and tripped by the single continuous pull of the trigger. Even during the Civil War, Remington, Starr, Cooper, Allen & Wheelock, Savage, and others had offered double-actions, usually in Navy .36 or smaller caliber. By the seventies, Remington's fine Double Action percussion Navy had been transformed into Remington's Double and Single Action Belt Revolver, .38 caliber, 6-inch barrel, costing somewhere around $15; and you could buy

SINGLE-ACTION REVOLVERS

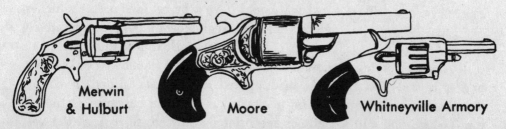

Merwin & Hulburt   Moore   Whitneyville Armory

a spare cylinder for "loose ammunition," meaning cap and ball, for about $3.50 more. This, by the way, was still a rim-fire gun. But the real Western double-action champions, the Colt and the Smith & Wesson, did not come along until the late seventies and eighties. Colt produced the Double Action Army .45, and the similar smaller "Lightning" Model in 1877, while Smith & Wesson's D. A. Navy, using the .44 Russian cartridge, and the slightly heavier D. A. Frontier, using the .44-40 shell, came along about three years later. These later revolvers, with their 6-inch top-ribbed barrels, flat barrel catches, break-open actions, and nicely shaped grips, were about the first to display the characteristic Smith & Wesson look now known and copied the world over.

But the Colt Double Actions were unique in the "rearing-horse" line. The barrel with its side ejector rod and cylinder looked much like the

Billy the Kid

Single Action, but the trigger was set in the middle of the much larger trigger guard, while the "birds-head" or "eagle-bill" grips look much more like something off a derringer or flintlock than they do like the grip of a modern revolver. And when you try them you either like them immensely or consider them terrible.

The .44-caliber Double Action, like the Single Action .44, was called the Frontier. It was also offered presently in .32-20, .38-40, and .41 by Colt, cartridges for the first two also being shells that could be used in a Winchester or Marlin rifle. You could get a barrel anywhere from 4½ to 8½ inches long, or even longer if you wanted to pay about a dollar an inch extra. A Double Action Frontier cost about $20. The "Lightning" models, lighter and differing slightly from the larger gun in the way the grip attaches to the frame, in lacking a lanyard ring and sometimes (especially with shorter barrels) an ejector rod, came in .38 and .41 calibers, and you could have a barrel as short as 2 inches. Here was your real hideout gun, comparatively easy to conceal. It was also a little cheaper.

There are certain undeniable advantages to the double-action revolver and it is said that Billy the Kid packed one in .41 caliber on certain occasions. Maybe he did, being a brash kid. But the one sure picture of him (which you will sometimes see printed reversed, so look at the vest buttons and don't decide he must have been left-handed) shows him packing a single-action, as did nearly all of the old-time gunmen and gun fighters alike.

Here again a very subtle point comes in. When you are betting your life on the immediate outcome, it is—or is it?—plumb amazin' how conservative you discover yourself to be; which is one good reason, of course, why any army is always so slow about adopting astounding new developments. With an expert handling the gun, the first shot can be got off almost as fast from a double-action as from a single-action, and for the rest of the load a good double-action is a split fraction of a second faster. But the gunman, and to an only slightly lesser degree the gun fighter, depended on that first shot. He had been conditioned by hundreds of years' usage of single-shot weapons—remember how they'd even fix the Army repeating carbines and rifles so you could "cut off" the magazine?—and he was very hesitant about hazarding the immediate certainty of the first shot for possible greater speed later. So he took a dim view of all double-action short-barreled weapons—but, lookut, not long-barreled ones. The same cowboy who swore at self-cocker pistols swore by his self-cocking Winchester, while the Army, doubly conservative, considered hand-cocked pistols and rifles both quite the McCoy clear up to the nineties.

"Fanning the hammer"

For very short range there was a two-handed way of using a single-action called "fanning the hammer," which at best is only a shade slower than a double-action. It consists in holding the pistol tightly in one hand, usually the right, and slapping the hammer back with the side of the palm of the other hand. You use both hands in this stunt, notice, and patently you're not going to hit anything requiring the least semblance of aiming. But if you're unloading at somebody inside the magic circle, say only 5 or 6 feet away, it's a lulu.

"Slip hammering" the gun—which means that the hammer spur has been altered and lowered so it will slide easily out from under your thumb and you can shoot without using the trigger—is slightly slower, say a quarter-second more for the full five shots, or thereabouts. But you can at least try to aim with this method. The disadvantage is that you've got the gun bobbing up and down like a walking beam, a good idea if it's percus-

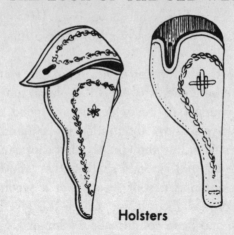

Holsters

sion and the copper caps may be blowing to bits and trying to fall in the works, but a time-waster and a distraction if you've got good metallic cartridges and are trying to concentrate on aiming.

In the matter of packing the revolver the Old West was equally conservative, and for the same reason: you don't experiment unduly with your life. At the end of the Civil War, the Army was carrying its revolvers in a flap-top holster, butt to the front, on the right side of the waistbelt, just about as awkward a fast-draw position as a man could devise. But because the hordes of young men being released from the Blue and Gray armies had become accustomed to packing and handling their short guns this way, in the immediate postwar civilian West they kept right on doing it: one, and sometimes two, revolvers, carried waist high in holsters that presented the butts forward. One drew by turning the back of the hand to the body, grasping the pistol, then corkscrewing it out with a lifting, twisting motion that brought the muzzle sweeping an arc up and across the stomach.

That sort of doing it the hard way didn't last long, however. The clumsy flap tops of the holsters had already been cut away or discarded. Nobody but a soldier, cop, or would-be suicide ever carries his man-hunting pistol in a flap-top case. Following the general lines of the Army holsters, the gun sheaths in this period, the late sixties and early seventies, were for the most part very plain, simply leather cases with belt loops sewed or riveted on the back; some of them with open bottoms from which the muzzle protruded; some closed. Some very fast shooting has been done from this sort of equipment, carried waist high. The next step was to reverse the gun positions in the holsters, so that the butts were to the rear.

Just who was the first fast-draw champion nobody really knows, but Eugene Cunningham's nomination of William P. Longley for the dubious honor I think will stand until a better comes along. Swift William was a Texan who flourished from 1865 to 1877, when he was hanged—for the second time, incidentally; the first time didn't take. He is usually credited with eighteen to twenty-six killings, depending upon who is doing the telling. But he was just a boy during the war, so maybe Wild Bill Hickok; Ben Thompson, the onetime marshal of Austin, Texas; maybe Jesse or Frank James; maybe William Clarke Quantrill, the guerrilla; maybe some man altogether unknown should be awarded the championship gun belt. All of these latter worthies were operating during the war. Or maybe it should go to that grimmest Tejano of all, John Wesley Hardin, two years Bill Longley's junior. Longley was born in 1851 and Hardin in 1853.

Legend gives John Wesley Hardin forty to forty-three killings, of which about thirty seem to be verifiable, and at least six or seven genuine quick-draw shootouts against men who were qualified to stand up and buck the tiger. This contrasts pretty strongly with the record of that far more publicized pistoleer, William H. Bonney, Billy the Kid. Of Billy's twenty-one notches, Cunningham considers only one to be a real contest, the rest pretty much bushwhacking sure things; and old-timers I can remember in New Mexico and Texas pretty much agreed. Ben Thompson is usually given about six to nine victims, "that many white men, anyhow"; Marshal Bat Masterson of Dodge City about four, Wyatt Earp, five; and the Lord knows how many for the legendary figures like Wild Bill Hickok or Buffalo Bill Cody. But these last you can probably divide by ten.

Most of these practitioners of the deadly art seem to have been proficient from all three of the standard positions which finally came to be accepted for carrying one's shooting irons. But the earliest position, almost beyond doubt, was with the holster carried waist high, on a plain belt, since this was the Army practice with the percussion revolvers. The next step, simple enough, was to loosen the belt, so that the pistol butt sagged closer to the hanging hand; and the weight of belt and weapon, incidentally, was supported more by the hipbone than by one's softer middle. It was also easier to tie down the bottom of the holster in this new stance, so that the gun could be unshucked the quicker. Finally the cautiously experimenting pistoleer began trying different positions on his anatomy for his artillery: under his armpit in a "shoulder holster"—which to begin with was only a belt holster strapped up there—or in his pockets, often leather-lined, either hip or front; or hanging from some kind of belt swivel; or tucked variously into the waistband of his pants, the bosom of his shirt or vest, or even in his boot top. Obliging cobblers and leather workers speedily provided the accessories for any and all of these variations.

The first gun belts, as we have noted, were plain, usually 2 inches (the Army width) to 3 inches wide, and with a plain tongue buckle. But belts with loops for cartridges also came in very early. The Army had them in heavy duck or canvas—so-called "Prairie" belts—for the .50-70 cartridges in use in 1870. These belts were 3 inches wide and had a plain bar buckle and short leather tongue (no brass belt plate, that is), an inner stiffening to keep the fairly flimsy material straight, and loops for fifty cartridges. The civilian gun belts, of course, were leather.

Introduced quite early was the so-called Mexican loop holster, in which the leather at the top and back of the holster is not cut off, but instead folded over and down, to provide a belt loop and a skirt beneath the body proper of the holster. The barrel part of the scabbard was usually just thrust through double slits in the skirt to hold the holster together,

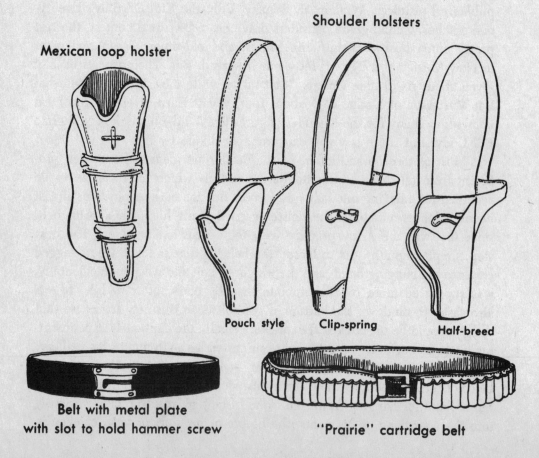

Mexican loop holster

Shoulder holsters

Pouch style

Clip-spring

Half-breed

Belt with metal plate
with slot to hold hammer screw

"Prairie" cartridge belt

although sometimes sewed loops were used. The simplicity and practicability of this idea are obvious, providing as it does a wide secure loop for the belt and a minimum of raw edges and sewing, or thonging. Where the edges had to be fastened together they were sometimes sewed with heavy thread, sometimes with a leather thong. You could make one of these holsters for yourself, with nothing but a knife, a nail, and a cowhide.

Sometimes the leather around the trigger guard was cut away; sometimes the edge was left straight. With a single-action, cocking the gun with your thumb as it comes out of the holster—maybe firing it too—the trigger is not so important right off. With a double-action, however, you want to get a finger on the trigger fast, so double-action holsters usually had the trigger exposed.

The set of the holster on the belt is also important. For the quick draw from the belt holster, experience soon demonstrated that the belt loop had better carry holster and gun at a slight angle, usually with the butt canted just a little to the front. So that when you slapped hardware, pulled your gun on somebody, you did just that literally, swinging your hand up and forward, cocking the weapon before the barrel cleared leather, and then swinging the muzzle forward and firing as it came level. This was the old gun-fighting technique.

Once again, notice, it makes a difference whether you're shooting at something or somebody close up, where you can depend on instinctive pointing, or outside the magic circle, where you'd darn sure better aim. In the former case shooting from the hip would probably get the job done and certainly be faster, while in the other the gun came out to eye level or thereabouts, then let loose. It could call for a neat bit of judgment.

For the "cross draw" you wore your gun, or guns, butt to the front, on the opposite side from the hand you intended using. Thus, if you were packing two guns, your right hand plucked the weapon on your left hip, while your left was drawing the gun on your right, your forearms crossing in the process. Notice that this was different from the way the Army used its left-hand holster, where by a double-jointed contortion you were supposed to extract a butt-front gun with your right hand from your right side.

Understandably, cross-draw harness usually carried the guns higher than the straight-draw outfit, and this was probably one reason the cross draw was preferred by some Northern gun fighters, while the drag-her-straight-out-and-shoot setup seemed to fit Southerners better. Down South you scarcely needed a coat a lot of the time, but up North you did. It's easier to dig under a coat to the left for a gun than it is to paw up a coat skirt on the right; and, if you hadn't thought of it, when it's really cold you have to keep that gun under cover and warm. If you don't, the oil thickens and it may freeze up on you.

There were also ordinances and objections against packing six-shooters in Western towns very early in the game, which was another reason for elevating your equalizers out of sight and, you hoped, out of officers' minds. They might spot your gun belt, of course. So there were other ways, too. You could just take off your belt and holster and stick your pistol down in the waistband of your pants, as Ben Thompson and Wild Bill Hickok usually did, or keep it in your hip pocket. Dallas Stoudenmire, dignified and deadly marshal of El Paso back when The Pass was really rugged, was said to have had his pockets lined for just such use. An early development was a holster to fit in the pocket, one with a belt loop and a large squared stiff skirt to hold the weapon just right for swift dragging. Another was a holster which hung inside your pants, held up by a ring which you looped over a suspender button.

But the Colt itself had one convenient piece that could come in right handy when you wanted to hideout the gun. Being heavy, a Colt Single Action is liable to slide right on through and descend into the lower depths if you just stick it in your waistband and trust. But the loading gate on the right side of the frame makes a perfectly dandy belt hook. You just flick the gate open and let it hang on your belt or waistband top.

If you didn't have any safe place to leave your belt and holster, as often happened when trail-driving cowboys came to strange towns, you could sling them over your shoulder, under your coat. Put the belt over your right shoulder and notch it up tight, so the holstered gun hangs right under your left armpit, and you have the original shoulder holster.

Bad Boy Ben Thompson is sometimes credited with inventing the shoulder holster, but I doubt it, because fighting men were already carrying firearms, even pistols, slung over their shoulders long before Big Ben came booming into fame. True, they were intended to be used as carbines when so fitted, but even Colonel Colt's Model 1848 Dragoons had come equipped with a detachable shoulder stock, which in turn carried a carbine sling ring. Considering what three or four pounds of six-gun and shells will do to your hipbone while you're pounding along in a saddle, I'll bet the idea of shoulder-slinging the pistol came easy.

Your belt holster probably would have a tie-down string or strap in the toe, which you could hitch to your belt and so improve the hang of the weapon under your arm. But next you'd probably design, as the pioneer pistoleers did, a regular shoulder holster, with a loop that went straight up over your shoulder, instead of slanting across your chest, and another breast strap, lower down, to hold the holster solidly in place. Then you'd have the original shoulder holster, pouch style, as it is called, which is still worn, still widely used.

The big trouble with this kind of shoulder harness is that it's likely to hang up your gun if you don't make your draw at exactly the right angle, neither too straight up so you tangle with your own armpit, nor too straight out so the gun binds in the pouch. A whole lot of good men, as well as bad ones, have got killed because of this. So the next step was to open the side of the holster, so you could yank the gun straight out. A clip spring, curving around the cylinder of the revolver, was generally added to hold the weapon in place. If you cut away all the front leather of the holster, just leaving the back and maybe the tip of the toe to hold the muzzle, you had the regular clip-spring shoulder holster. If you left the front leather or most of it, just adding the clip spring and keeping the seam open, you had a half-breed shoulder holster. A leather flap folding loosely over the hammer was sometimes provided to keep the hammer spur from tangling in the shirt, and to help keep sweat from reaching and rusting the gun. This is not only the most convenient way to pack a weapon; it is just about the best way to keep it hidden but available pronto. So, from the Old West to modern gangsters, yes, and peace officers and even Army aviators, you find plenty of shoulder holsters.

Some of the Texas Rangers, and, following their style, other officers too, liked to have a metal plate with a slot in it fitted to their belts. Into this slot they slipped the stud head of a special extra-long hammer screw with which they replaced the regular screw in their Colts. The stud stuck out on the left side, above and just back of the trigger guard, and when it was inserted into the horizontal belt-plate slot the gun swung, muzzle down. There wasn't any holster. You could flip the gun free of the plate and shoot, or, if time pressed, just swivel the muzzle up and let fly without ever unhooking. But it does seem an awfully casual way to carry a weapon.

Swivel holsters, with a sort of universal joint between belt loop and pouch, so the wearer could just flip the pistol level and shoot through the open toe without ever unleathering, were another novelty. So was the Wes Hardin vest, or holster vest, supposedly invented by the outlaw, with the guns in pockets on each side, butts pointing in and the guns nestling against the short ribs. And still another famed gun fighter carried his stub-barreled Colts in his front pants pockets, from whence he was as swift as any in extracting them. But the shoulder holster and the belt holster, set for either straight or cross draw, were by far the preferred styles.

Now for the little tricks of the trade. Naturally when a man might need his six-shooter any minute, and need it bad, he wouldn't have any flap, safety strap, tie string, or whatever holding the gun in the holster. But you did need some way to keep the revolver *in* the belt holster, especially when you were riding a rough one. This was accomplished, or at least tried, by molding the holster leather as closely to the gun as possible, while still allowing smooth, fast extraction. Using the actual gun model that was to be carried in the holster, or an exact form, the holster makers would soak and shape the leather over it, fitting it as carefully as a fine glove might be fitted to a hand. The "box fit," just right to keep the gun in, not too tight to slow the draw one iota, was the ideal for gun scabbards.

The inside of the holster might be greased, oiled, or tallowed to smooth the draw, and a small wad of paper or knotted bit of whang leather in the bottom of the holster was thought to help. Sometimes the large front sights would be replaced by smaller round beads, to avoid any chance of their hanging up the draw and the fireworks. The bottom of the holster would be tied or strapped to the leg, particularly if one carried his artillery swung low.

The average cowboy was no gun fighter, and, often as not, packed his six-gun just any way, cleaned it maybe once a season, and left it, more often than not, in the bunkhouse or chuck wagon. But the gunman or gun fighter practiced daily, with all the painstaking care of a concert pianist, and out of this practice came a number of stunts that you hear about but which I doubt ever played any serious part in real gun fights. The principal tricks were the "roll"; the "road-agent's spin" or "border roll," which is the reverse of the regular roll and may possibly have figured in a real incident or two; and the "border shift," which again may possibly have seen serious use somewhere. To these we might add fanning, which we have already discussed, and which probably did see service in barroom brawls more than once.

The road-agent's spin is a trick supposed to be hot stuff when somebody gets the drop on you and demands that you hand over your pistol. To make the trick work, the aforesaid somebody needs to be a congenital idiot. He lets you draw your revolver, turn it upside down and seemingly start to hand it to him, butt up and pointing toward him, barrel down and pointing toward you. But you, you clever boy, have your forefinger hooked in the trigger guard. Just as the sucker reaches, you flip the gun, so that the butt spins over and smacks into your hand. Then you shoot the guy. And if he'll let you get away with this he deserves it.

John Wesley Hardin, in his autobiography, says he pulled this trick on Wild Bill Hickok in 1871, when Hickok was marshal of Abilene, Kansas,

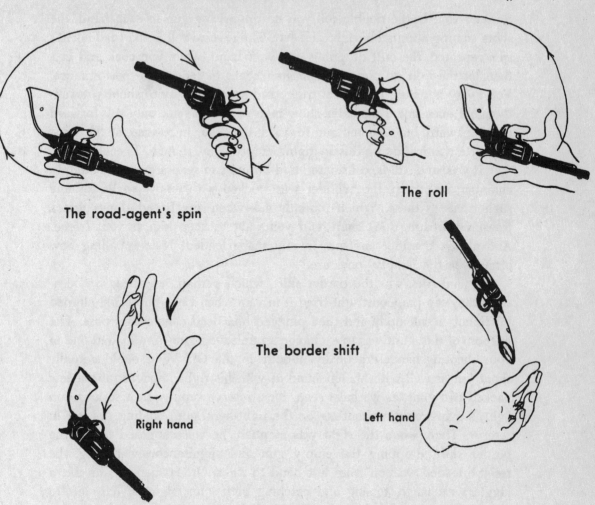

The road-agent's spin

The roll

The border shift

Right hand

Left hand

and possibly he did. Hardin, by the way, does not name the trick; he simply says that he "reversed" his guns. The name seems to have come considerably later, as many Western details did.

The proper way to disarm an opponent, of course, was either to make him unbuckle his belt with his left hand, and let his hardware drop, or extract his fangs yourself, from behind, while he held up sky.

The roll proper is purely an exhibition trick, and I can remember the itinerant-medicine-show "doctors" performing it for our edification when I was a youngster growing up in the Old Chickasaw Nation, Indian Territory. In this, the reverse of the spin, you roll the gun forward, the butt coming up, the barrel dropping, and as you do, you cock the hammer by letting the spur slide under your thumb. Then, if this isn't a dry run, you fire, either at a target, or, more often, just into the ground 6 or 8 feet in front of you. In the double roll you do this with a gun in each hand, the shots coming alternately right and left. The reverse roll is the road-agent's spin repeated, the butt dropping into your hand, when you cock and fire, then let the butt go down and around again to repeat the performance. Very, very hot stuff, and a real tricky and extra-fine way to shoot yourself; though I once saw a medicine-show man who could not only roll forward and backward, but also one gun forward, the other in reverse, at the same time. He was just doing this snapping empty guns, though, I recall.

It was, and still is, considered bad business to snap a gun on an empty chamber, so usually the cylinder was stocked with empty shells for any such tricks as these. Which reminds me—when any friend shows you a treasured firearm, don't snap it, if you want to keep him as your friend. And always consider any gun in any shape loaded! It is appalling how often even the "empty" ones are.

A final trick was the border shift, which perhaps was tried on occasion—they say Jim Courtright tried it in vain when Luke Short first clipped his thumb accidentally and then plugged him dead center a-purpose. The purpose of this stunt was to exchange an unloaded gun for a loaded one in your shooting hand. Practically nobody in the Old West could actually shoot just as well with his left hand as with his right, though quite a few packed two guns, as we have seen, for a reserve supply. In a serious gun fight, a man would concentrate on the right-hand gun, holding the left in reserve. Then, when the right was emptied, he was supposed to try the border shift, dropping the empty gun and simultaneously tossing the reserve loaded weapon from left hand to right. Or, fancier yet, he did a juggler's exchange, tossing and catching both guns, right to left, left to right. I have seen this done, but I don't believe anybody ever tried it in a real serious gun fight. What were you supposed to do with the empty gun after you caught it?

Those are about all the standard tricks, though there were others galore. "Can rolling," for example, was the delight of happy-go-lucky cowboys in town on the loose. You found an empty tin can and kept it rolling by hitting it, or, better yet, hitting just under it so it would jump crazy, until your cartridges, your can, and your enthusiasm were exhausted. Or you might take a half-brick, throw it underhand straight away from you, draw, break the brick, and break at least two more pieces before they hit the ground. That was considered to be pretty fair country shooting.

The famous Ed McGivern, pistol expert of Lewistown, Montana, could hit a tin can tossed in the air five times in around one second. And I know of one FBI man who is credited with walking into a hotel room,

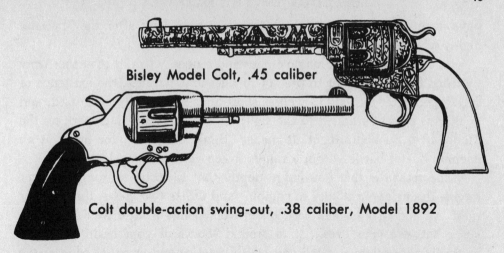

Bisley Model Colt, .45 caliber

Colt double-action swing-out, .38 caliber, Model 1892

right into the muzzle of a leveled revolver, with the badly wanted gent behind it all set to shoot. The FBI expert drew and shot him, very effectively, before the bad gent could think to pull the trigger. I don't know how long it took. But that's shooting, on anybody's clock.

Now for a few that don't really qualify as Old West guns but ought to be mentioned. The Bisley Model Colt, the single-action with the long, more smoothly curving grip, flatter hammer, and larger trigger guard, didn't come along until 1896 and production was discontinued in 1912. This was the real "hogleg" Colt, though the nickname has since spread to just any old single-action. Colt also produced one lot of Double Action Army .45's with very large trigger guards and triggers, intended for use with gloved hands in Alaska. But just about this time, 1902, there was trouble in the Philippines, and the big .45's were sent out there, so this model is called either the Alaskan or the Philippine Colt.

Double-action revolvers with solid frames and swing-out cylinders, the form we generally visualize when we think of a revolver today, began to appear in 1889 with the so-called New Navy models, in .38 caliber. In 1892 the Army decided to abandon the old Single Action Colt in favor of the new faster-loading actions, and adopted both Colt and Smith & Wesson double-action swing-out .38's instead. They looked much alike, except that the Colt has a square butt and the S. & W. a rounded one. But they weren't very powerful and the cylinders rotated the wrong way, to the left, so that, particularly in the Colt, the hand or pawl sometimes pushed the cylinder just a little too far, failing to line up the chamber with the barrel. Then, when you fired, part of the bullet went through the barrel, part didn't. This trouble was soon corrected, but the conservative Old Westerner would have none of the swing-out double-actions, even long after they became highly reliable guns.

As a final note about magic circles and ranges, when in 1873 the Army switched from .50-caliber to the .45-70 rifles and carbines, the existence of such a perimeter for long as well as short guns was tacitly recognized, and a "B" was presently added to the sight scales at the 260-yard mark on the Model 1879 Buckhorn sight. It means "Battle Sight . . . for firing at an enemy's line of battle within a range of 400 yards, aiming low."

The reason is that you judge depth—that is, distance, range to your target—through your ability to combine and utilize two views, that of your right eye and that of your left, taken from points a little way apart, the space between your eyes. Up to around 480 yards your brain will automatically triangulate and tell you (with practice and error, of course) the distance. But over 480 yards it won't, no matter what range your high-powered rifle has. Modern telescopic range finders extend the stereoscopic depth in which one can estimate the range. But there were no range finders on the frontier.

Prairie schooner

VI

TO GET FROM HERE TO THERE

NOWADAYS our picture of the Old West in motion is of horsemen; of pioneers riding in covered wagons, or on quaint-looking trains, or even on glamorous steamboats. While there were all such, and we look at them later, it's amazing, when you dig into the records, to discover just how many walked—walked all the way to Oregon, or California, or wherever, and maybe pushed a handcart to boot! Hitching and hiking, it would appear, were two separate operations in the West. You hitched up the team to the wagon, yes. But you didn't ride in the wagon to drive the horses; instead you hiked, shank's mare, right alongside.

It wasn't always that bad, of course. When your feet absolutely wore out you could catch a ride on one of the team horses, maybe, or on the "lazy board," a stout oak plank that pulled out from the left side of the huge Conestoga freight wagon.

Most modern Americans have never seen a Conestoga except in the movies. But every day of our lives we commemorate the big wagons, just the same. Because it was the Conestogas and the weary feet of their drivers that really laid down the first rule of the road in America: *Keep to the right.* In other countries, as you probably know, the rule varies. British traffic keeps to the left, with the driver on the right, so that he can use his whip freely. That was the reason for placing the driver of horse-drawn vehicles, stage-coaches, phaetons, and the like in the right-hand seat, and we Americans also followed the custom with most of our horse-powered outfits and early automobiles. But in ancient Rome the other way, left-hand driving, was the custom. In the Italian countryside the driver rode on the right and traffic passed to the left and in the city the postilion rode the left wheel horse and traffic passed to the right. In America, a similar confusion developed. Even by the last half of the nineteenth century, no set rules had emerged, and traffic in American cities, to say nothing of that on Western trails, was more a whoop and a snarl than anything else. But if you are going to ride one horse of a team occasionally, as the freight-wagon drivers did, you'll choose the left-side horse because he's the one you can conveniently get on and off, mounting and dismounting, as you must, from the near side of the horse. And you'll also guide right and pass right so you can watch clearance.

In the period from 1865 to 1900 the Conestoga wagon was vanishing from the American scene, because it was too big and bulky for the rough West. But from the early 1700s to the late 1850s the big wagons had carried most of both goods and immigrants heading West. There were still plenty of them operating in the sixties, and they were a brave sight to behold.

The Conestoga had originated in Lancaster County, Pennsylvania, in the very early 1700s, and Lancaster County was the center of the Conestoga-building industry until the very end. Typically, the huge vehicle was 26 feet long, 11 feet high, weighed, empty, from 3000 to 3500 pounds, and required the work of four men for about two months to build.

The bed was boat-shaped, the center sagging, the ends arched upward, like a gondola, so that the load would tend to shift toward the center, if it shifted en route, and not awkwardly against the endgates. The bed was usually about 16 feet long, 4 feet wide, and 4 deep, with sturdy white-oak lumber for the frame and poplar for the sideboards. Flooring and sides were nearly an inch thick. The endgates were hinged at the bottom, so they could be dropped for loading, and held in place by heavy chains.

Curving atop the big bed, some six to sixteen wagon bows held up the wagon cover, of white canvas or homespun, puckered with a draw rope to close the ends, and laced down to the wagon sides. Since the Conestoga was boat-shaped, the front and rear bows slanted outward sharply and the wagon cover was much longer than the running gear.

Underneath, the big vehicle was equally sturdy. Heavily ironed and

Conestoga wagon

braced, its bolsters and axles were of hickory, the hubs of black or sour gum, almost impossible to split, and the rims of the wheels anywhere from 2 to 10 inches. A 4-inch rim was the usual size, with the front wheels ordinarily 3 feet, 6 inches, in diameter, the rear ones 4 feet, 8 inches. Heavy iron tires, ½ inch thick, usually made of two pieces of iron welded at the joints, encircled the felloes (the fello is the wood rim part of a wagon wheel), and the art of making these tires, just big enough to set on when expanded by heat, neither too tight nor too loose when the cold-water bath shrank them to set, was a very neat bit of blacksmithing skill.

Like all good wagon wheels, these also "dished" outward slightly. That is, the wheel was like a very shallow bowl, thanks to some more precise work, this time by the wheelwright. The wheels were held on the axles by linchpins, resembling big cotter pins, or sometimes by nuts. When it left the wagon works, the Conestoga was always brilliantly painted, with bright red running gear and a Prussian-blue body. The great snowy cover completed the national colors.

Ordinarily there would be a tool box ironed to the left side of the wagon, back of the lazy board, which pulled out in front of the left rear wheel. Here you'd carry the usual gear of a frontier freighter, a hatchet or

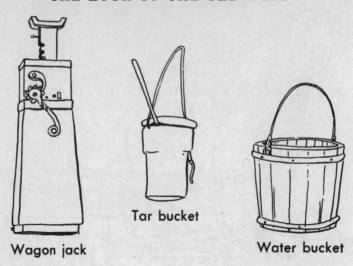

Wagon jack   Tar bucket   Water bucket

ax and some nails, an auger, some rope, perhaps a few extra linchpins, kingbolts, and strap iron. The wagon jack might be here, but since it was big and clumsy, its usual place would be hanging from the rear axle, alongside the tar bucket with the pine tar or other lubricant for the axles. These jacks were customarily made by the same smith who had "ironed" the wagon and might carry his name, or initials, or the name of the wagon owner, and might even be ornately decorated, Pennsylvania-Dutch style. They worked with a lever handle, much like an old-fashioned pump. And they had to be pretty sturdy, able to lift 3 or 4 tons. They were used when greasing the wheels.

Typically, three teams (that is, six horses) were used with these wagons. The front team was called the lead team, the middle one the swing team, and the rear one the wheel team.

A hundred years ago, the horses would have been Conestoga horses. The breed is now extinct, or virtually so, but it had a proud lineage. It traced back to the Flemish stallions that once had carried armored knights. According to some accounts, William Penn himself sent the first stallions to Pennsylvania to be bred to Virginia mares and so produce this New World horse. The big horses weighed 1800 pounds or more, averaged 16 hands high, and could lug that behemoth of a wagon 12 to 18 miles a day. Which is lots of horse and lots of horsepower.

They worked in a heavy but very simple freighting harness, a stout leather collar with iron hames (these are two curved pieces which fit over the leather collar and carry the tugs, or loops to which the traces are attached); a girth around the body just behind the front legs; a back strap,

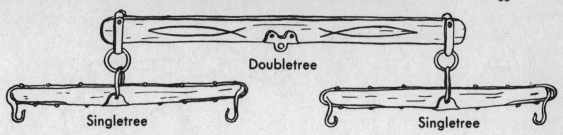

Doubletree

Singletree Singletree

running from the collar along the top of the back to the crupper (the piece that went back to encircle the tail); plus some more straps called breeching, which came down over the haunches to support the traces. These traces were the tow straps, or usually chains in the Conestoga harness, coming horizontally from the tugs on the hames around the collar through loops on the bellyband or girth and through more supporting loops in the breeching to attach to the ends of a singletree, which, in turn, attached at its middle to the end of a doubletree. Thus the power of two horses, each pulling at the end of the stout doubletree, was combined and applied at a single point to the wagon. The idea of all this was to equalize the pulling power of the teamed horses.

A typical Conestoga bridle carried blinders, pieces of leather sewed to the cheekstraps beside each eye, so that the horse could not see back, or very much to the side, but only ahead. The bit was usually a plain bar, or perhaps a snaffle (the difference is that the snaffle is jointed in the middle), with the long driving reins directly attached and leading back through supporting loops on the collar. In the case of the lead team the reins also were supported by loops on the swing-team harness.

The wheel team had backing straps attached to their harness, heavy wide horizontal pieces across their buttocks, against which they could throw their weight to help slow or stop the wagon. The hames on their collars supported pole straps, or chains, to hold up the front of the wagon tongue, a heavy pole which extended between them, from the front of the wagon up to about even with their noses. Since only this team could exert power to back or brake the wagon, these usually were the sturdiest horses in the outfit.

The doubletree of the wheel team connected by a swinging pivot, the doubletree hammer, to a framework just in front of the front axle. This axle, in turn, was pivoted to the wagon. The wagon tongue was rigidly attached to the axle; that is, as far as any horizontal play was concerned. So, by turning the wheel team, the driver could turn the wagon tongue,

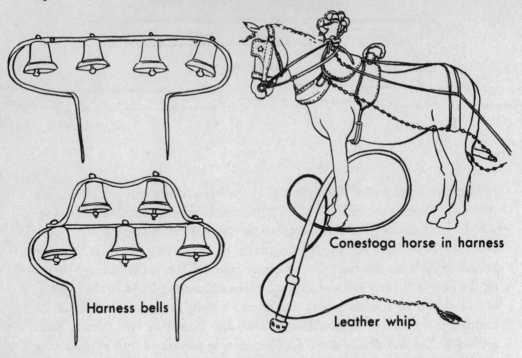

Conestoga horse in harness

Harness bells

Leather whip

which, in turn, steered the front wheels and so the wagon. It was simple, though it sounds complicated in description.

The doubletree of the swing team was fastened to the end of the wagon tongue, and from it also a chain went forward to catch the doubletree of the lead team. Additional teams could be added in front, if necessary, simply by extending the chain. In going around a turn, however, the horses would have to step over this chain and back again as the going straightened out, and sometimes there was trouble.

Fastened above the collars of at least one pair of horses would be a small set of wagon bells, of brass or iron, five or six of them in a metal or wooden frame. These jingled merrily as the horses plodded along. This is where the expression "I'll be there with bells on" originated. If the Conestoga freighter got stuck and had to have help, by road custom he forfeited his bells. But in the West, with the constant threat of Indians, you usually did not advertise your presence unnecessarily, with bells or anything else.

The six big horses would cost at least $1000, probably more. You would make anywhere from 6 to 20 miles a day, depending on load, terrain, and weather. Oxen could pull a Conestoga, of course, in which case you had a bull train, cheaper but also slower than horses. Or you could use mules. It would take about ten mules to do what six big Conestoga horses could accomplish.

Each wagon had a heavy brake, a crossbeam just in front of the rear wheels, under the wagon, with an 8-inch block of hickory on each end as a shoe. Sticking up on the left side of the wagon was a long brake lever, usually with a rope attached to the top. By pulling this lever the driver could press the brake shoes against the iron tires on the rear wheels. If the slope was so steep that brakes were not enough, he would "deadlock" the wheels by running his chains around the rims, from one wheel to the other.

These were the typical Northern freighting monsters. Now let's go South and see what they used down there. In the Southwestern country, they'd had even greater behemoths than the Conestogas, believe it or not. They'd started with the Mexican oxcart, a dainty little dish with wheels 7 feet high, 20 inches thick, and 7 feet apart!

This traditional freight vehicle of Mexico was technically a cart, with only two wheels. But what wheels! They were made solid, from three pieces of wood. The middle piece was 7 feet long, 3 feet wide, and 20 inches thick at the hub, tapering to 10 inches at the rim. Attached to each side of this centerpiece were the side pieces, cut in semicircles and held to the centerpiece by long wooden pins, big ones, at least 3 by 5 inches in cross section, passing through holes bored clear through the three sections, rim to rim.

The hub, or nave, was a huge sloping hole, at least 6 inches in diameter on the outer side and 8 inches or more on the inner side next the body. Through this went the axle—there were no such technical niceties as skeins, wheelboxes, and such, of course—the spindle-shaped ends providing at least an inch of tolerance. That is, a 7-to-5-inch spindle in that 8-to-6-inch hub hole: real close-fitting! The wheel was held on by a heavy wooden

Mexican oxcart

linchpin thrust through a hole bored in the end of the axle. Later this pin was sometimes made of iron. The axle itself, of stout live oak or pecan wood, would be at least 8 inches thick, and long enough so that when the wheels were put on they would stand 7 feet apart.

On this tremendous running gear was placed a heavy wooden bed, averaging 6 feet wide and 15 feet long. It was fastened to the axle with wooden pins and rawhide thongs. You could build yourself one of these *carretas* with only the tools of the farthest frontier; you didn't have to have any ironwork at all—bolts, nails, straps, pins, or whatever!

Before you put the bed on, you attached the tongue, another huge timber that fastened directly to the center of the axle, extending on back to the end of the bed, and projecing some 12 feet in front of it. This, too, was secured with wooden pins and rawhide.

For the bed itself you provided a heavy floor and then sideboards to suit your fancy. Sometimes they were solid boards, sometimes just rails and stakes. The big cart, however, was usually covered with a thatched straw roof, so help me, held up by wooden standards set in the sides of the frame. The original house trailer! Forward, the long tongue kept the vehicle from tipping over, while in the rear a stout leg hinged to the bottom edge of the bed dragged on the ground and prevented—well, usually prevented— a backward flip. The cart could carry 2½ tons or more of freight, though its two-wheeled underpinning did require a very neat balancing of the load. It was ordinarily drawn by five or six yoke of oxen, that is, ten or twelve animals.

The oxen were harnessed to the cart with huge wooden ox yokes, a curved beam set on the animals' necks, just behind the horns, and usually lashed to the horns with a broad rawhide strap about twelve feet long. Curved wooden ox bows sometimes were added, which went down around

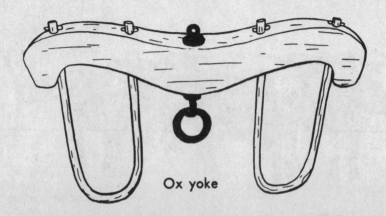

Ox yoke

the oxen's necks and attached to the yoke simply by being poked through holes. The yoke of the first pair of oxen was attached by a loop or hole directly to the front end of the tongue, while the additional yokes, on up front, were connected to the same point via rawhide ropes. Typically the driver walked. These carretas were very, very slow, of course. And they had one other unfortunate feature: they were noisy.

The gigantic wheels and poorly fitted spindles were never really lubricated. Why trouble, when oxen were so cheap and you could always hitch on a few more? So the great wheels wore, wobbled, wavered, and screeched to the highest heaven and you could hear them for miles. When they got too hot the carter would maybe stick a prickly pear in, to wet the wood and perhaps lessen the noise a leetle, señor. These huge juggernauts were common in Mexico and the Southwest until at least the seventies.

A somewhat smaller version, the Chihuahua cart, carrying about half the load and requiring only three yoke of oxen, was also popular for freighting, especially on the more rugged routes. These were often seen in the plazas of old San Antonio, El Paso, or Santa Fe during the sixties, seventies, and even later. Sometime in the seventies better wheels, in diameter about 4 feet, started rolling in, with iron used for boxes and tires, and spokes, instead of solid disks. These were made in both Mexico and New England for the Southwestern trade. A. Staacke of San Antonio was perhaps the first importer of these better cartwheels, and Staacke also is credited with introducing the prairie schooner for freighting in the Southwest and northern Mexico.

The prairie schooners, developed from the Conestoga, were smaller but still too heavy and clumsy for mountain work or badly broken country. They had a bed 14 feet long, 4½ feet wide, with sides 5½ feet high. The hind wheels were 5 feet, 10 inches, the front ones a foot less in diameter.

Solid iron axles carried spindles 3 inches in diameter, and the rest of the running gear was in massive proportion. The prairie schooners weighed 4000 pounds and could carry up to 7000 pounds of freight—for example, sixteen bales of cotton in one load. On the sides of the heavy, usually doubled wagon covers the owner's name was customarily painted, or the wagon's number when the vehicles were in a train, as ordinarily they were. They were drawn by mules, rather than oxen, at least in Southwestern usage, 8 to 10 mules to the wagon. Like the Conestoga, the prairie schooner usually had a blue body and red wheels.

On these Western wagons the driver ordinarily rode on a wagon-box seat which clipped over the top edges of the wagon bed, near the front. Quite often this seat had elliptic springs under each end, so that the jolting of the wagon would be at least partially softened for the driver. Sometimes these seats were quite elaborate, carved and cushioned according to the fancy of the owner, who, after all, spent quite a bit of his life there. They were of course detachable, set just far enough back to place the driver's feet comfortably on the footboard, angling out above the headboard, the front endgate of the wagon.

The prairie schooner was usually driven from the right-hand side, and projecting up on that side was a heavy iron brake lever, working in a ratchet frame. This lever manipulated a brake beam, set laterally underneath the bed just in front of the rear wheels and equipped at each end with a heavy rub block, a shoe which pressed against the tire of the wheel when the brakes were applied. The driver could lock the brake in the ratchet frame and leave it locked, which was one way of tying down a possibly restless team when he wanted to leave the wagon.

As in the Conestoga, he also carried chains with which to deadlock the wheels when necessary. On steep slopes he might drag a log, or a whole tree, behind, as further braking. This was called a "Mormon brake." To prevent the vehicle's pitching over sideways on steep slopes, ropes were fastened to the axles when required, passed over the top of the load, and held by men walking on the upper slope.

The prairie schooner was decidedly top-heavy, clumsy, and hard to handle in anything like broken country. But it was widely used. Mexican-made versions of this wagon had no sideboards, just stakes, with a rail or two to hold the load, and their enormous wheels had tires 6 inches wide and an inch thick. These, typically, would be drawn by fourteen mules, working four abreast, except for the pair on the wagon tongue. Such a wagon could carry 10,000 pounds, even over the terrible Mexican roads.

In contrast, the U. S. Army's freight wagons could carry around 3000 pounds and used six mules, sometimes fewer. But these lighter, smaller wagons were far more roadworthy and maneuverable. An Army train might be of almost any size, but the average professional civilian freighter's train would be from ten to twenty wagons—enough men and animals, that is, to provide reasonable security, but not so many as to make the unit unwieldy.

In the more northern areas forage was not generally a problem, but in the dry Southwest quite often it was; and to find grass for 140 to 150 mules was bad enough, without making the number 400 or 500. A typical South-western wagon train, with a dozen wagons, would carry a crew of twenty-three or twenty-four men, ten mules to each wagon and perhaps twenty to twenty-five extra animals, just in case. Even so, that's about 150 animals. And it must be remembered that to keep a horse or mule in good marching order you need to feed him about three times a day; and it takes him about an hour to fill his belly, even with fair to good grazing. Trains usually carried grain for their animals, feeding the mules in long canvas troughs so that there would be no waste. But even so, grass usually had to be the mainstay. And grass sometimes was right hard to come by.

The train ordinarily would be divided into sections, with a *caporal* (or a captain up North) as train boss, and a *capitan* (a lieutenant up North) for each section. Typically a train would move at about 2 to 2½ miles an hour over fair going; much slower, of course, in mud, broken ground, or heavy sand. A bull train would average perhaps 12 miles a day; a mule train 15 to 20. Usually, and especially in the Southwest, the train would move only in the mornings and late afternoons, "nooning" during the heat of the day. At daybreak the oxen would be yoked up or the mules hitched and the train would travel until about 10 o'clock. Then it would swing into corral, the stock would be watered, if possible, then fed. You always watered first, before feeding. And you had to water sometime during those first three or four hours' march if you expected to keep your motive power happy. But once you were nooning, with the stock grazing, the *cocinero* (cook) would whomp up a meal for the men—sowbelly, beans, shortcake, and coffee, most likely—and the siesta would stretch out until two or three o'clock, when you'd hitch up again and start the second drive of the day. This would last until about sundown or until you arrived at your selected camping place, where there was water if it was at all possible, and go into corral again.

You always corralled when you stopped, to provide a convenient stock pen, even if Indians weren't expected. There were various ways of doing this. In the Southwest the wagon trains corralled by sections. At the wagon boss's command the first section, in the lead, would swing to the left in a big arc calculated to bring the first wagon back to the road just as the rearmost wagon was leaving it. The second section would swing to the right, to curve back and meet the point. The result would be an oval of wagons, about 70 or 80 feet wide by 120 or 130 long, with two main openings, front and rear, which would be closed by ropes.

In dangerous country, as the wagons halted, the teams would be swung sharply inward, so that they would be inside for control and protection. But at an ordinary halt they would be swung outward for more convenience.

In the more northern areas, where Mexican freighting customs were not followed, a brisker system was in vogue. The train probably would corral by alternate wagons, the first wagon turning right, the second left, the following wagons similarly alternating until the circle was formed, the wagons closing up until the tongue of one overlapped the wheels of the next wagon in line. Well-trained drivers could go into corral quickly with this pattern. Each driver carried a rifle, usually in a scabbard or in a sling on the near side of the wagon where he could reach it, and ordinarily he also had a revolver, these weapons being provided by the employer. Extra stock would be in charge of a wrangler, which is probably an American corruption of the Mexican *caverango,* hostler. The wrangler, in turn, might have an assistant, especially for night herding, which gave him the title of night hawk. The drivers' assistants were called swampers, especially on the "jerkline" outfits, in which the swamper was on the wagon, handling the brake, while the teamster rode the near wheel horse. The jerkline itself, incidentally, was simply a single rein, sliding through loops until it reached the bit of a lead animal, who was trained to respond to jerks of the line, the other animals following his lead.

Both mule skinners (mule-team drivers) and bull whackers (strictly those who drove oxen, though the term was sometimes slang for any kind of freighters) used bull whips, which in the sixties and seventies cost a dollar or two and were plentifully available in any wagon yard or harness shop, if the wagoner did not make his own, as he often did. Typically a bull whip had a short hickory handle, 2 feet or so long, a braided body from 12 feet to as much as 20 feet long, then finally a buckskin popper. An expert bull whacker could knock a fly off the ear of an ox 20 feet away without bringing blood. He could also cut the eyes right out of a human opponent's face or slash him to ribbons; provided, of course, that the victim didn't charge right in where the whip could not be used. Duels sometimes were fought with bull whips. And they could be cracked with the report of a pistol.

Some bull whackers, however, preferred an ox goad. Both oxen and mules being valuable, the goad wielder or whip popper seldom actually injured his animals. But his language notoriously was enough to scorch even a mule's thick hide.

Sometimes, where the going was fair, two or more wagons would be hitched together, the tongue of the "trail wagon" or "caboose" being run under the bed of the lead wagon and secured. On the other hand, if the going was very bad, teams might be "doubled" on a single wagon—that is, oxen or mules added until the vehicle did move.

Even in the black darkness of an early-morning start a good outfit could be yoked or hitched up and ready to move within 5 or 6 minutes after the caporal cracked his whip and bellowed his stentorian, "Catch up!" or, in the Southwest, "*Vámonos!*" The next command would be, "Stretch 'em out!" and off you'd go in a volley of popping whips, oaths, and, "Gee up, thar! Gee up!"

Actually, the command "gee," addressed to oxen primarily, means "turn right." "Haw" means "turn left." And "whoa" I suppose everybody still understands. But all these, and particularly the additional embroidering commentaries, were strange language indeed to the Indians. To them, very soon after encountering the first wagon trains, cattle became "wohaws," and wagons, "goddams."

For very long hauls with slow freight, such as mining machinery not urgently needed, oxen were best. They were slower, but surer, and also cheaper, since they could travel on grass alone. But they had to be shod, and shoeing them was quite an art, since they were cloven-footed. Sometimes iron, sometimes rawhide, would be used for their shoes. Mules were much easier shod but needed grain to keep going. That had to be carried, cutting the payload down by just that much. But they were faster and you could trim down the long ox-grazing stops and cover more ground between waterholes. Which was something to think about in a land where, at best, it was often a right smart way between drinks. On some routes, of course, you had to carry water, in barrels on the wagons, for the stock as well as the men, and that was more expense and trouble.

Aside from the emigrants and cattlemen supplying their own ranches, freighting in the Old West was generally done by professional contractors, although some large traders and merchants had their own trains. Freight rates were figured on the difficulty as well as length of the haul, but they'd be, say, around $20 a ton for up to 200 miles on the level plains, but maybe double or even triple that for mountain work.

One other amusing detail about wagon trains before we let them go.

When wagon trains met in a narrow place, or where there was only one good track, it was plains custom for the unloaded train—or if both were loaded, for the lighter procession—to pull off and let the heavier go by. But who's carrying the mostest is a neat subject for argument sometimes. So there were occasions when both trains just camped in the trail and sat there for anywhere up to a week, sulking out the weighty problem. They were sometimes indeed hogs on ice, wagon freighters.

There were lots of wagon makers in the country in the booming period after the Civil War. Some of the famous makes were Studebaker, very popular, made by the Studebaker Brothers Manufacturing Company, forebears of the present Studebaker automobile makers; Shuttler, another popular make; Whitewater; Milburn; Moline, made by the Moline Wagon Company; Fish Brothers—this company boasted proudly that their hubs, wheels, and running gear were of the finest Wisconsin oak; Kansas; Mitchell; Fort Smith; John Deere, another famous company still very much in business; La Belle; Jackson—the list could go on.

In the late sixties and early seventies a good wagon cost from $150 to $200 or more, depending on where you bought it and how many extras you wanted. A spring seat cost around $20. The wagon cover was $10 or $12. But with a loaf of bread about a nickel and beefsteak 10 or 15 cents a pound, a wagon cost real money.

The Army used lots of Studebaker wagons in the West, both during the War and afterward, and these Army wagons usually were painted blue, with black wheels and running gear. Red, white, and black (the old imperial colors of Germany) were popular as wagon colors in Texas, where many Germans were in the freighting business, and also up in the Dakotas and the Northwest generally. Commercial wagons came in a variety of colors, generally red, green, or yellow, or some combination of these three. The maker's name was ordinarily stenciled on the side.

So much for the wagons generally, the heavy vehicles that carried our durable forebears and their plunder and possibles. There were assorted specialized wagons, huge ore carriers, mail wagons, mountain wagons, and others. But certainly we want to know what an Army "dougherty" ambulance or wagon was like, and a buckboard, a jump seat, a buggy, a wagonette, and of course a stagecoach and its lighter companion, a mud wagon. These vehicles were seen often in the West—clear up to the days of the automobile.

The Army had begun the Civil War with ambulance carts for the wounded, horrible two-wheeled affairs, drawn by a single horse or mule, and with space for four stretchers inside. These were replaced by light four-wheeled spring wagons, that is, wagons with springs between axles and bed,

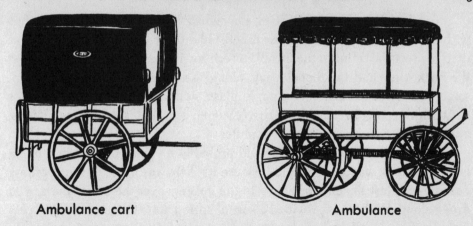

Ambulance cart   Ambulance

thus reducing the jolting of the wounded occupants. After the war this ambulance evolved into a sort of carry-all for Army personnel, sick, wounded,
or otherwise. Strictly speaking, this was the Army ambulance of frontier days,
a light wagon covered with a permanent canvas top. It was entered from the
rear and had seats along the sides, benches which could be used for beds
for wounded men, while straps for still more stretchers hung from the top.
The canvas sides could be rolled up. They carried a green Maltese cross
and a large U. S. until the late eighties, when the Medical Department
finally adopted the Red Cross. Sometimes the medical caduceus emblem
would also be on the side near the front. There were two carriage lamps or
lanterns, one on each side just behind and above the driver's seat, which
stretched transversely clear across the front. The vehicle was drawn by two
or four horses or mules and had a foot brake like a wagon.

Much more famed in frontier annals, however, was the dougherty
wagon or ambulance, often just called the dougherty. This was built more
like a coach, with side doors entered via a hanging iron step plate, two or
three transverse seats, like a stagecoach, for the passengers inside, in addition to the driver's seat up front under a sort of awning projection of the
roof, a permanent roof, canvas side curtains which could be rolled up or
strapped down snugly, and in back a boot, a chain-supported platform again
like that on a stagecoach, in which baggage could be carried.

Instead of having a flat straight floor like a wagon's or an ambulance's,
the dougherty had a bottom which arched upward in a half-tunnel or well,
just back of the driver's seat. This was to give the front wheels more room to
turn without rubbing the body. The front was open, like a buggy, with only a
dashboard between driver and team. Four horses or mules usually supplied
the motive power, and the vehicle could carry as many as fifteen or sixteen
passengers.

The Army also had wagonettes, somewhat similar to the doughertys, but with seating arrangements almost exactly like those of the hotel hacks that used to meet the trains in the little Western towns, back when. Entered from the back, they had two bench seats along the sides, a flat permanent top, sometimes with a rail for baggage, glass side windows, and more glass between the passengers and the driver's open seat, two side carriage lamps, a foot brake, two or four horses or mules.

Civilian ranchers and such would probably be going around in a buckboard, or buck wagon, so called because its floor was made of long springy boards, with just the ends attached to the bolsters over the axles; and as you drove along, the boards provided a sort of spring action, or, as the West preferred to say, "bucking" effect. There were one-seater two-passenger buckboards, and two-seater four-passenger ones, much like buggies and surreys, respectively. Usually the seats had their own longitudinal springs, like wagon seats. Typically a small railing or low box siding enclosed at least the back, for light luggage. And depending on the load and the going, the buckboard was drawn by one animal in shafts (these were curved poles that went along both his sides and hitched to his collar), or by two on the regulation pole. Usually in the West you'd see a team of two animals to a buckboard.

Buggies, the real old stand-by of horse-drawn America, east and west, were, like the automobile, first thought up abroad but perfected here. The name was first used for a two-wheeled English vehicle intended for one passenger. Just who made the first American buggy nobody knows. But they were introduced somewhere around 1826 and speedily arrived at very much

Buckboard

Buggy

the form we remember, with the perch (the spring-vehicle name for a reach or coupling pole), the axletrees, and the body reduced to very light weight, and the wheels also slenderized, so that if the buggy turned over, one ordinary man could right it and two could lift it clear off the ground. The American buggy, unlike the English, was four-wheeled, with the front wheels smaller than the rear ones. Only rarely would a buggy have brakes. The body rode on transverse springs, and very often the wide padded seat had a calash folding top of leather or heavy painted canvas. (The calash was an older type of vehicle, a sort of convertible coach, that had sported such top gear.) For bad weather a large waterproof storm curtain, with slits for the reins and small mica glazed windows ("isinglass lights," they were called), buttoned to the sides of the top, draped over the curved dashboard in front, and provided protection for the passengers. In the rear curtain was another mica window. A whip socket was provided on the right side of the dashboard for the buggy whip, which was about 6 feet long, only moderately flexible, and with a small braided lash or popper.

Buggies were made in many areas and for many different kinds of service. A Concord buggy would probably come from Concord, New Hampshire, a famous vehicle-making center. A Texas buggy was a stout vehicle designed for punishment on Southwestern roads. The drummer's rig would doubtless be a sturdy buggy, perhaps with brakes, and drawn by a team, though buggies were usually drawn by a single horse in shafts. Not to be too strictly technical, a surrey was a sort of two-seated buggy, and a jump seat could hardly be called anything but an adjustable buggy, since it was merely a light vehicle whose one seat could be shifted to make room for a second seat, that is, a buggy converted into a surrey. There were, however, some-what heavier forms called jump-seat wagons.

With these light carriages you would probably use a driving harness, with a breast collar, merely a broad leather band across the horse's chest, instead of the heavy neck collar and iron hames of the heavy hauling harness.

This was the sort of rig you'd rent from a livery stable, if you had no transport of your own. For an evening it might cost you $1, for a whole day

Jump-seat wagon

Four-passenger surrey

Sulky

Platform spring wagon

Six-passenger rockaway

Family wagonette

$4 or $5, depending on where you were and how far and fancy you wanted to go. A feed barn might also have rigs for hire, but generally this was, as its name signified, merely a place that would stable and feed your animals. Finally, a feed yard, or wagon yard, which you'd find in most Western towns of any size, would be a lot where you could pull in and stop for the night, a sort of frontier tourist court. You could sleep in your wagon, or on the ground, or sometimes there'd be bunks. But always there would be feed troughs, grain, and forage, water for stock; and practically always a little red-eye for the driver.

The glamour carriage of the Old West, of course, was the stagecoach. This was another importation from Europe which reached its highest development here in America; the heavy lumbering coaches of the old countries had been with us in Colonial times. American stagecoaches were built in many places, Troy and Albany, New York, Salem and Worcester, Massachusetts, among them. But in the 1820s the stagecoach makers of Concord, New Hampshire, rolled to the fore, and thereafter their famous product, the Concord coach, was the *ne plus ultra, the* final word in coaches all over the world. These coaches were imitated even by the first railroad cars! If you had a Concord coach, particularly one made by Abbott, Downing & Co., you had the best.

In the sixties and seventies such a coach would cost from around $900 for the coach alone, and on up to just about whatever you wanted to pay for

Abbot, Downing & Co. coach

extras. Concords varied in details, just as Rolls Royces or Cadillacs do. One typical example which operated in the Southwest weighed 3000 pounds and could carry a 4000-pound load. Its woodwork was choicest hickory, its metal, save for brass trimming, all steel. Its axles were steel and the spindles 2½ inches thick and 14 inches long. Its cushions inside were built over coiled steel springs, padded with horsehair and covered with the very best brown calf leather. Its body swung on leather thoroughbraces, heavy long straps, rove through stout steel stanchions lifting above front and rear axles, right and left. Layer on layer on layer of live leather gave a velvety, hammocky swing and cushioning to the body that has scarcely been equaled even by the best modern springing.

Inside were three seats, two facing forward, the third facing back. In some coaches the middle seat could be lowered to form a bed, so that if there were not too many passengers, they could lie down and catch some sleep as the coach rocked along. Each seat was big enough for three people without crowding, and three more seats could be provided on the roof, which was covered with the very heaviest of painted waterproof duck. The coach could carry twelve to fifteen passengers without crowding and on occasion packed in as many as twenty-three or twenty-four.

The doors were on the sides, entered with the aid of hanging steel step plates. Some coaches had glass in these doors, and glass also in the small quarter-windows in the frames on each side of the doors. You can imagine just how long this glass lasted on Western roads. But the windows beside the front and rear seats were open and protected by canvas curtains, which rolled up and down on a stout slat, fastening with eyes and turnbuttons when down, or held rolled up by leather straps.

Inside the coach on each side were tug straps, to which the passengers next to the windows could cling. The seats were quite close together, and those in the front seat riding backward quite often had to "dovetail" their legs, as the process was called, with the legs of those in the center seat riding forward; dovetailing was an arrangement looked on with high disfavor by the Victorian ladies of the period.

Outside, the coach was very fancifully painted with much red, gold, and yellow; it had floral and vine designs in the panels, and, usually, the stage's destination—Deadwood or whatever—on the door panel or above it. The name of the stage company, plus the particular stage's number, was on the panel under the driver's seat. The body of the coach was ribbed and paneled, and, since the bottom of the vehicle was curved like the bottom of a boat, the side ribs curved also, coming to a prowlike point under the driver's seat and a somewhat blunter stern in the rear. The driver's seat was

Deadwood stagecoach

set high on the front, outside, so that he perched a good 6 feet from the ground, the forward end of the coach top providing a shoulder-high rest for his back. Making the driver's seat a part of the body, so that the driver too got the benefit of the springing, was an American idea; in the earlier European stagecoaches the driver's box was part of the chassis instead, and he took a beating accordingly.

Under the driver's box was a leather-shrouded "boot" for baggage, and directly beneath his shelflike seat was sometimes another smaller compartment in which were carried such valuables as the strongbox, a stout money chest, often chained and padlocked as well. In the rear of the coach was a hinged, chain-supported platform, also leather- or canvas-hooded—another boot for heavier luggage. Railings around the top provided space for still more luggage.

The driver, or whip as he was often called, drove from the right-hand side of the box, where a powerful foot brake was provided. On his left, in troubled country, rode an armed guard, a shotgun messenger, sometimes hired by the stageline, sometimes provided by the express companies as a traveling agent in direct charge of valuable express shipments. These messengers typically packed a pair of six guns *and* a sawed-off shotgun loaded with buckshot, a truly lethal combination.

The stage was drawn by four or six horses. The harness was called rigging. A pair of leather reins from each of the teams came back to the driver's expert hands, so that he manipulated four, six, or on occasion even eight "ribbons," no mean feat. Each rein was split at the forward end. The right rein's split ends linked to the right side of each horse's jaw, the left rein's ends to the left sides, so that a single pull directed both animals. Usually the driver had a long-lashed whip as an additional aid, but sometimes he contented himself with the reins themselves as crackers.

The stage had a pair of square-sided oil-burning coach or carriage lamps, set in brackets right and left, just back of and below the driver's seat. They provided some light at night, though it must have been precious little. But the driver's eyes were keen, or at least so you hoped, and you knew the horses up front there could see, even when to you it was dark as the insides of an owl. Some stagelines did not travel at night; others did, especially on the important mail-contract routes. You could, if you wanted to, go from St. Louis to San Francisco in about 25 days, traveling night and day, sleeping, if you could, on the stage. The fare was about $200. There were inns, stage stations, or road ranches where you could stop for meals, or a night's rest, and every 10 to 20 miles a swing or relay station, with fresh teams for the stage, and at the end of each run a replacement for the driver. Average time of stagecoach travel was about 35 miles every eight hours.

At a stage station you would find a stationmaster in charge, a handful of hostlers to care for the animals, and perhaps a rough eating house or restaurant. The buildings would be of logs, whipsawed lumber, sod, or adobe, depending on location. There'd probably be a tin basin on a bench beside the door where you could wash up, aided by some soft soap in a side dish, soap that would curl the hide off a hippo. A roller towel that had seen better days and a more or less toothless comb, detained by a rawhide string,

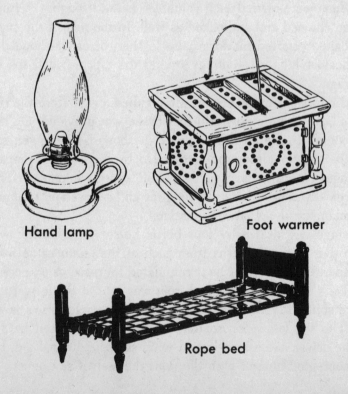

Hand lamp

Foot warmer

Rope bed

would help you complete your toilette. Inside there'd be a big fireplace, acrid sputtering tallow candles, or maybe coal-oil (seldom called kerosene) lamps, which might explode, oil refining being what it was at the time. Your meal would be the inevitable hog and hominy or beef and beans of the frontier. There'd be something rugged to drink, certainly, and maybe a tattered deck of cards on the puncheon table to separate you from your change; and bedbugs to keep you company when or if you retired.

Your bed, if you had one instead of just a bunk, would probably be a roped bedstead, with stout cords running to wooden pegs on the side rails and ends, forming a sort of net with about 9-inch squares. On this was placed a bedtick stuffed with "prairie feathers," meaning grass, and atop that blankets. No sheets, of course.

Life at one of these isolated stage stations was a pretty rough and dreary endurance contest at best. And stage stations were a favorite target for Indian war parties, always in search of more horses. So the stage probably wouldn't tarry too long en route, stopping over only when forced by complete exhaustion or the weather. And it took pretty horrible weather to stop the stages.

They were stout fellas, our Western forebears! If it was cold, they just muffled themselves in shawls, overcoats, blankets, and buffalo robes, and maybe had the stage attendants shove in a footstove, a metal and wood box containing sand or ashes and live coals, which tucked in on the coach floor under the passengers' feet. Sometimes a large brick, or chunk of heated soapstone, substituted for the coals. There were overshoes made of buffalo hide with the hair left on, to buckle over your regular footwear. Somebody'd be bound to have a flask, of course—it was standard traveler's equipment.

If it was so muddy that the big coach couldn't roll, perhaps the stagers would ring in a mud wagon. This was either a lighter, smaller, simpler version of the big Concord stage, or, more often, a wagonette. It lacked the doodads of the big vehicle, having just canvas sides and top instead, and two or three seats inside, carrying about half the load of the big coach. Usually its motive power was supplied by mules. There was a single boot for luggage on the back, and more baggage could be piled inside with the passengers. But it wasn't a lordly vehicle like a coach: it was a hack, a delivery wagon, and it looked like one. It got you there after a fashion, and that was about all you could say for it.

There were records of much better than the average speed of 35 to 40 miles in eight hours, and lots of blowing about "lightning stages." On the better roads, back East, champion whips had at times recorded speeds of around 10 miles an hour for 100 miles and even more, which was really

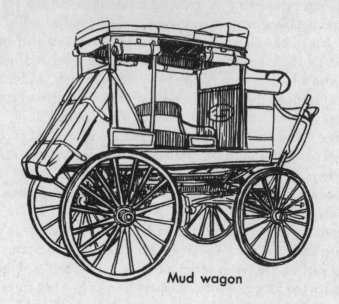

Mud wagon

traveling. But in the West, where there were goat trails for roads much of the time, 35 miles in eight or nine hours was traveling too. After all, you had to count in all the up-and-down and right-and-left motions as well. Riding in a Western stagecoach was better than walking, undoubtedly, and it did get you there, dead or alive. But it was without too many regrets that the most hidebound Old Westerner saw the first iron horse come puffing over the horizon, to start the old stages on their way to the Wild West shows and the movies. If he couldn't have steamboats on the prairies—and that, now, he did regret—he was plumb ready to try the train. It was so much less painful, to say nothing of being so much faster. Golly, 20 miles an hour!

Before we climb on our first iron horse, however, let's have a look at the river steamboats, which did play a notable though steadily diminishing part in the transportation saga of the West during the period we are covering. Unfortunately there are not too many navigable rivers in the West; the ones that are navigable run for too much of the way mostly southward, where the traffic wants to go east and west. But there are some, like the wide Missouri, the lordly Columbia, the Sacramento, the Rio Grande. And there are a lot more that the shallow little stern-wheelers used to navigate—today you just can't imagine it—even the Trinity, up to Dallas, and the Red, into Oklahoma!

The little Western boats were mostly stern-wheelers, and for a very good reason. When they bumped into a sandbar, they just turned around and dug a channel through with their big wooden wheel. Or they walked

Colorado River stern-wheeler

over the bar—"grasshoppering," it was called. Long heavy spars were carried vertically on derricks near the bow, one on each side. When the boat stuck on a bar, the ends of these spars were dropped to the bottom, the tops slanting forward. Then, with block, tackle, cable, and capstan, the spars were used like push poles or crutches, to lift and hop the boat forward, while the paddle wheel splashed furiously. After each hop you reset the spars and did it all over.

They were on the Rio Grande, the little boats, where Captains Richard King and Mifflin Kennedy were combining steamboating with ranching, and gathering together their gigantic ranch properties. The King and Kennedy steamboat *Ranchero* had taken a leading part in the fight at La Bolsa, in 1860, between old Rip Ford's Texas Rangers and Juan Nepomuceno ("Cheno") Cortinas's Mexican guerrillas. A movie-style fight, too, with cannon on the boat, fighting cavalry ashore! The little boats swarmed on the Missouri, feeding Fort Leavenworth, Independence Landing, Kansas City, St. Joseph, Omaha, and a hundred now forgotten jumping-off places for the Western trails. They'd even turned into mountain boats—not goats— clambering up to Fort Pierre in South Dakota and even to Fort Benton, clear up in the heart of Montana in the Rockies. It cost 12 cents a pound for freight from St. Louis to Fort Benton, 2300 miles of dangerous water away, 70 to 100 days up, about 20 to 40 coming back. Boats were on the Arkansas, serving Fort Smith on the border of the old Indian Territory, and Fort Gibson inside the Territory. The *Tahlequah,* named for the capital of the Cherokee Nation, the *Argos,* and the *Fort Smith* were among the boats plying between these points and New Orleans in 1870. Boats were on the

Red River, where old Captain Henry Shreve, father of Shreveport, Louisiana, had first developed the real American river steamboat, a flatboat hull drawing not more than 5 or 6 feet of water, and sometimes less than 30 inches, with light powerful engines and two main decks. They were on the Far Western rivers, the Columbia, the Sacramento, even the Colorado! There was a day when you could take a steamboat from Yuma, Arizona, to Callville, Nevada, and for a fare of no more than 12 or 15 cents a mile.

A little 190-foot boat even got in on the most famous Indian campaign of all, Custer's last fight. It was the *Far West*, Captains Grant Marsh and Davie Campbell, and from its cabin (it was tied up at the mouth of the Rosebud on the Yellowstone) the fiery Custer strode out with his last instructions, on his way to gory immortality.

A river steamboat of the sixties or seventies cost anywhere from $20,000 on up to build, and could be bought secondhand for from $5000 up. On the Mississippi, on the lower Missouri, or out on the Sacramento in California, there were regular floating palaces that had cost anywhere up to a quarter-million to construct, with worlds of carved wood, ogee molding, gilt and scarlet, crystal chandeliers, red plush divans, all the luxuries of a grand hotel. The Western boats were smaller, rugged working boats, for

Custer's *Far West*

Mississippi River steamboat

freight and immigrants. Still, large or small, the steamboats were all fairly similar in construction.

As you came up the stageplank or staging from the bank, you stepped onto the main deck, which resembled a warehouse, or a large open shed. In the center of this, forward, was the housing for the boilers and engines, and below the deck were holds, entered by hatches, for additional freight. Wagons, animals, chickens in coops, household goods, sacks, bales, boxes, barrels, stacks of cordwood for the roaring fireboxes under the boilers (which would average about a cord an hour consumption)—anything and everything might be found on this deck. Deck passengers, so called, made the trip here, living in their own wagons, or sleeping on the planks. Here was the cheapest steamboat passage.

The roof of this carry-all deck was the boiler or cabin deck, because here, on the second floor as it were, you found the hot stuff among the boat's passengers and the fancy accommodations, a long, central lounge or saloon, and around it the individual cabins, called staterooms, for first-class passengers. The front part of the saloon was the Gentlemen's Cabin, for male passengers only, except at mealtimes, when tables were set up and meals served here. The rearmost third or fourth, usually separated from the forepart by folding doors, was the Ladies' Cabin, for female travelers. Into this sanctum no mere male penetrated, unless he was a preacher, or married or otherwise closely related to one of the ladies, in which case he was permitted to intrude briefly.

Except at mealtime there were no women—well, no *ladies*, anyhow—in the Gentlemen's Cabin, because this was a horridly masculine place. It had a bar or buffet, white-coated Negro waiters scurrying with drinks, card tables, the inevitable professional gamblers who infested all river boats, battalions of brass cuspidors and sand-filled boxes serving the same purpose, oceans of cigar smoke, rivers of tobacco juice, and even juicier language.

The staterooms surrounding the saloon are sometimes said to have been so called because originally they bore the names of the states instead of numbers. They opened into the big dining room, and some of them also had outer doors giving into the narrow promenade between the staterooms and the outer guardrail, or guards. The roof of the cabin deck was the hurricane deck, having no covering, though in the central part forward it did have the texas, cabins for the ship's officers, and quarters for the white deckhands and also usually the Negro waiters serving the passengers. The texas was named after the Lone Star State, either because it was annexed to the staterooms, or because it was a larger cabin or stateroom—authorities differ.

Atop the texas was the pilothouse, a small many-windowed structure where the pilot, czar of the boat, rode in lofty grandeur and attended a wheel that might be as much as 10 or 12 feet in diameter, the bottom half extending through the deck into the texas below. Bells with bell ropes, a whistle, and a speaking tube to the engine room provided him with communication. Along the back of the pilothouse was ordinarily a long bench for visiting pilots and other notables. But otherwise, compared with a seagoing vessel's bridge, for instance, the river boat's pilothouse was dismayingly bare. In the eighties and nineties, as the government charted and marked the rivers with lights, and electricity came in, the river boats changed also. But on the early boats, the navigating was something a pilot did with his head, a phenomenal memory, and an uncanny sixth sense that got him out of all sorts of holes.

Sometimes just one, but usually two, lofty flaring crowned stacks sent their columns of woodsmoke heavenward just in front of the texas. Swung between these stacks would be assorted gingerbread, often the initials or insignia of the boat or of the company to which it belonged. High up on the stacks, right and left, would be the passing lights, big red and green lanterns. On a river steamboat the red light was always on the bank side, whether this was left or right, port (or larboard, as the left side was usually called on the rivers) or starboard. Steamboats did run at night, especially on the lower reaches of the rivers. But, coming down the upper reaches, especially of such a treacherous stream as the Missouri, they preferred not to attempt the most dangerous stretches in the dark. With the mighty current thrusting you on, you never knew just what might happen, whereas, going against the current, you could inch along or even stand still. In pitch darkness the passing lights of a boat ahead showed where the bank was, which was important. Illumination was provided by fancy brass cabin lamps, square-sided deck and hold lanterns, and, for loading, torch-baskets, which were iron cages crammed with blazing pine knots, on the end of a sharp-pointed iron staff, to be thrust into the bank.

The crew of a steamboat generally included a captain or master; two pilots, who were really the lords of the boat once it left the bank; three or four engineers; one to three mates; one or two clerks; a steward; a deck crew of thirty or forty; and a cabin crew, the twenty or thirty aristocrats serving the cabin passengers. The pilots were top dogs in wages, drawing from $300 to $400 a month up to $2000 a month for extra-perilous trips. A captain drew about $250 a month; mates, engineers, and clerks somewhere around half that.

The firemen, who fed the roaring fireboxes, and the roustabouts, who did the heavy work of handling cargo, loading and unloading, were usually Negroes. Unlike the cabin crew, these deck hands usually bunked anywhere they could manage on the main deck, and down in the hold under the boilers was one favorite spot.

A pilot often would have a cub, a greenhorn working for nothing, and even paying the pilot anywhere up to $500 to be taught the trade. The cub helped in the steering, pulling down on the opposite side of the big wheel as the pilot directed. The pilots alternated watches, four hours on, four off, the watch from midnight to four o'clock being the after watch and from four to breakfast the dog watch.

The pilot could jolly well sink the boat if he wasn't careful, or even blow it up when he was trying to be extra-cautious. Boiler explosions on steamboats were frequent; and sometimes I wonder if maybe that wasn't one of the reasons for all that extra and distracting elegance on the steamboats—fancy meals, fancy drinks, whatnot. On the big river boats, the meals—golly! Two kinds of soup, three kinds of fish, seven sorts of roast, seven entrees, five choices of cold dishes, choice of thirty desserts, seven kinds of candy, raisins, almonds, pineapple, oranges, bananas, figs, apples, dates, prunes, filberts, peanuts! That was living! You didn't fare quite that well on the mountain boats, of course, but you were far from starving.

It wasn't too speedy a way to get anywhere, but it was luxurious and, considering, pretty cheap. Depending on the boat, the competition, and the times, the fare was 2 or 3 cents a mile, sometimes more, often less; and the boat generally carried up to 250 pounds of baggage free. It cost about $300 for the 2300-mile trip from St. Louis clear out to the gold-field excitement at Fort Benton, Montana. As for time—well, the *Robert E. Lee*, racing from New Orleans to St. Louis, 1218 miles, in 1870, averaged about 13 miles an hour, though you could do better than that running downstream, of course. The run from Kansas City to St. Louis, 450 miles, was made once or twice in around 16 hours, an average of 25 miles an hour, probably the top speed ever made by a pioneer steamboat. Upstream, it took about 48 hours to make the same trip, fare $25 in the seventies, if you're interested. But about 7 or 8 miles an hour was a good, even optimistic, average.

But even before the Civil War the iron horse was champing at the bit, and after the war, it promptly doomed both steamboat and stagecoach as major carriers. The railroad could, and in most cases eventually did, go where you wanted to go, when you wanted, and, for the times, breathtakingly fast.

America had had steam locomotives since the 1830s. At the close of the Civil War there were 35,000 miles of American railroads in operation, although some in the devastated South were probably not actually operating. But the tracks were all east of the Missouri and most of them east of the Mississippi. In 1865 they went no farther west than St. Joseph, Missouri, where the Hannibal & St. Joseph made connections with the famed though short-lived Pony Express (and in 1862 put on the nation's first mail car, incidentally, with Fred Harvey as one of the mail clerks). But by 1870, just five years later, there were nearly 53,000 miles of railroads in the nation, and 23,540 miles of them were in the western states.

By 1880, in spite of the panic of 1873 and the ensuing years of depression, railroad trackage was up to more than 93,000 miles. It boomed to

The first mail car

163,597 miles by 1890, with the bulk of the new construction in the West. Even in 1870 the railroad had come a long, long way from its modest American beginnings at Baltimore, where, in 1830, for 9 cents you could ride a whole 13 miles, the entire "railroad system" of the nation.

For one thing, they'd "adjusted" the fares by 1870, making it considerably more expensive to go places on the cars. The Union Pacific had started by charging 10 cents a mile for passengers, as compared with about 3 or 4 cents on the roads in the North and 5 or 6 in the devastated South. But you were getting more for your money, on all the railroads: sleeping cars and diners, better brakes and more safety, to go with all that speed. And after May 10, 1869, when the lines of the Union Pacific, building westward, and the Central Pacific, building eastward, met at Promontory Point, Utah, you could go from Omaha to Sacramento in five days, as compared with about a month by stage and 150 to 200 days by ship around the Horn. That is, you could if your train didn't happen to get snowed in for "some weeks," as General G. M. Dodge, chief engineer of the Union Pacific, unhappily recalled as happening to some half-dozen trains west of Laramie in the winter of 1869-70. Luckily they'd thought to include a boxcar full of provisions, plus a big extra stove for each train, and one train had a whole opera company aboard, which obligingly entertained. Everybody survived, even the opera.

You could go from coast to coast in six and a half days for $173, first-class fare, plus $2 a night for sleeper ($2 a day, too, and you were expected to tip the porter at least 25 cents a day), while meals at the stations were around $1 and terrible. From Omaha to San Francisco the first-class fare was around $100 in the seventies, second-class was $75, and a new "emigrant" service, in accommodation cars somewhat but not much better than cattle cars attached to the freight trains and arriving like freight, eventually cost $40 per head, or $65 coast to coast.

But you could also have luxury, even in 1870. For extra fare you could ride the Union Pacific's much-publicized Hotel Train from Omaha to Ogden, with Pullmans, dining car, sometimes even a smoker. The Central Pacific,

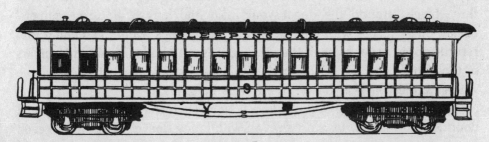

The first Pullman car

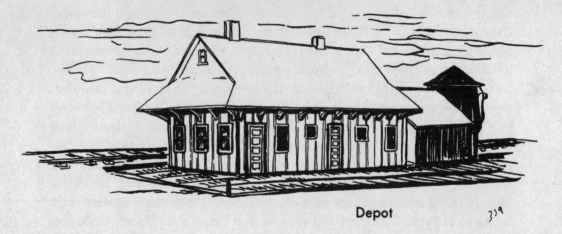

Depot

hauling you from Ogden to Sacramento, had its own Silver Palace sleeping cars and fed you at station restaurants, generally a little cheaper than east of the Rockies, though.

As for speed, when it wasn't snowing and the railroads really wanted to extend themselves, they could get up and step, even in the seventies. In 1876 another theatrical outfit, not the snowed-in opera company, went from Jersey City to San Francisco in a little less than 84 hours,[1] which is right fast rolling, even today. But the usual speed of the times was somewhere around 16 miles an hour.

No matter; let's take a trip on a typical 1870 train. They guaranteed you a colorful experience, no matter what else you missed. The station was a rough wooden depot ("dee-po"), with a waiting room lined with wooden benches, heated by a potbellied stove, and lighted by oil lamps. It would probably be swarming with westward-bound emigrants, many of them foreigners still in their quaint European costumes, innocent of a word of English. Adjoining would be a restaurant or railroad eating house, where you could get meals for 50 cents to a dollar, and they'd pack you a lunch basket for 50 cents. You could get food lots cheaper than this in the cities, you understand; these were railroad prices. In a big town, for about two or three blocks around the depot you'd also find a rash of ticket-scalpers' offices, dingy places with loud signs and gaudy flags, where you could buy return-trip tickets or some of the passes that were handed around like cigars in those dear, dim days. The price would be just about what you and the scalper agreed on. So, you see, there were bargains.

If you escaped the scalpers and bought from the station agent, you'd doubtless find him in his shirt sleeves, with fancy sleeve garters above each

1. Martin D. Stevers, *Steel Rails* (New York: Grosset & Dunlap, 1933), page 175.

elbow and paper cuff protectors, like gauntlets, shielding his own paper cuffs. He'd doubtless have a paper eyeshade, celluloid still being on its way. He'd have a big railroad watch on a fat chain across his middle. And you and he would consult the railroad's own timetable, and I mean it was the railroad's own time too, because there wasn't anything standard about it.

In the 1870s there was only local time in this nation, and each railway had its own variety. The result was that there were more than seventy different kinds of railroad time, all in use at once. The newspapers would obligingly publish tables of the various local railroads' times for travelers' use, and you can just imagine how helpful that was, on top of the mysteries of each road's own timetable. The local jewelers would set your watch for you, but they generally had differences of opinion too. Some places, trying for uniformity, fired a noon gun, and others, adopting the old railway highball system, dropped a large ball from the top of a high, centrally located mast, at precisely high noon. But who was to determine just when noon was?

When you started traveling out of a town, for each 9 miles, east or west, your watch lost or gained about a minute. It was a mess, as you can see, and eventually, in 1883, the railroads and then the country as a whole adopted our present standard time system, with Eastern, Central, Mountain, and Pacific time zones, 5, 6, 7, and 8 hours, respectively, slower than Greenwich, England, time. Boundary lines between the zones were largely determined by railroad division points. And the time zones were and are checked and kept on time by telegraph.

A highball, by the way, was an early railroad signal, a large red metal ball, hoisted on a pole in front of each station. All the way up it was indeed a "highball," telling the engineer to sail right on through. Down, it was a "lowball," meaning stop. The expression "to highball," meaning to get or keep going, has persisted to our day.

In safety systems, as in the matter of time, the early railroads were pretty much rugged individualists, and although the block-signal system had been introduced into the country as early as 1863 by the United New Jersey Canal and Railroad Companies (later part of the Pennsylvania system), many other roads had their different ideas, as well as financial problems. The old time-interval system, which merely spaced trains so many minutes or hours apart and then depended on flagmen, lanterns, and torpedoes to avoid collisions, was not supplanted for a long time. As a matter of fact, the old flags and torpedoes are used even yet, even on lines with completely automatic signal systems. Like everyone else who deals with power that can kill you quick, railroaders tend to be conservative. But standard train signals were adopted in 1884, a standard system for inspecting rail-

SIGNALS

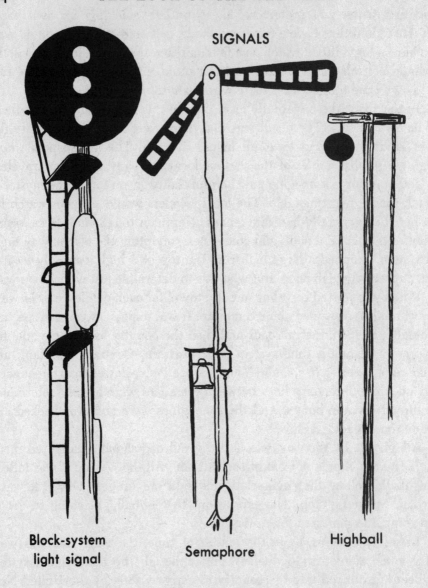

Block-system   Highball
light signal   Semaphore

road watches in 1886, and standard rules and orders for all trains in 1887.

Back in 1870 our little train would still be pretty much a free agent. It probably would have red lanterns on the rear, and, of course, a big headlight up front, a monstrous oil-burning affair of much brass and glass which emitted about as much light as a burning pine knot. These lights, sometimes with added lights and flags by day, green to denote a train running in several sections, white for an extra train, are called markers; they distinguish a train from just some cars and an engine, maybe stored there for the winter or something. The train would have several brakemen, to go forward and back,

Early train

on foot, with red lanterns, flags, and torpedoes, which were big percussion caps to fix on the rails to warn other trains, should the train break down.

It might or might not have the new Westinghouse air brakes. These, invented by George Westinghouse and first used in 1868, in the beginning merely used compressed air, manipulated by the engineer on the engine, to set all brakes on all the cars on the train. This worked for short passenger trains, but was slow for long freight trains. So in the middle eighties Westinghouse came through with a device whereby the engineer's releasing the air pressure in his cab instantly set the brakes all down the string of cars. These air brakes have been standard equipment ever since. If they didn't have any on our train, then periodically we'd have a brakeman charging through our car, to set the brakes by hand, turning the big wheel on each car. Which took considerable running and doing.

And here's our engine. Almost certainly it was what was known as the American type, or a 4-4-0, as the later Whyte system of classifying locomotives by the layout of their wheels would have put it. This means the engine has four big driving wheels, two on a side, and a four-wheel pony truck (little wheels, two on a side) up front. There are no trailing wheels at all under the cab. Good at taking sharp curves and sticking to uneven track, the American was a very popular type of engine all over the country clear up to the turn of the century. On a freight train, the engine might have been a mogul, a type originated by the Baldwin Locomotive Works just after the war. Mogul engines had six driving wheels, three on a side, and a front truck with only two wheels. In either case, the engine would probably be bright with much brass and paint and would have a name, like a ship, rather than a number, though numbers were coming in. Hurricane, Tiptop, General McPherson, Texas, Colorado were the names of some of the engines on the transcontinental run in the early 1870s. The engines which met at the famous meeting of the rails in 1869 were the Union Pacific's Roger, No. 119, and the Central Pacific's Jupiter, No. 60. And they exhibited also the difference most laymen would notice in locomotives for years more: a large flaring, balloon- or funnel-shaped stack on the Central Pacific engine;

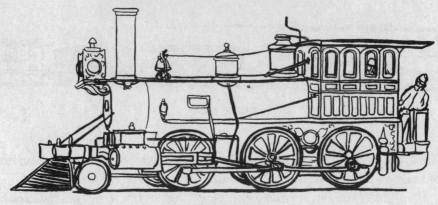

Mogul engine

a tall straight stack, but with a funny-looking crownpiece, on the Union Pacific iron horse.

The crownpiece was a spark-arrester cap, and the funnel stack on the other engine was principally for the same purpose—to try, at least, to catch the blazing sparks and cinders being hurled out in a veritable fire storm by the burning wood in the fireboxes below. The cars behind were wooden, and there was tinder-dry grass alongside the tracks. The railroads generally didn't get converted to coal until the eighties and nineties. They would not really lick the spark menace until the Diesels came along, sixty years later. Inside that big flaring stack was a deflecting cone, to spread the holocaust as widely as possible, and on top an iron net or screen. Well, at least it did spread out the sparks.

Now for the engine crew. Quite often in the seventies the engineer would still be called an engine driver and the fireman a stoker. They'd probably be wearing woolen shirts, and woolen caps or slouch hats, and very likely one of them at least would have on a vest as his outer garment. Quite a far cry from the neat striped overalls of today's engineers.

Back of the engine would be the open tender loaded with wood, and back of that maybe a U. S. Mail car, a railway post office, since they'd started during the war, or a combined mail-and-baggage car. Behind these would be the passenger coaches, probably not more than three or four, since passenger trains weren't very long in those days. The cars were wooden, except for running gear, and from 44 to 54 feet long, with open platforms on the ends and only a light iron rail to protect the passengers from falling into the swaying, clanking void between the cars. Coaches were connected by a primitive link-and-pin coupling, which the switchman had to go between the cars to operate and which very frequently got him killed, until at last

an automatic coupler was developed. In wrecks the open platforms had a
nasty habit of climbing up and smashing into the next car in line, mashing
any poor passengers too near the door. The enclosed vestibule, introduced
by Pullman as a safety device, was not added until 1887. The seats would
be wooden, upholstered in red or green plush. A potbellied stove would
provide heat (steam heat, piped from the engine, dates only from the late
eighties), and coal-oil lamps would provide light. Pintsch gaslights came
along in 1883, Pintsch gas being an oil product, and electric lights in the
late eighties and nineties.

This train would probably have only day coaches, and you'd eat at the
stations. But you could have luxury, if you wanted it, at an extra price. There
were Hotel Trains, as we've noted, the de luxe stuff, with a diner that was
out of this world, Turkey carpets, inlaid woodwork, fancy hangings, wall
mirrors, snowy linens, a mile-long menu, and prices to fit. The Hotel Trains
carried some day coaches but mainly they hauled Pullmans and Silver Palace
sleepers, the latter the Central Pacific's competitor to Pullman, and both
unheard-of magnificence out on the plains. There'd be about three each of
Pullmans and Silver Palaces, two coaches and a baggage car. Quite a train
for the times.

There were other kinds of sleeping cars, including, as we've noted,
tourist cars furnished by the railroads and hauled by the freight trains often
as not. And some other companies were making first-class fancy sleeping cars
in the seventies, real competition for Pullman: the Wagner Palace Car; the
Mann Boudoir Car (a boudoir was the term of the time for what we now
call a compartment); and even a Union Palace Car. All were absorbed by
Pullman by the 1890s.

George M. Pullman, the name that means sleeping car to us, was an
enterprising Westerner who built his first sleeping car in Chicago in 1858.
It was at least better than the canal-boat-style sleepers, complete with low

The Pioneer, as it appeared in Lincoln's funeral train

bridge, that the railroads themselves were supplying. It had ten sections, a stove at each end, and two washrooms—though you did have to use a roller towel and pump your own water with a miniature farm pump. But Pullman himself wasn't satisfied.

The Civil War delayed his plans for a while. But in 1864 he built a new sleeping car, the Pioneer. It was 54 feet long, 10 wide, with a roof high enough so you could even wear a top hat, larger washrooms, fancy uphol-stery, polished woods, real sheets, its own conductor, a porter—service! A berth cost you $2 a night—over and above the regular first-class rail fare, you realize. And you had to tip the porter. Pessimists said the traveling pub-lic would never stand such stupendous charges, and the railway men said the durn car was too big and wide anyway to clear the bridges and station platforms then in service—did George expect them to rebuild the whole railway system? If so, let George do it!

Then a momentous event occurred—the assassination of President Abra-ham Lincoln. Strange, that the death of a president should change all the railroads in America, but that was what happened. The martyred President's body was brought home to Illinois in the President's own car, with the best railway equipment the nation had, and in the train was Pullman's Pioneer. Now the bridges and platforms had to be altered to fit.

In 1867 the Pullman Palace Car Company was organized, eventually to put its cars, complete with conductors and smiling porters, on almost all the railways of the land. In the same year Pullman launched his first dining car, the President, a combination sleeper and buffet. The next year he was oper-ating dining cars as well as sleepers, and the next, when the Union Pacific–Central Pacific transcontinental line was completed, he had a whole flock of "luxury" cars ready. The early Pullman cars were named, as they still are.

There had been eating houses at the stations, of course, virtually from the beginning of railroad travel. They had, for the most part, a deservedly bad reputation. But there was a pioneer ready to fix that too, the same Fred Harvey who served as mail clerk on the first railway post-office car. Maybe he didn't like the meals he had to endure along the way. Anyhow, in 1875 at Topeka, Kansas, on the Atchison, Topeka, and Santa Fe line, Harvey opened the first of what would soon become the most famous of all railroad café systems, the Harvey Houses. Presently Harvey would take over not only all the other station cafés along the line, but also the dining-car service for Santa Fe, and his food, service, and pretty waitresses would become known all over the world.

Now the rest of the train crew. Engineer and fireman we have met. The conductor, master of the train, probably would be garbed in a frock coat

Trainmen's caps

in the early seventies, and with his inevitable whiskers would look very much like Prince Albert on the modern popular smoking-tobacco tin. A long, double-breasted frock coat was called a Prince Albert, in honor of the highly respected consort of Queen Victoria. Our conductor might be wearing a small, dark, soft, slouch hat, especially on Western trains, but, more likely, he would be wearing a trainman's cap, a straight-sided pillbox affair with a bill. Quite like the headgear railroaders still wear, except that the peak was flatter and squared off at the corners, the sides softer than now. This type of cap, and the bell-topped variety with a drooping, rounded, leather vizor, stiff band but no stretcher in the floppy top, were European importations, particularly affected by German immigrants, of whom, thanks to the revolutionary troubles of the forties and fifties in the Old Country, there were a great many in the American West of the fifties and later.

The conductor would doubtless be wearing a turndown stiff collar and a bow tie with ends tucked under like a gambler's. Along with the inevitable

The first Harvey House

watch and chain he would have a ticket punch, since the modern ticket system, with serially numbered tickets to aid in checking and to discourage counterfeiting, had started just before the war. The conductor's punch, by the way, then as now not only cancels the ticket but also identifies the conductor taking it, since each punch makes a different-shaped hole.

The history of tickets is interesting in itself. On the early stagecoaches, just as on shipboard, passengers were booked rather than sold tickets. That is, they paid their fare to the station agent or booking clerk who entered their names in a book, giving a copy to the stage driver. This practice was also followed on the early steamboats, with the agent ashore or the clerk on the boat booking the passengers. But it was so clumsy and so easy to evade that tickets soon came in, crude coupons, which made it easier to check on passengers, but were still easy to counterfeit. Then came the serially numbered tickets and finally, sometime in the middle of the period we are covering, the first connected trip tickets.

The brakeman, next member of the train crew, would be less formally and probably more heavily garbed than the conductor, since he had to get outside more, but he too doubtless would have a trainman's cap with a brass badge marked BRAKEMAN, distinguishing him from the conductor, who usually had a similar plate marked CONDUCTOR. Porters and waiters, usually Negroes, would have white jackets, or, in the very plush dining cars, waiter's cutaways. Meals in the dining cars, by the way, were $1 and up, and on some of the Far Western roads became rather famous for their quality.

And as for speed! We need to remember that the traveler of the 1870s had neither automobiles nor planes for his comparisons. He was used to boats, wagons, coaches, oxen, horses. A horse at a hand gallop moves only about 15 miles an hour. A wagon makes about 2 to 2½. A steamboat would do perhaps 10, and a stage 5 or 6. A railroad train, at 25 miles an hour, was simply scorching the earth. There were, seriously, some grave fears entertained that human constitutions could not stand the speed.

Not that the early steam boilers couldn't do considerably better than that on a halfway decent track. They seldom had the track, pioneer railroad construction being what it was. But in 1893, during the Columbian Exposition at Chicago, an American-type locomotive, the New York Central's No. 999, did a verified 112½ miles an hour on a stretch between Batavia and Buffalo, New York. That is traveling, even for today.

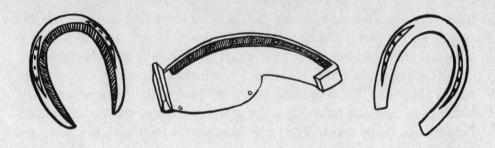

VII

HOOF TRAILS AND WHEEL TRACKS

AS YOU begin to get an over-all picture of the Old West you come to see it in the image of a great loom. True, there was much variation, where local designs were being worked out. But in the great pattern of the West, from the Mississippi to the mountains, the woof of the weaving was the tracks of the traders, the gold seekers, the sodbusters, the businessmen. These ran east and west, crossing the eternal warp made long before by the Indians, the buffalo, the trail herds and herders, which went north and south.

Between them, the hoofs and the wheels contrived to weave the fabric of a society which even its neighbors, the eastern and western coastal areas, do not understand. In the East, too many of the threads run the same way— up and down—and the North tends to fear and disparage the South, while the South resents and rejects the North. New York cross-weaves with Europe as much as with interior America. And the West Coast is a golden, island world of its own. But in the Old West—which begins at the Mississippi (despite Fort Worth's claims) and ends somewhere in the Rocky Mountains —American threads cross each other with peculiar American purpose. It is not something to be understood, but rather absorbed. You do not learn it. You live it.

Sometime in the dim past the ancestors of American Indians had come drifting from the north down the Great Way of the Winds, between the river and the rocks, all the way to the tropical forests. The buffalo, life tide of the land, shuttled annually back and forth from north to south in giant herds, and the Indians followed the buffalo. (Not that it was quite this simple, for the Plains Indians were, and still are, almost as cross-woven as were and are the whites of the land, a fact not generally appreciated.)

Now look at the trails. There were two main kinds which we may identify by the traffic that dominated them, the hoof trails of the wild animals, the Indians, and the ranchers, and the wheel trails of the traders, miners, farmers, and businessmen. The hoof trails, for the most part, run north and south. And the wheel trails go east and west. After the manner of our objective generation, we have mapped and defined the wheel tracks very exactly, while permitting the hoof tracks to fade almost into oblivion.

Let's take the wheels first. As my friend and colleague, Stanley Vestal, the Western historian, begins his classic, *The Old Santa Fe Trail*,[1] a hundred years ago there were three great ways from the river edge of American civilization into the mysterious West.

One, the Oregon Trail, went up the Platte River, over South Pass, and eventually on to the forests of Oregon and the north Pacific coast.

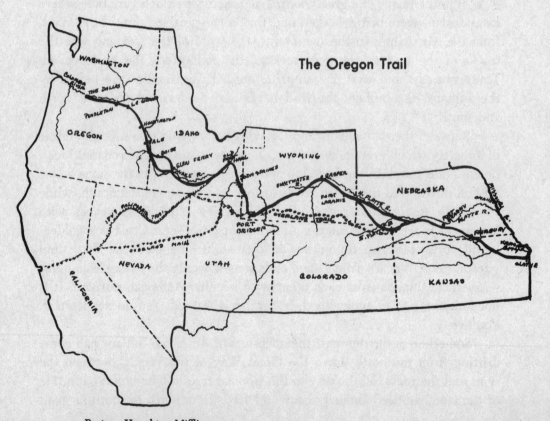

The Oregon Trail

1. Boston: Houghton Mifflin, 1939.

The second route was the Missouri River itself, also traversing the Great Plains, and heading up into the Rockies. This too was a wheel route, if you will—paddle wheels, side and stern, on steamboats.

The third, stretching from the Missouri to Santa Fe and thence on to California, was the Santa Fe Trail.

When the iron trails broke through to the Pacific, they repeated these patterns with variations and amplifications. The Union Pacific-Central Pacific made it across the middle in 1869, establishing what you might call the Oregon Trail of the railroads, even though the magnetic pull of forty-niner gold did draw it just a leetle south!

The Atchison, Topeka, and Santa Fe, largely following the Old Santa Fe Trail, reached Santa Fe from Kansas in 1880, and California in 1883.

The Southern Pacific, backtracking west to east, was in Deming, New Mexico, and El Paso, Texas, by 1881, to connect with the Santa Fe there, and by 1883, buying and building, it had gone on east to San Antonio, Houston, and New Orleans. This was the famed Southern Route, not too far from where John Butterfield's Overland Mail stages had swung from San Francisco and Los Angeles to Forth Smith, Arkansas, where they separated, some to go to Memphis, some to St. Louis.

The Northern Pacific, building from the Superior-Duluth area through Bismarck, South Dakota, toward Portland, Oregon, and building east from Pasco, Washington, at the same time, to speed the work, completed its line in 1883.

The Great Northern, driven by James J. Hill, former steamboat freight agent, went through from St. Paul to Seattle in 1893. Those are the iron trails.

Now let's look for the hoof trails, mainly running north and south; already these are mystical, just as there is an unmistakably mystical feeling about the Great Plains themselves. There is something solid and enduring about a wooded area, a sense of company. But on the plains, the early traveler was always tortured by loneliness and isolation, by the constant awareness of his own small self asking the question, "Where am I?" So it is with the hoof trails today.

Men and horses by the thousands, cloven hoofs by the millions, passed along these roads, beating their traces far and wide and deep. But where were they then, where are they today? In Oklahoma and North Texas, right on the ground, we have been arguing that question for a generation. Perhaps we'll never really settle it.

But, with apologies to those who distinguish them slightly otherwise, here in outline are the great hoof trails.

They start in South Texas where, in the coastal area between the

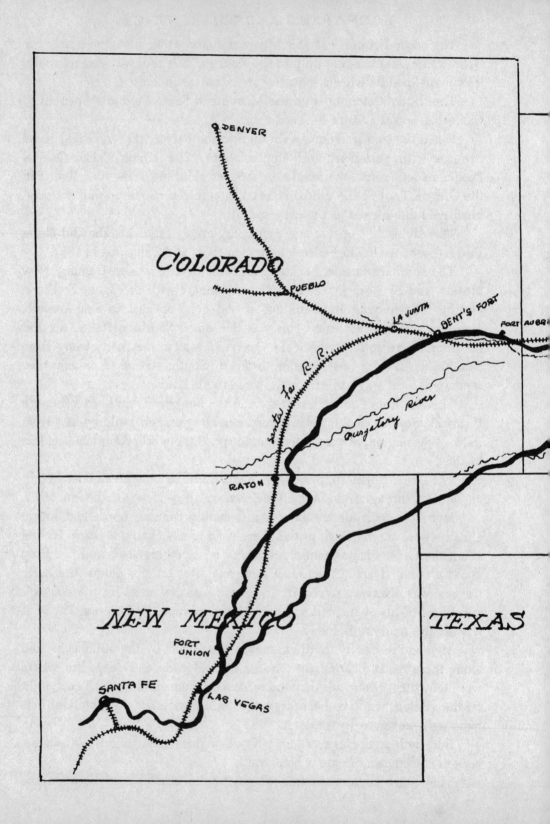

The Old Santa Fe Trail
and the Atchison, Topeka, and Santa Fe Railroad

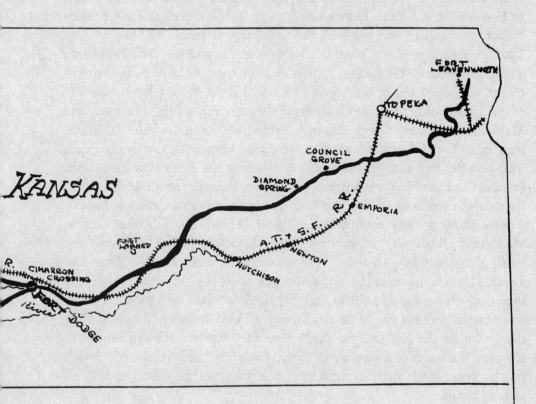

Colorado and Rio Grande rivers, the Western-range cattle business had its beginnings in the two generations before the Civil War. In those years you could leave St. Louis, go west to Sedalia, Missouri, thence south and west to Fort Smith, Arkansas, thence angling across the corner of the Choctaw Nation over a road laid out with the assistance of Jesse Chisholm to Fort Towson, where at Fort Towson Landing you crossed the Red River into Texas. This was *not* the famous Chisholm Trail, though the Scotch-Cherokee trader, already noted in the 1830s as a trail blazer, helped lay it out.

Another route from St. Louis came through Springfield, Missouri, and Maysville, Arkansas, thence through Tahlequah, capital of the Cherokee Nation, to Fort Gibson, where it made connections with the Texas Road. This was the first and greatest route connecting the Lone Star State with Missouri and the North. It entered the Indian Nations (now Oklahoma) at the extreme northeast corner, between Baxter Springs and Chetopa, Kansas, it went slanting away southwest, past Fort Gibson, through what is now McAlester, Oklahoma, on through Boggy Depot to Colbert's Ferry, just north of Preston (now Denison), Texas, where it crossed the Red River into Texas. This was the main route of emigrants into Texas from the North, and they were swarming down it as early as the late 1820s and early 1830s. It was also the route of the Missouri, Kansas & Texas Railway Co. (originally the Union Pacific Railway, Southern Branch), which reached Denison in 1873 and the hands of a receiver in 1874. It was also the first trail northward for the Texas cattle drivers, right after the war; and they too ran into all sorts of trouble.

The difficulty, at least as far as the trail drivers were concerned, lay in the fact that this early road had been laid out by the wheel people. And they're different from the hoof-trail people, just as the woods Indians were and are different from the Plains Indians. You see, when you're on foot driving a wagon on which you ride occasionally, you want to be in or close to timber. But when you're mounted, and driving half-wild cattle or horses, timber is the last place you care to be.

Because the early travelers coming from the east were essentially foot travelers and woodsmen, they were afraid of the great open spaces. They settled in the timber but left the plains alone, even calling them the Great American Desert. The horse-and-cow men, when they got to timbered country, found nestors and sodbusters, who were their natural enemies. "Nestors," by the way, were probably given this name ironically after the old Greek counselor named Nestor in the *Iliad*, meaning "wiseacres," and not because of any connection with nests. When the Texas cattlemen of 1866 were trying to drive up the Texas Road, they met with the East Kansas nestors around Baxter Springs. The Kansans said, probably with some justice, that the Texas longhorns had ticks carrying Texas fever and they wanted no part of either the men or the beasts. They had set up a deadline for Texas cattle and were enforcing it with rifles and shotguns.

It was practically an act of war, a blockade, and this was just the country for it. The Civil War might be officially over elsewhere, but it would be going on for a decade or so more in this border country, where the ex-Southern guerrillas from Quantrill's band and the ex-Northern Jay-hawkers once led by Jennison and Lane would continue to spread violence for years.

The trail drivers couldn't get through, and you can't sell a steer if you can't get him to market. So they milled around awhile and then tried the next best thing, swinging their hoof trail west. They were aided in arriving at this brilliant solution by a Yankee of Springfield, Illinois, one Joseph G. McCoy. Young Joseph could not see why longhorns and iron rails should not go together, almost as naturally as ham and eggs. He found that the Kansas Pacific railroad was building west through Kansas and had even reached Salina, which was full of nestors too, all wanting no part of Texans or tick trouble. But there was a lonely little whistlestop a bit farther east, called Abilene. And, heck, Abilene would take a chance on anything!

The Kansas Pacific wouldn't, though, and neither would the connecting Missouri Pacific. But the Hannibal & St. Joseph was a bit smarter, or at least more daring. McCoy got a grudging agreement from the Kansas Pacific to build a siding, *provided* the Hannibal & St. Joe would take on the horrible task of actually carrying those Texas ticks with cows attached. The Hannibal & St. Joe did; it took them right on up to Chicago, instead of to St. Louis, thus making Chicago the greatest meat market in the world.

Then McCoy set out to steer the steers into Abilene. This was in 1867. The year previous, perhaps a quarter-million Texas cattle had tried trekking north. Because of the nestor troubles McCoy succeeded in enticing only about 35,000 to his nice new pens. That was enough. The next year there were longhorns by the mile, Texas was out of the timber, and the trail-driving boom was on. And while it lasted there was never anything quite like it in all history.

The route these herds followed was the Chisholm Trail, laid out in 1865 by Jesse Chisholm, leisurely driving his loaded trade wagons down from about the present site of Wichita, Kansas, to barter with the Indians on the Washita River near Fort Cobb. Jesse was not a cowman, at least not primarily; he was not John Chisum, the Texas cattle king; and he was not

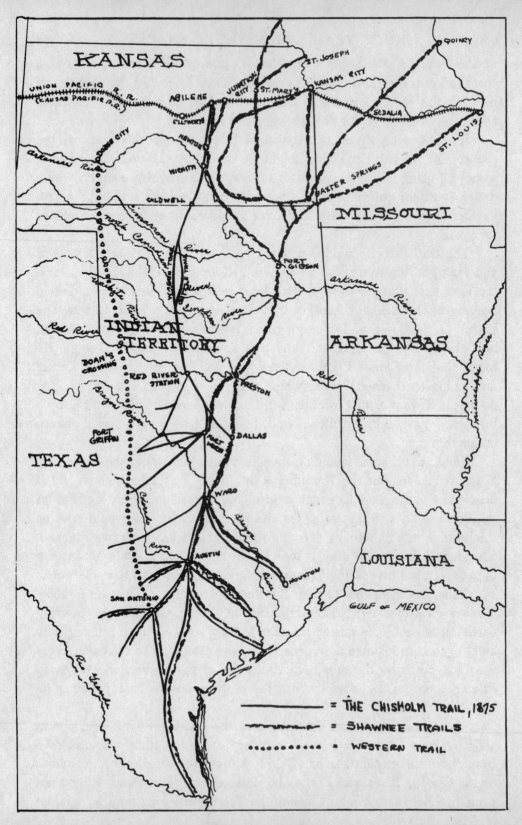

Cattle-driving trails

even the first trail blazer over the route. Lieutenant Colonel William H. Emory, commanding the Union troops that had garrisoned Forts Cobb, Washita, Arbuckle, and Smith, had gathered his men at the outbreak of the war in 1861, and, guided by the noted Delaware Indian, Black Beaver, had retreated to Kansas over approximately the same trace. There'd been nearly a thousand in that column, with wagons and animals, so they must have left quite a track. Chisholm, four years later, merely backtracked it. He did not even blaze the rest of the way to the Red River and Texas, about 80 miles, the way the trail ran, from the Washita.

But the Chisholm Trail it became, one of the most famous trail names in all history. As the drivers used it, the Chisholm entered the Nations (as the Indian Territory was called) at Red River Station, about 100 miles west of Colbert's Ferry, on the old Texas Road. The old station is almost due south of present Waurika and Ryan, Oklahoma, and U. S. Highway 81 pretty much retraces the route. From Red River the Chisholm went crawling due north, crossing the Washita River just east of what is now Chickasha, Oklahoma, the South Canadian at Silver City, splitting here into two forks. The west fork, used also by the stagecoaches, passed through Fort Reno, while the east fork went by present Yukon, about midway between present El Reno and Oklahoma City. You realize that most of these flourishing metropolises weren't present when all this was going on and wouldn't be until after 1889 and later, when the government started opening up Oklahoma for white settlement. The forks joined again at Dover, on the north side of the Cimarron River, and the single trail went on then through present Hennessey (where Pat Hennessey was killed by Injuns in an attack on his freighting train in 1874), through Enid, Pond Creek, the Salt Fork of the Arkansas, Sewall's Ranch, then, angling north by east into Kansas, to Caldwell and Abilene.

The trail traveled in part through the Chic and Choc Country, as the lands of the Chickasaws and their closely allied kinsmen, the Choctaws, were called. These two nations were among the Five Civilized Tribes (the others were the Cherokees, Creeks, and Seminoles). They didn't care a whole lot for the idea of providing free passage and free pastures, too, for a lot of Texans. So they did various things, including the passage of a tax of 10 cents a head on all tourist longhorns.

For this and other reasons, yet another cow path presently developed across the Nations. This one was known as the Western Trail, the Fort Dodge Trail, the Fort Griffin-Fort Dodge Trail, naming both ends, and at the last the Dodge City Trail. This multi-monikered road was not the westernmost trail, but was about 100 miles west of the Chisholm Trail. It was established partly by trail herds coming in from West Texas, partly by other trail outfits sliding west to escape those taxes, fences, and nestors. It entered Indian Territory at Doan's Crossing on Red River, just north of Doan's Store (established in 1878 by J. Doan, though the crossing itself had been in use for several years previously) in the bend of the Red River just north of present Vernon, Texas, and slightly southeast of Altus, Oklahoma—just a little way upstream from the mouth of the north fork of the Red. The trail followed that north fork for a while, then went on north through the lands of the Comanches and Kiowas, the Cheyennes and Arapahoes—"wild Indians" or "blanket Indians," quite different from the Five Civilized Tribes to the east. It went on past lonely places with colorful names like Soldier's Spring, Rock Crossing, and Cedar Springs, a noted watering stop; then to Buffalo Springs, on over the Cimarron, just over the line in Kansas to Deep Hole Crossing, Chief Dull Knife's old camping ground, and thence into Dodge. The railroads were building west too, spewing sodbusters along their lines, so the railroads kept shifting the cattle terminals westward to stay out of barbed wire and civilization. Starting as it did at the old buffalo-hunters' and outlaws' hangout, Fort Griffin, this trail was tougher than the Chisholm. According to cowboy tradition, the very first herd over it was "wet" cattle, surreptitiously acquired by illegal means in Mexico, hotfooting it north for the Nations with a Texas posse on its heels.

Still another trail, even farther west, was established in 1866 by Oliver Loving and Colonel Charles Goodnight, and it ran west, not north, at least to start. Hopping off from old Fort Concho, now San Angelo, Texas, the Loving-Goodnight herds trekked west to the Pecos River, hitting it at Horsehead Crossing, then trailing up its brackish bitter waters clear to Fort Sumner, New Mexico, and eventually into Colorado. In 1868 this trail was extended clear on into Wyoming and the northern ranges. It was a toughie, this Goodnight, or Goodnight-Loving Trail, because from the Middle Concho to the Pecos was a 90-mile dry drive, no permanent water. There were Comanches and Lipans as well, along with white outlaws, all beef-hungry. Many a longhorn, to say nothing of cowboy and cayuse, just didn't make it.

In 1884, taking alarm too late, the cattlemen tried to get a National Cattle Trail set aside, a 3- to 6-mile strip extending from the Red River to Canada, with homesteaders and sodbusters and their dang barbed wire strictly excluded. But it never panned out, and after the Big Blizzard of 1886 had put its cold crimp in the cattle business, it didn't much matter anyhow. Trail-driving days were about over. By 1893 the real free Old

West was gone, since in that year the government gave out the last of its good land for free homesteading, and in the next four or five years even the northern ranges were pretty well filled up. The old days had vanished, and with them the old hoof trails.

These, then, were the hoof trails, and where they went after passing the Nations, dark heart of the West—to Kansas or on north to Colorado, Wyoming, Nebraska, the Dakotas, Montana, even Canada—doesn't matter. The Nations, the Kansas line (the Kansas quarantine), and Parallel 36 North, the Colorado quarantine line made famous by the classic cowboy novel, *North of 36*, by Emerson Hough[2]—these were the real barriers. Once north of them you were in Yankee country, brisk, bustling, with plenty of Yankee energy and Yankee cash to stock ranches, build cities, string railroads, start packing plants and factories—all the thousand and one things the nation needed.

Now let's look at the men, the horses, and the cows that broke the barriers and went up the long trails.

The trail drivers began their gatherings away down in South Texas in the *brasada,* the brush country, between the Nueces, "deadline for sheriffs," and the Rio Grande. To know what that country was really like, you'd just have to go down and get scratched by those thorns, get yourself really blooded. Even the inimitable J. Frank Dobie, past master at bringing the Old West back to life, cannot quite do full justice to those stickers.

Into those sun-baked thickets the Spanish and Mexicans, and after them the Anglo-Saxon Texans, had chivvied their longhorned cattle and thorn-scarred caballos, and at the close of the Civil War the place was literally busting with beef. Some of those steers were 10 to 12 years old; hundreds of thousands of them had never been branded. There wasn't any law and order to speak of above a whisper, and all you needed was a rope and a running iron—which you could improvise, with a cinch ring and a couple of sticks to hold it—to brand yourself rich. Though, of course, the man who owned those cows, or claimed to, might just up and hang you high as Haman, and with your own rope, if he caught you exercising your hot-iron artistry.

But there wasn't too much chance of getting caught, not in those thickets! And up No'th they paid real money—$20 a head or so—for those steers. In Texas you could get them for between $5 and $10, even if you paid for them, and, as the trail drivers discovered when they got around to calculating it out, it cost about a dollar a mile to trail a sizable herd up to market. One buck for the whole herd! You could make money that way.

2. New York: D. Appleton & Co., 1923.

And money was one thing Texans didn't have plenty of, back there in 1865-66, right after the Surrender. As Texans saw it, the Union hadn't licked the Lone Star State, hadn't even successfully invaded it, and the last battle of the war, fought at Palmito Hill near Brownsville on May 12 and 13 (more than a month after Appomattox), had ended with the Confederates advancing. But that still didn't make Confederate money any good any more, and so, as the Texans came riding home, from Terry's Texas Rangers, from John B. Hood's old outfits, and such, they just naturally shifted from watching out for Yankee bluebellies to looking for Yankee greenbacks. And what more promising than selling 'em cows?

They went out on cow hunts, as they called roundups down in the brush country in those days. And, remembering that brush, you know why. You never round up anything in that stuff; you hunt it down.

Getting ready for a cow hunt, you drove or "choused" in your string of cowponies, of which you'd need six or seven at least. You'd be wearing your *brasadero* rig, so let's look at that, head to toe.

The hat or sombrero was not too big, because the limbs and thorns would tear it all to where Confederate money had just gone. It generally had a barbiquejo or bonnet string, meaning a chin strap, which had better not be too tight, or too tough either, or it might hang and break your fool neck. Like the chin strap on a modern Army helmet, it was a dubious addition. But if you lost your hat, you couldn't go back to find it in that doggone brush.

Around your neck would be a bandanna, close-wrapped to keep it from
flopping and catching in the brush. In the stickers it was some protection
to the throat. But don't let the romanticists kid you, the main reason cowboys wore bandannas was because most collars, if any, on early shirts
looked like hell and left an expanse of turkey neck bare to whatever and
sundry. With decent collars, the bandanna either got tucked inside to make
the open collar look a little dressier, or it went into a pocket where it
belonged. The shirt itself would be hickory or linsey-woolsey—or maybe
wool in the wintertime, because the cold can penetrate worse at freezing
point along the Bravo than it does at zero in the mountains. Over this shirt
you'd have a tough leather or duck brush jacket, once again to keep those
thorns from taking you all apart. Incidentally, you'd sometimes be called a
brush popper.

On your legs you would have the stoutest pants you could find, and
quite possibly, even in the sixties, the original California cowboy sports
wear, Levis. These weren't "overalls," mind you. A dyed-in-the-wool old-
time cowboy wouldn't be caught dead in nestor overalls. They were "pants,"
and made by a firm destined to become as famous in the West as Stetson
or Colt.

Levi Strauss, a member of a New York tailoring family, heard the
siren call of California gold and shipped out for the diggings, via clipper
and Cape Horn, in 1849. He financed his way in part by selling cloth to
his fellow passengers and arrived at length in San Francisco with practically no lengths left, except a bolt of canvas he had thought he'd sell for
miners' tents.

But the miners didn't need tents in sunny California; they needed
pants—rough, tough pants, hard-rock pants, the tougher the better. So
Strauss tried making some out of his tent cloth, and found he had struck a
gold mine without ever lifting a pick. He sent rush orders home to his
family in New York for all the duck and denim they could buy. And Levi
Strauss & Company was on its way to fame and fortune.

"Levi's pants," soon known just as Levis, were tailor-made jobs, or at
least tailor-designed for the job in hand, and the quality of the product
was scrupulously maintained, both by Levi and by his successors. They
were low-waisted, snug in the hips, with slim tapering legs; they were
comfortable in the mines and in the saddle, and they wore like iron. Early
in the game Strauss settled on indigo-blue dye, both as the best color he
could find and as a hallmark for his product. Sometime in the sixties he
adopted the idea of copper-riveting the pockets and strain points.

Shortly after the war, Strauss expanded operations into Texas. At first

Levis were sent by ship from California to Galveston and Indianola, Texas seaports, but factories were established later in the Lone Star. The copper rivets, the leather label on the waistband, the orange thread with which the blue denim is sewed, and the oilcloth ticket identifying the garment as a genuine Levi Strauss—all were in use by 1870 and were patented or copyrighted until about 1908. Levis were, and still are, *the* Western pants.

So under his chaps the brush hand would be wearing Levis—or else homemade trousers, which was about as likely. The pants would fit tight enough to stay up by themselves, or he might have a gay Mexican sash to hold them up and keep his belly warm, or he just might have galluses, with the buttons on the outside of the waistband, and not elastic, by the bye. Or, if he was a real old-timer like a Mountain Man, he might even be wearing buckskins, hunting shirt, and leggings and moccasins.

Injun leg coverings were leggings, not pants. Up under the shirt they just ended, with no crotch and no seat, and around your middle you wore, if anything, a separate breechclout or cloth. One of the troubles missionaries and Indian agents in Oklahoma used to have was keeping their wild wards from cutting all the important parts out of the pants a benevolent civilization was trying to force them into. I mean blanket Indians, of course, not the Civilized Tribes.

Levis

But there never was more comfortable footgear fashioned than properly made Indian moccasins, provided one didn't try to walk too far in them. And what Plains Indian or white Texan ever wanted to walk? But even so, your early *vaquero* (Mexican for cowboy) would most likely be wearing boots. They were his first real trademark.

The boots would probably be calfskin, coming up to just under the knees, cut off square at the tops and perhaps with "mule-ear" tugs hanging down on each side. Or there'd be canvas loops inside to help pull 'em on. And around the bunkhouse or somewhere on the place were bootjacks, homemade at first, just a board with a notch in it to fit around the back of the boot, so you could yank the boot off while standing on the board with the other foot. Later, as life grew more luxurious, so also did the bootjacks, and you might have an iron beetle (the boot fitted between the antennae), or maybe a steer, or even, if you

BOOTS AND SPURS

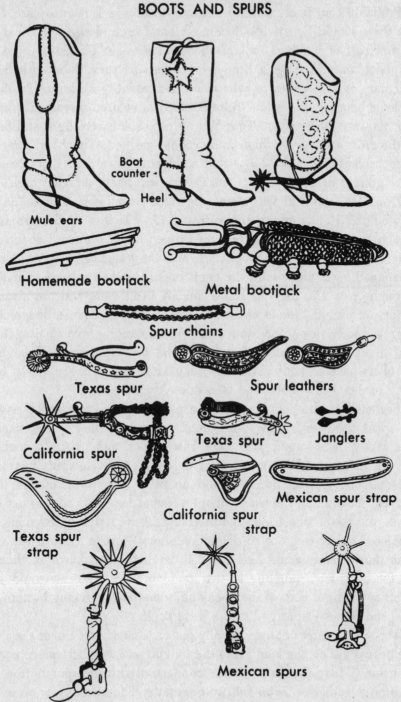

Mule ears

Boot counter

Heel

Homemade bootjack

Metal bootjack

Spur chains

Texas spur

Spur leathers

California spur

Texas spur

Janglers

Texas spur strap

California spur strap

Mexican spur strap

Mexican spurs

were a bachelor and just plumb incorrigible, an inexpressibly wicked Naughty Lady.

Probably your boots would be square-toed, and I mean square. Sometimes there would be a wide decorated band around the top, or at least the front half of it, like a jockey's boot. This might be red or blue on a black boot, or yellow on a brown one. Perhaps there'd be cutouts, too, Lone Stars or horseshoes or whatever, and possibly elaborate scrolls. Or the whole boot would be fancifully stitched in colored thread. But usually the boots were rather plain. Toes had no cap. Soles were light and flexible and the arch was curved high and wooden-pegged. The heel, sometimes straight, sometimes underslung—that is, sloping inward so that actually it hit the ground darn near under the instep—was about 2 inches high.

Don't let them kid you about the reason for heels, either. "So your foot wouldn't slide through the stirrup"? Or, "To dig in the ground for leverage, to hold a wild one after you'd roped him"? Maybe. But the Army in flat heels, the Injuns in moccasins, and the gauchos of South America all managed, right along with the gents on stilts, when it came to handling the rough ones. The truth is, those cowboy heels were and are a mark of position, an insignia, like a colonel's eagles or a policeman's badge. When you get a good pair on, they shove you up into another world altogether, a world that's not as mean and petty as the flatfoot pedestrian landscape most of us have to hoof it through, day after day. They're wings to the spirit, those cowboy boots—and who doesn't want wings?

Fastened on the boots would be a pair of spurs for which you would have spent some real money, ten bucks or more. They would likely be Texas style, hand-forged jobs with rowels not more than 3 inches in diameter and more likely 2 inches or under. Texas-style spurs were fairly plain and heavy, with the heelband about 1 inch wide, maybe lightly engraved, maybe not, the shank about 2 inches long and not curved much if at all, the rowel wheel blunt-pointed and in the shape of anything from a 5-pointed star to a 17- or 18-pointed sunburst. Just in front of the rowel, on the shank, there would likely be a little chap-guard barrel or thumb to keep the chap from tangling in the steel. And the leathers would go on buttons at the front ends of the heelband, sometimes swinging buttons, on a staple, sometimes just forged to the band itself.

The spur leather or strap, usually cut on a curve to fit over the instep, came in two pieces, the long piece the tongue and the short piece carrying the buckle. Where the tongue piece connected with the spur button there was often a leather or metal *concho* or rosette. The buckle was often worn on the inside of the foot, where it would be less likely to catch on limbs and brush, and the decorative concho was on the outside.

The early spur often had two buttons on the heelband, one for the spur strap, the other for another tie-down strap that went on down around the arch, just in front of the heel, to hold the spur firmly in place. Sometimes heel chains, permanently attached to the spur, would take the place of this strap, and these, worn loose, would clink pleasantly as the wearer strode along. Sometimes they'd just leave this heel strap or chain off, and just let the weight and fit of the spur hold it loosely down.

Add a pair of janglers, little bell-clapper pieces to clink against the rowels and make cheerful noises as you rode along, and you were really well heeled. And you could walk in these Texas spurs, by the way, since they sat high, on the counter of the boot rather than the heel, and you could, if you wished, just leave 'em hitched to your boots when you peeled to your socks. With a California spur you generally didn't do this.

The Californios, in that golden world of their own, hadn't been troubled much with Anglo-Saxon influence until the time of the Mexican War. Even now the California cowboy seems a lot more Spanish or Mexican in his getup than are his hossbacker compadres on the other side of the Rockies. Wearing low-heeled shoes in his earlier incarnations, the California vaquero had on them a pair of straight-shanked spurs he had to take off every time he lit down from his saddle, because the darn things had rowels anywhere up to 6 or 7 inches in diameter, practically as big as steamboat paddle wheels. There were spikes on these monstrosities too, often as sharp as nails. And lots of Californians kept on wearing them even after adopting the universal cowboy boot, because in a way they were insignia too, going back through Mexico and Spain to the stickers the knights had worn on their armored heels and had had to win the hard way, the spur being the mark of knighthood.

Ever since the days of Rome the mounted man has been the noble, the aristocrat, of Western civilization, which is the main reason you get into such big arguments over boot heels, spurs, saddles, hosses, and such. The American cowboy, in reality, was the very last of the hossback aristocrats, a member of just about the only aristocracy a good man could get into entirely on his own merits.

Spanish and Mexican spurs, "chihuahuas" as they were often called in the Old West, also had huge sharp rowels, though the heelbands and shanks were often more on the Texan than the Californian style. Actually it was the other way around; we got the cowboy spur from Mexico. It is Latin in its antecedents and a knight's spur by origin, only slightly modernized. The Anglo-Saxon spur, which came riding West to hook up with it, was basically the military spur, generally of brass, where the cowboy's was steel; shank curving upward, though the cowboy's was straight or down-curved; small sharp rowel, to the cowman's huge blunt one; firmly strapped low on the heel, while the range style was hung relatively loose and high, almost on the ankle. And no real old cowpoke would have been caught dead in any "English" Army-type spur.

Over the boots and pants, when he was in the saddle, the old-time cowboy would be wearing chaps (pronounced "shaps"), American short for *chaparrejos* or *chaparreras,* which in Spanish-American means leather breeches, though the root word itself is *chaparro,* the evergreen oak. A chaparral originally meant a thicket of evergreen oaks, of which you find plenty in South Texas. And when you mix them with about eighteen jillion kinds of thorny mesquite and cactus, you need leather breeches if you aim to do any penetrating. Chaps are like Indian leggings, with no seat; usually each leg is separate, or the two are laced together only in front, or maybe just held with a bit of whang string.

Leather breeches, I suppose, are practically as old as the idea of pants themselves. But the cowboy variety really started, down in Mexico away back when, with a sort of skirt or apron. These were big flaps of tough leather called *armas* that fastened over the front of the saddle and hung

Armitas   Chaps

down on each side. When you climbed aboard you tucked them over your legs like a robe. And when you got down they stayed on the saddle. There is something to be said for this arrangement, but at best it is clumsy and leaves part of your anatomy defenseless. So the next step was to take the leather aprons off the saddle and put them on the man.

These were called *armitas*, "little arms," both words coming from the Spanish *arma*, weapon, which included shields. The armitas were leather aprons, two of them, hanging from a belt around your middle and coming down to your boot tops, and provided with thongs along the sides so you could tie them around your legs. Actually they were chaps of a sort, but they too were clumsy and slow to get in and out of. So, although you could see armas and armitas down in Mexico and along the Bravo and probably quite a few in California, by trail-driving days the American cowboy east of the Rockies had adopted the real chaps. These were a pair of leather legs reaching from his spurs to his waist in front, and to the seat of his pants behind, held up by an attached waistbelt.

At the start, these chaps were closed-leg chaps; that is, the legs were permanently sewed, quite often with fringe down the outer seam, like Indian leggings. And Texans just after the Civil War called them leggings, not chaps. There wasn't much love lost between Texans and Mexicans in those days, and though a Texan might adopt a good Mexican idea, he'd give it an American name. But, since these closed-leg or shotgun chaps were hot, and clumsy to get on and off, there were also wrap-around open-leg chaps (or leggings, as you prefer), which hooked or buckled or tied together somewhat like armitas.

On these chaps the inside part, between your leg and the horse, just comes back and connects with the outer flap, or wing, where you see the line of conchas or rosettes, and you can unsnap your chaps and back out of them. This style leaves more or less of a loose flap, extending on back from the leg for further protection. The style came to be called the Texas wing chap because it was at first a characteristic Texas style. Later the chaps makers began to cut away the lower part of the inside leg, curving it so it wouldn't catch on the stirrup so easily, and this was called the Cheyenne leg. (Cheyenne was a great town for originating cowboy styles, a sort of frontier Paris.) Originally the chap was worn fastened all the way down, except that the knee buckle might be left loose for comfort. Nowadays it's generally left open from the knee down. Those with a big, flaring wing are called bat-wing chaps. And you could, if you wished, have wings on closed-leg chaps as well.

Up in the northern ranges the closed-leg style was preferred because it was warmer. These were often called shotgun chaps because they looked kind of like a double-barreled shotgun. You could get you a pair complete even to the choke in the barrels—the bottoms narrowed to keep those icy northern winds from blowing up your legs.

Remember that the cowboy was *not* considered a style-setting, glamorous figure in the Old West, not even by himself. Two things had to happen before the Western horseman would become the beau ideal, the peerless knight of American song and saga, and those two things were just beginning to happen in the sixties and seventies. First, the cowboy had to cross trails with the sodbuster, the horseman tangle with the man on foot. Hated though he was, the cowboy was still a romantic figure to the farmer—who knows how much of the legend comes from the daydreams of farm boys? And then the jongleurs, the minstrels, the storytellers, and the showmen must make capital of the drama. And Ned Buntline, Buffalo Bill, Major John Burke, Pawnee Bill, Badger Clark, Jack Thorp, Frederic Remington, Owen Wister, Emerson Hough, and their innumerable fellows have done a swell job of that.

But in the meantime, very slowly, the glory gear and trappings must be devised and gathered, for the white rider did not have the gauds of his red opponent—the war bonnets, decorated coupsticks, and such—nor even the charro color of his Mexican compadre to the south. Looking back, three-quarters of a century later, we tend to fall into anachronism, like the Renaissance painters who naïvely dressed the Biblical characters on their canvases in medieval armor and costumes. This is not such a horrible crime as I might be making it appear, since one of the major aims of good art is to persuade the observer that he is, somehow, a part of the picture. But that is illusion. It's more fun, in the end, to know what was real.

In the Old West a number of things were remarkably different from the way later artists, writers, and movie producers have re-created them, and among them, certainly, was the lingo. There are all sorts of Western terms now current that were seldom or never heard then.

For one example, the word roundup, and even the action it denotes—gathering together all the cattle or horses in an area in one big herd—were strange to the Old West. Instead you heard of a "cow hunt," or "gathering cows," and the outfit engaged in the hunt was a "cow crowd" or "bunch." Even the idea of an annual roundup was Eastern, imported from the Southern mountain country where for generations the mountain folk let their stock run loose and about once a year got out with the neighbors to bunch the stock up and sort it out, just to see what they had. In the period around the Civil War the idea came west and the cattlemen adopted it. The term has hung on long after fences and barbed wire have made it pretty mean-ingless.

Or buckaroo. It's a northern corruption of *vaquero,* and it had to wait until the northern ranges had been stocked and northern cowboys had their chance to mess up Spanish even more than had the Texas cowhands, with their Tex-Mex, which, incidentally, is a language in itself.

Or cowpoke, or even cowpuncher. You'd probably have got poked in early Abilene for calling a rider that, because the original pokes or punchers weren't cowboys at all. They were pickup vagrants who rode the cattle trains and punched the cattle with long poles, thrust between the bars, to get them up on their feet; a downed animal in a railroad car is likely to get injured or even killed. But by the late eighties and nineties the terms had got respectable, maybe because so many real cowboys had ridden the "rattlers" (trains) in as punchers, just to see the big town.

Ramon F. Adams, Western historian, has made a lifetime study of these Western terms and their origins, and his dictionary, *Western Words,* is a must for anyone interested in writing about or even understanding the Old American West.

You want to remember that the Western cowman was a conservative. When he found something that worked pretty well, he hung on to it, because it was generally his life and his money he was betting. And until the "Bill shows" and then the rodeos started demonstrating what a helluva feller the cowboy was, he never even thought about duding himself up much, especially not out on the range. Save for the working specialties he had to wear, like chaps and spurs and maybe a pistol, he wore just about what everybody else did in his time. His working pants were blue or brown, denim or duck; his dress-up pants, when he wore them, most likely black broadcloth, blue serge, or "gambler's stripe," a black material with a fine white stripe, much affected by gamblers, which came in either wool or cotton. His working shirts were gray, or maybe blue. His hat was black, or gray, or just possibly brown. The only touch of color about him would be where the ordinary man wears it now, in the scarf around his neck. And that, most likely, would be a red or blue cotton bandanna. Blacks, browns, grays, and blues were the standard colors, not only because they showed dirt less, but also because dyes were pretty poor back in those days.

But the old-time cowman had two flashing examples to try to live up to. They were the Mexican vaqueros, and the Plains Indians. You never saw anything gaudier than a bunch of Mexican cowmen on dress parade, unless it was Plains Indians. The Mexicans had sombreros worth maybe 500 pesos per each, silver buttons big as 'dobe dollars, silver-mounted saddles, rainbow Saltillo serapes, and horse trappings just out of this world. And the Plains Indians, with their buckskins, feathers, and beads, put on a mighty fine show too—and some of 'em still do, as you can see if you go down to Anadarko some summer for their big fair and parade! The white male has had his feathers trimmed too durn much in this dreary world!

Now if you could just dress up fancy free, like the cowboy, after the shows started giving him the idea! You could get a pair of chaps and put conchas all down the legs—these are really just washers, used originally to keep a thong from pulling through, but in nickel or silver they can be mighty pretty—and then maybe add your initials, your brand, or whatever, in nailhead brads on the wings.

You could have the pockets made of different-colored leather. Generally chaps have two pockets, one on the front of each leg, patched on like little

Pawnee chief   El Charro

purses, though sometimes the pockets are inside and have vertical openings, like the side pockets on a modern pair of pants. You could carve and decorate your chaps belt—generally it buckles over your left rear where a fancy buckle wouldn't do much good, but you can wear one on your pants or pistol belt, of course.

Or you can go real fancy and make your chaps out of something other than just old cowhide. For hard service there's nothing better than cowhide and even in cold weather it's windproof, which is what you want for service. But you can use goathide with the hair left on, or bearskin, and there was at least one gay caballero who actually did have a pair of genuine tiger-skin chaps. He was King Fisher, of South Texas, and an unfortunate circus that happened into his bailiwick, down Uvalde way, unhappily supplied the tiger.

Wolf, sheep, horse, and cougar or panther or catamount or mountain lion or puma (which are a lot of names for the same cat) were other possible sources for snappy chappies, and the Mexicans and Californians had been doing things with these for quite a while, even before the war. But the American cowboy didn't really go for fur chaps, angoras (made from Angora goat hide), or woolies (sheepskin) until he got up on the northern ranges in Montana, Wyoming, and the Dakotas, all of which were largely stocked from Texas. When you were riding out in a blizzard up there fur chaps made sense. But elsewhere, and in warmer weather, they were seldom seen, except in shows.

Out on genuine open prairie, where there wasn't any brush, your cowboy probably wouldn't wear his chaps, except maybe for protection from the cold. As soon as he got out of brush country he'd shed that brush jacket too, in favor of a vest. The vest is another curious cow-country garment that needs elucidating. If you are looking at a modern weskit, the reason anybody would want to wear that doggone thing as a work dress just plain escapes you. But when you look at the old-time vest, and also see what else there was to wear, it begins to make sense. Vests were the best choice they had.

Actually they were following a very old tradition that goes back to armor and knighthood, just as did their saddles and spurs. The idea of a jerkin, a short, usually sleeveless garment made of leather or heavy cloth, was ancient among horsemen, the knights wearing them as padding under their mail, while for the humbler riders the leather served as cuirass and armor. Leather jerkins lasted in the American Army at least until World War I, where they had them made of heavy leather, wool-lined, sleeveless, and stiff as a banker's upper lip. Probably tough enough to stop musket

Cheyenne leg   Batwing   Texas leg

Woolies   Chaparrejos

bullets, too. Well, a vest is really a sort of abbreviated jerkin, and in Colonial times the vest was a waistcoat, really a sleeveless coat with lapels and pockets. You wore this waistcoat with a heavier topcoat, actually an overcoat, atop it. And don't forget, the Civil War period was a lot closer to those Colonial styles than we are. Vests, in Civil War times, were still practically coats, with heavy linings, pockets, lapels, everything except sleeves. And sleeves, for a rider's jerkin, you didn't want anyway.

Besides, when you went into a frontier Western store, what else could you buy? There weren't any Eisenhower jackets, Cossack coats, windbreakers, or whatever. If you wanted a waist-length coat you took a vest.

The old-time cowboy might not have had any undershirt on at all. Even in the towns, back in those days, the heating arrangements were pretty crude and you might say localized: big blazing fireplaces or pot-bellied stoves that cooked you quick if you stood close, while over on the other side of the same room you could have a fast freeze. So clothing was arranged so that you could put it on or take it off, button or unbutton, without having to retire to your boudoir to do so. The cowboy might not have any undershirt, but his overshirt would probably be as thick as a modern overcoat, and with a double-breasted shield front to boot. Like as not, it would have no pockets at all. Thus a vest, worn buttoned when you were cold, open when you got warm, and also supplied with pockets, was a right convenient garment. Riding, it left your arms free. If they got cold, you could wrap them around yourself.

In addition to the store-bought style of vest there were also fancier ones, Indian- or Mexican-made, sometimes beaded and elaborately stitched, with decorations made of porcupine quills or inlays of cloth. These Western-made vests were usually leather, sometimes lacing, like a hunting shirt or, later, buttoning down the front. But the vests you'd see on the range would ordinarily be just cloth, the prosaic sort you found in the stores.

Except in really cold weather, an old-time cowboy seldom wore an overcoat or even a sheep- or blanket-lined short coat, though he might have a blanket-lined jumper, waist length and with sleeves. But he did carry a slicker, which served him as a greatcoat as well as wet-weather apparel. Usually yellow, and strapped to the cantle when not being worn, the slicker was a voluminous affair with wide long skirts, and a slit and gores in the back, so that it could cover the whole saddle, as well as the man. It cost around $4, got stiff as rawhide in cold weather, and had a bad way of getting sticky in hot weather, especially after you'd had it a couple of years or so. Early slickers often had no pockets, but later there were two side pockets with slit openings so you could reach your pants pockets inside, as in modern Army overcoats. Typically the slicker closed with big buttons and a fly front. With a couple of wool shirts under it, you weren't too bad off in dry cold. But if it was damp—boy, you can freeze to death in damp cold quicker, and at a higher temperature, in a doggone slicker than in any other garment ever devised by man.

Sometimes you might see a Texas or Arizona cowboy with a Mexican *poncho* instead of a slicker, and this does have its advantages. The poncho is a finely woven serape which either has a slit cut in the middle to stick your head through, or has been woven with the slit in it, and it will shed water. It's made of fine wool, or wool and linen, and it's warm. But usually Mexicans or Indians wore these, and Texans didn't like Mexicans or Indians, so Texans didn't wear 'em.

Now for another piece of gear that has just plain vanished from the modern Western scene. On his hands, in cold weather, and quite often in warm as well, for protection against rope and rein burns, your old-timer would have gauntlets. Fine buckskin, light brown or gray, with stiffened, flaring cuffs, 7 or 8 inches long and about as wide.

These gauntlets roughly followed the Army pattern. But the cowboy version, very often made by Indian women, was fringed with fluttering leather, beautifully beaded on the back, sometimes even with colored porcupine quills worked into the patterns. You could buy these gauntlets around Indian reservations and trading posts, and of course there were the commercial varieties in the regular stores. They would be decorated with Lone Stars, cattle brands, flowers, geometric designs, swastikas (the swastika is a very, very old emblem and the American Indian had it ages before the Nazis: nor is it true that the Indian swastikas all went the other way from the Schicklgruber style, either), flags, eagles, coats of arms. Sometimes the design would be worked out in colored stitching, sometimes in leather inlays or overlays, sometimes in nailheads. But most gorgeous of all were the beaded ones, with glass trade beads about the size of small radish seeds, every color in the rainbow, sinew-sewed on by patient Indian women. Very often the whole outer side of the cuff, and the back of the glove as well, would be covered with intricate designs.

Ordinarily the cowboy gauntlet was not lined, though the cuff might be, in order to add to the stiffening. When you were on horseback, or driving an open wagon or coach, the huge cuff served the very useful purpose of not letting cold wind blow up your sleeves. When a cowboy removed his gauntlets, he stacked them and hung them over his belt, since they were much too large to pocket. Which probably, as much as anything else, was the reason for the gauntlet's disappearance. It was too easy to lose and too clumsy to carry around.

While we're in the neighborhood, leather cuffs were bands of leather,

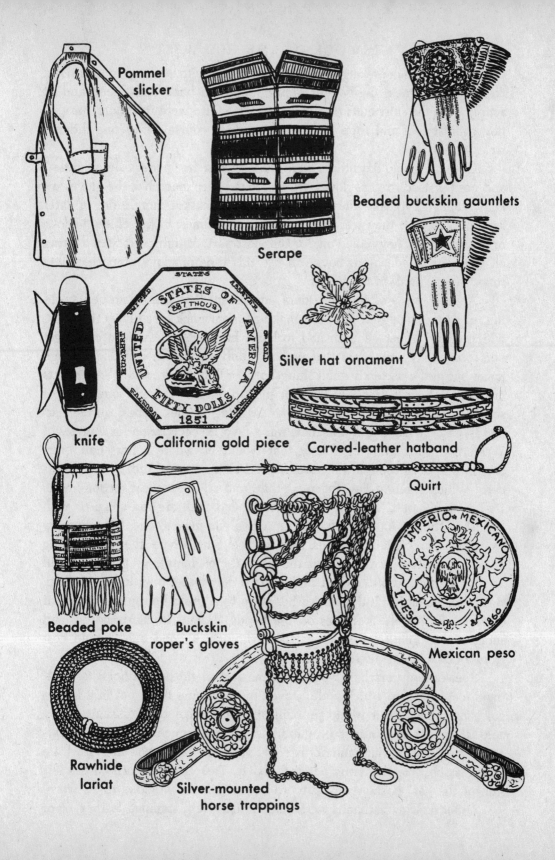

Pommel slicker

Serape

Beaded buckskin gauntlets

Silver hat ornament

knife

California gold piece

Carved-leather hatband

Quirt

Beaded poke

Buckskin roper's gloves

Mexican peso

Rawhide lariat

Silver-mounted horse trappings

usually 6 or 7 inches long, carved or stamped with assorted decorations, flowers, geometrical designs, or nickel spots; the band ends laced and fit snugly over the shirt cuffs on the wrists. They also were mainly for protection against rein and rope, and were worn, of course, when one did not wear gloves.

Even in the old days there were those who scorned the flashy gauntlets and used instead ropers' gloves, which looked very much like the gloves we know today. Typically they were made of buckskin, horsehide, or later kangaroo leather; they were brown, gray, sometimes, in horsehide, yellow, or smoke color. They pulled on, for the most part, or tightened with a string on the back. Modern cowboys still use this type of glove, since handling ropes is very hard on the hands.

Another piece of frontier-riders' equipment that seemed to be vanishing for a time, though it has been making a comeback recently, is the quirt, which every proper vaquero had to have, back when. And you could get you some really fancy ones that were not only an aid when riding a rough horse but also a perfectly good slungshot in a fight. The cowboy's quirt was ordinarily about 2 or 3 feet long, of plaited leather, though sometimes of stitched buckskin or woven horsehair. Making bridles, ropes, quirts, hatbands, and the like out of horsehair was a favorite occupation for inmates of Western prisons, and very likely that would be where a horsehair quirt came from, even though the storeman did claim it was "Indian" or "Mexican." Which it might have been, at that, and still have been prison-made! Its handle, or butt, would probably be loaded with an iron spike or with buckshot, thus giving you a handy sap when you needed one. Usually there would be three plaited bands, one at the butt where the wrist thong attached, another at the end of the 5- or 6-inch handle or grip, and still another at the end of the quirt body where the popper or cracker attached, this latter being just a double leather strap that could be replaced when it cracked off. Tassels or fringes on the bands, designs in the braiding, and such, offered infinite possibilities for variations. A good quirt would cost from a dollar up in the seventies.

Speaking of horsehair, your old-timer just might have a horsehair hatband too, from ½ to 1 inch wide, woven by a genuine Injun not in a hoosegow, in which case it would probably be natural-colored horsehair; or by a Mexican, when it might be gaudily dyed red, green, yellow, or whatever. The horsehair hatband adjusted to your hat via a knot and two little white tassels, like the Army hatcord tassels. Tassels were worn on the left side of the hat, as the Army hatcord was originally intended to be worn.

Other cowboy hatbands were made of carved or stamped leather, or of

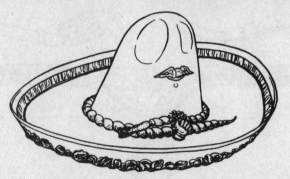

Gold-and-silver-trimmed sombrero

beaded leather, which was another Indian item, or sometimes of rattlesnake
skin. There's a natural glue in snakeskin; you can press it tight wherever
you want it and it will stick. Cowboys used snakeskins to decorate all sorts
of things, even to make neckties. The early hatbands were not silver-
mounted, though later ones might be. The Navajos and Zunis, who are the
great silvermakers among the Indians today, did not learn to make silver
until about 1870 and didn't set turquoise or any other kind of stones in their
silver until about ten years later. So the old-timer didn't have much Indian
jewelry.

When Indian silver came along, the cowboy might have a Navajo silver-
mounted bridle, with big silver conchas on the headstall, silver plates on
the headband, jinglers on the bit, and a *naja*, a little silver ornament like a
crescent moon, points down and with tiny hands or knobs on the points,
hanging in the center of the horse's forehead. This trinket was a real old-
timer, a horse amulet to ward off the evil eye. The Romans fastened its
like to their bridles, and after them the Moors, the Spaniards, the Conquis-
tadores, the Mexicans, clear on down a couple of thousand years to the
Navajos and the American cowboys who bought from them! You sometimes
see the same amulet on Navajo necklaces.

Another trifle I remember, because my Dad used to buy some Navajo
silver in New Mexico, was the tobacco canteen. They made 'em of rawhide,
of brass, or of silver, little fellers shaped like an old, round Army canteen,
complete with stopper and chain and maybe three inches across. You carried
your tobacco in them, flake or granulated, of course, cigarette makings that
would pour. The tobacco wouldn't get sweat-soaked or wet in the rain,
which it might in a muslin sack, and when you saw a man with one of those
little boxes you knew he was from the deep Southwest, the mesa country
or the border. I haven't seen one in years and years, but, just remembering,
I can smell that black Mexican tobacco and the cornhusks.

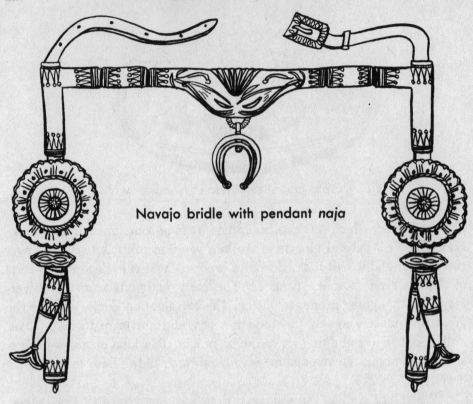

Navajo bridle with pendant *naja*

That was about as close to a canteen as your old-time cowboy ever got, because he never carried a water canteen. There'd be a water barrel on the wagon, if he got dry. Or he depended on what he could find, which was sometimes pretty awful. What cattle, and especially buffalo, can do toward making a pond of water into "buffalo tea," as the old-timers called it, is something. If he were riding a far piece by himself, the cowboy might pack some "airtights" along, generally canned tomatoes, to supply him with fluid. That is, if he wasn't scared of tomatoes—some people still called them "love apples" and suspected they were poison.

What would he have in his pockets? Well, for one thing, almost certainly a big stockman's knife, if he didn't have a sheath knife on his belt, probably a bowie. The pocketknife would likely be two-bladed, with a stag or wood handle, looking much like the knives cowmen carry today. He'd use this for the thousand and one things an outdoorsman needs a knife for, including, in his case, castrating calves or colts at the branding fires, and "kneeing" outlaw cattle, which meant cutting a tendon in a knee joint, so the animal was crippled and couldn't charge anybody thereafter. After which he might cut his meat and pick his teeth with the same blade, sho!

He'd probably have a pencil or a stub of one. He probably wouldn't have a wallet or billfold, since Confederate money had taught him an acute suspicion of all paper currency. But he would have a poke, a purse or pocket bag with a drawstring, probably buckskin and Indian- or Mexican-made. In this he'd keep his money if he had any, which would be silver or gold—U.S. cartwheels, big Mexican 'dobe dollars, or maybe even Californian gold pieces, because there had been private mints out on the Coast coining gold pieces all the way up to huge, 50-dollar slugs, many of them eight-sided instead of round. They were still circulating, back then, but if you have one now, hang on to it! Collectors will pay you plenty.

The trail boss in charge of the outfit on the road would doubtless have a supply of hard money for operating expenses, not much since there wasn't too much to buy, but he might have to pay a hand off, make good for a nestor's fence, or add some provisions. He would very likely keep the money on the wagon in a leather morral or nosebag. Money thieves weren't very bad on the cattle trails; rustlers might run off your cows, but you could just leave money lying around loose and chances were nobody'd bother it. As for Indian visitors, the Civilized Tribes knew about money all right but, by and large, they had an amazingly high standard of honor, and the "wild" Indians didn't even know what money was for.

Only exceptionally would the cowboy have a watch. They were expensive, hard to take care of on the trail, strictly non-waterproof and non-shock-resistant in those days, and anyway the Westerner would have been taught from childhood how to tell time from the sun and stars. The swing of the Big Dipper around the North Star made a particularly fine clock—*El Reloj de los Indios*, "the Clock of the Indians," the Mexicans used to call it. By watching the pointers, the two stars on the front side of the cup that point to the polestar, they could tell the correct time within 15 or 20 minutes. Or, if the night was cloudy, the riders on guard counted time by cigarettes! I have heard of South Texas land measurements made with the same unit, so many cigarettes north, thence so many cigarettes east, meaning the distance a man would ride while rolling and smoking that many. Or, if not that, by timing the songs, or, if not that, then by guess and by gosh.

The night watch over a herd was divided into three reliefs or guards, and sometimes on cloudy nights the first guard would be mighty short and the last gosh-awful long. But not often. There is some sort of curious mechanism inside a man that will tell him the correct time, if he but learns to listen to it, that will wake him right on the dot when it's time to go, and the old trail drivers knew it.

Nor did they need a compass. That also is provided, deep inside a man, if only he will listen to its still small voice. The physiologists, I believe, have decided it is part of the inner ear, with its semicircular canals and delicate organs of balance. Whatever the mechanism is, wild ducks have it, and cats, and salmon and eels in the sea. I know it was an inherent quality of the real old-time Westerner. As one of them said to me once, they were never stuck on the dead center of futility because they never stopped at a dead loss. Some of the trail outfits used to point the tongue of the chuck wagon at the North Star each clear night so that they'd start off sharply oriented next morning, but I don't think they needed to. I think they'd have known anyway.

The rest of his loot or plunder—the Mountain Man would have said "possibles," and some old cowmen still did in the seventies—the cowboy would carry in his war bag, which was just a sack, usually canvas, that went along with his bedroll on the wagon, unless he was changing jobs or moving solo from here to there. In the war bag would be an extra shirt or two, spare socks, maybe a change of underwear, a reserve supply of tobacco, an extra box of cartridges, the bill of sale for his personal horse, a letter from home or from his girl—things like that.

And a straight razor and shaving brush. You could use any kind of soap, and you didn't really have to have the brush either—you could singe your whiskers off or pluck them out one at a time, as Indians did, with a couple of shells or pieces of wood for tweezers, though this was considered kind of drastic. So you had a razor, straight. There weren't any safety razors in old-time cowboy kits, or anywhere else for that matter. Safety razors came along with effete civilization. There were guards you could put on straight razors, though, if you had the palsy or were shaving on a train, to keep from cutting yourself too badly. But the first satisfactory safety razor as we know it, the hoe-type whisker chopper, came along only in the nineties, and then it had a blade that was just a chunk of straight razor, which you honed and stropped. No old-razor-blade problems on the trails.

As a matter of fact, there wasn't much whisker problem either, because, like as not, you just didn't bother to shave from the time you left South Texas until you hit the rail town in Kansas and found a barbershop. And you bathed, if at all, in the creeks.

The subject of bathing brings me to another group of the period, the surviving Mountain Men and their immediate descendants. Time has begun to invest these hombres with a glamour not so evident, so far as I have been able to find out, to those who were close enough to smell 'em. To be brutally frank about it, the Mountain Men generally stank so bad that even their frontier contemporaries (who bathed maybe two-three times a year themselves, so they couldn't have been too particular) complained about it. They were beaver trappers and butchers, and as with the later buffalo hunters, similarly engaged, not even the strongest soaps could remove the odor of their profession. When they came to town, other men gave them a wide berth.

Nor was it their odor alone that made them frontier pariahs. True, there were among them men of culture and breeding, even some with fine intellects. But, as a general thing, the Mountain Man had quit the settlements and elected instead to live with the Indians and wild beasts because, for one reason or another, he had had to. He was a misfit, a ne'er-do-well, a renegade, an outlaw. By and large, the rendezvous of the trappers were drunken orgies, and, with only a few exceptions, their dealings with the Indians, and especially the Indian women, were disgusting and disgraceful.

But the Mountain Man proper, though still surviving, was not an important figure in the period we are covering. His real heyday was from about 1820, when the Western trapping business really got going, to about 1845, when his bloody industry had decimated the beavers, when men were beginning to wear silk hats rather than beaver hats, and the Mountain Men had to turn to other avenues for a living.

Individually, he persisted into the post-Civil-War period as an "Old Scout," genuine or otherwise, often serving as guide for cavalry columns, emigrant trains, and such. He continued to affect the old-time costume: fur cap, long hair, whiskers, buckskin hunting shirt, leggings, breechclout, and moccasins. Sometimes he still carried the pre-Civil-War Plains rifle, so called. This was a modification of the traditional Kentucky rifle, and had developed when the American frontiersmen had emerged from the woods onto the plains, being at first flintlock, then later caplock, with shorter barrel (25- to 35-inch) than the Kentucky (which typically carried a 39- to 40-inch barrel or an even longer one), large caliber, .46, .48, .52, or even bigger, as compared with the Kentucky's average of about .32; half stocked to the Kentucky's full stock. The idea was to get a rifle which was easier to handle on horseback, and with greater shock power to drop the larger animals, and more distant human enemies as well. The Hawken brothers, Jake and Samuel, of St. Louis were famous makers of Plains rifles in the thirties and forties, and among other gunsmiths, mainly in Pennsylvania, where most of the "Kentuckys" were really made, were Golcher, Deringer, Henry, Oldham. Since these guns were made by hand, by individual gunsmiths, there were many makers' names.

With his Hawken, or Golcher, or whatever rifle, your Mountain Man would have a powder horn slung around his neck, a rifle bag or bullet bag, about 8 by 10 inches, leather, often with the hair left on, to carry his bullets, and about his waist a wide belt for his butcher knife and pistol. Additional plunder, or "possibles," he carried in a large leather haversack called a possibles bag, and still more in parfleches, rawhide cases or bags slung on his pack animals.

Some of the Mountain Men who were still around in the seventies, serving as guides and scouts for whoever would hire them, did have a most amazing knowledge of the West and its wild inhabitants. But there were others who were Grade A frauds, who hung around towns, let their hair grow long, told large lies to tenderfeet, and often, after the manner of mankind, got their falsehoods believed while the truths were forgotten. In the nineties practically every Western town had at least one of these old fakers, cadging drinks around the bars and telling of how he'd fit with Custer. Long-lived, those Mountain Men.

VIII

SHORT HORSES AND LONGHORNS

LONGHORN cattle are just about gone out of this world now, replaced by plain Herefords and moo cows and such. But they were proud bovines in their day. Some of those tremendous heads had a spread of horns about 9 feet, and, as the old-timers said, a jaybird had to carry rations to fly from one horntip to the other. Some of the great-great-granddaddies of those steers fought the United States Army, on their own initiative, under their own leaders, and at least to a good draw.

You have to know something about the ancestry of the longhorns to appreciate them. They could look down their noses at our own Pilgrim Fathers, for one thing. Their forebears had arrived in America a good century before the *Mayflower* with its little band of potential First Families. The Andalusian cattle of Don Gregorio de Villalobos first trod Mexican soil in 1521 and were old, old settlers by the time those shorthorns up No'th arrived. They were of the same proud stock that produced the great black bulls of the Spanish and Latin-American bull rings. They came with the Spanish conquistadors, and by the time the first Anglo-Saxon American settlers reached Texas, the woods were full of cattle and little Mexican ranchos raising, as much as they raised anything, Spanish "black cattle" (though they weren't always black), "mustang cattle" (meaning strays), "cimarrónes" (meaning wild ones). And they were really rugged, those sharp-horned bulls. Take a shot at one of them and miss a vital spot and he was quite likely to turn and kill you for your discourtesy. The frontiersmen were almost as leery of them as they were of Comanches.

These cattle were thick in the brush country of South Texas and in New Mexico and Arizona. During the Mexican War, the Mormon Battalion under

Colonel Philip St. George Cooke, marching from Santa Fe to California, actually fought a battle with a small army of these black cimarróns in Arizona, the bulls charging out of the brush right in the face of musketry fire. And Lord help you if you were caught afoot in their bailiwicks. They'd kill you, just as soon as look at you!

Having inadvertently provided horses to the Plains Indians, particularly the Kiowas and Comanches, the Spanish and then the Mexican colonists never did cope successfully out in the open with the Injuns thereafter. Their ranchos and villas and little towns came only to the edges of the plains country, but no farther. The Anglo-American would have had no better luck had it not been for the invention of the six-shooter and the repeating rifle, because what a Comanche Indian could do with his short powerful bow and a quiverful of arrows you just wouldn't believe. From the back of a racing pony he could let fly up to twenty arrows a minute, a regular rawhide machine gun. And he ranged from hell to breakfast, so you never knew where or when to expect him. In the brush, or timber, or rocks, you could maybe contrive to handle him, but he much preferred catching you out where he could ride rings around you and shoot you ragged.

So the first Anglo-American settlers in Texas and the Southwest followed the same general pattern as the Spanish, crowding into the timbered areas, and letting the bare prairies alone. They brought with them their own cattle, Missouri and Kentucky and Tennessee strains for the most part, long domesticated and much more apt to turn out patient oxen or gentle moo cows than *ladinos*. The wild black cattle didn't think very much of these effete intruders either, and were inclined to get them out into the brush and gore them, or just plain walk 'em to death. But in time the strains mixed, and the result was the longhorn.

The longhorn was not as mean as the cimarrón, and he was larger and heavier, a better beef animal and at least as sturdy as his outlaw sires. He had long legs and a long, limber tail, and he came in just about every color of the cow rainbow, perhaps most often some hue of red, brown, or yellow, but there were also brindles, "gruyas" (*grullas*, mouse-colored), duns, blacks, whites, creams, and every conceivable combination. An animal violently splotched with different colors was called a paint, and one with a line stripe down his back—which the old Texans often called a lobo (wolf) stripe, since it was a distinguishing mark of wild cows, horses, even burros— was called a lineback. Regardless of their color, they could run like deer, swim like sea lions, and fight like catamounts; and to help in this latter endeavor they had about the most fantastic horns ever to grace the head of a critter. Though probably the average spread wasn't more than 4 or 5 feet, there were plenty that went 6 and 7, and old-timers "remember" them clear up to 13 feet! Well, take it or leave it.

Usually the horns of a cimarrón pointed forward. But the ornaments of a longhorn, though they generally did arch forward more or less, might grow in just any old fashion, like the handlebars of a bicycle, or curving upward like a sacred cow's, or a lyre-bird's tail, or with curve on curve, or even one horn up and one down. I remember seeing one head whose owner, so they told me, had starved to death because his horns, sweeping downward on both sides, at last had quite prevented him from grazing. And the famous Buckhorn Curio Store, formerly the Buckhorn Saloon, in San Antonio, is full of weird examples of just what could be done in growing horns.

At about the age of four or five, when the longhorn was considered to be getting his full growth, though he'd keep putting on weight for years longer, little wrinkles would begin to grow up from the bases of the horns, and the older the steer got, the more the wrinkles would show, giving rise to the term "mossy horns," meaning old-timers. A full-grown young steer would weigh 800 to 900 pounds, while a fat old mossy horn might go as high as 1500, or even more.

In time, the cattlemen of the Southwest discovered that you could drive a full-grown Texas longhorn north and he'd put on weight and get amazingly

Texas longhorn, with mossy horns and ear crop

bigger on northern grass. In the sixties and seventies there were millions and millions of acres of lush free grass up in the northwestern territories. So it was not only for the immediate markets, for the packers and their buyers in the railroad towns, that the Texas trail herds went northward. It was also because of those empty northern pastures, and finally because of the demand for feeder cattle for the farm pens in Iowa, Illinois, Wisconsin, and Indiana, for beef to be fattened on corn. Denied expansion elsewhere, the South, or at least the cattle-raising part of it in Texas, would find its room for expansion in the north.

But here, as we have seen, the blind prejudice of the sodbuster against the stock raiser made itself felt, with all sorts of rumors of the evils of Texas cattle. Some of these beliefs ultimately burned the very men who had started them. But it must be admitted that some were not entirely without foundation.

Some Texas cattle undoubtedly did carry cattle ticks, insects which in turn carried the dreaded Texas fever to northern farm cattle. And beyond dispute, some few of the Texas trail drivers did need a good permanent hanging! But assuredly the sins of the few were far outweighed by the virtues of the many, and here with the hammering hoofs was a golden flood of prosperity, for everybody. No matter, some people couldn't see it.

Baxter Springs, Kansas, for one, got out with shotguns, insisted on remaining a narrow-minded wide place in the road, and got its wish. Had it been otherwise, today it might well be one of the great cities of the Midwest. Abilene, pulled up from nothing by Joe McCoy and the trail herds he tolled into its rude stock pens, smugly decided in 1872 that it wanted no more of these uncouth Texans and their cows. It actually sent circulars down the trail, informing the Texans they weren't welcome! Texans took the hint and went elsewhere, and then Abilene howled dolefully when it discovered the departed cowmen had taken also the prosperity and future of the town.

Now the trail herds themselves. The early herds, or at least some of them, were mixed—steers, bulls, and cows—which must have been one heck of a combination to try to drive. The Mexicans seldom castrated their animals and I'm sentimental and noncommercial enough to ride right along with them there. But gelded animals are easier to handle, put on more weight, and produce a better quality of meat; so an Anglo-American rancher usually gelds his bulls, save, of course, those kept for breeding purposes. Strictly speaking, any castrated animal may be called a gelding, though ordinarily the term is reserved for horses, while a castrated calf becomes a steer, and an unsexed lamb a wether. Ordinarily calves are gelded while quite young, 6 to 8 weeks, and colts at around a year or more. An animal unsexed after it has reached maturity is called a stag. Unsexing a female animal, called spaying, is a much more difficult operation, and although sometimes it is done, to produce better beef animals, or to quiet a fractious mare, it was very rare in the Old West.

While we're in the veterinary business, dehorning cattle is quite an art, too. If you catch your calf very young, in the first week, you can rub his little horn "buttons" with a bit of caustic potash and prevent the horns from growing at all. It isn't much of an operation. But if you wait until he gets horns you have to saw them off, or use heavy dehorning clippers, and that's quite an operation since the animal not only objects but may bleed to death. Cauterizing with a red-hot iron was the usual way to stop the bleeding.

Of course the old trail driver didn't worry one bit about dehorning his charges. But he did sort his herds out, into all-steer herds, or at worst steers and cows ("she-stuff"), just as soon as conditions in Texas permitted him to do so, before starting his long trip north. A herd mixed with cows was a pain in the neck, because the cows would be dropping calves practically all the way up the trail. Since the little fellows couldn't travel and their mothers couldn't be left behind, if the calves couldn't be given away to somebody along the way, they had to be killed. Rough as they were, cowboys hated that. On the other hand, many a later prosperous stock farm, especially in North Texas, Oklahoma, and Kansas, owed its beginnings to giveaway calves some thrifty settler had scrounged from trail herds passing by.

Unless a trail herd was under one brand, which ordinarily it wasn't, it was customary to road brand the animals—that is, give them all an extra insignia to identify them on their journey. Owners of the various brands in the bunch would usually give the trail boss bills of sale describing their

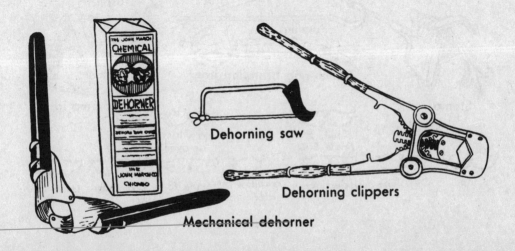

Dehorning saw

Dehorning clippers

Mechanical dehorner

contributions, so that if he got into trouble up the way he'd have some legal papers, as well as powder and lead, to back him up.

Brands, again, would make a book by themselves. The original Conquistador himself, Hernando Cortes, conqueror of Mexico, is said to have been the first man to run an American brand, on both his cattle and his human slaves. His cow brand was three "Christian" crosses. From this beginning, the Spanish and Mexican cattle brands developed into some of the most elaborate and fanciful designs imaginable. When the Anglo-American ranchers came along, their brands were much simpler.

Brands were applied with a running iron in the old days, which meant just practically any old piece of iron you could heat in a fire, contrive to hold on to somehow—even a saddle cinch ring, held between two sticks, would do in a pinch—and so write your own, or more honestly, your employer's ticket, on the side of your calf. You'd roped, thrown, and tied said calf before attempting this artistic piece of leather burning, naturally. Later on, when the full possibilities of this free-hand art had been realized, particularly by owners coming up shy of calves, carrying a running iron in your saddlebags could be a grave social error. Stamp irons were preferred instead. A stamp iron is simply one with the brand already shaped on the end by a blacksmith. Some of them had long iron handles, like a poker, and others a short prong which you imbedded in a wooden handle. They made a much sharper, clearer brand.

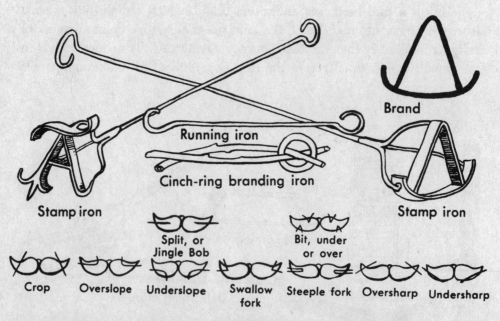

Brand

Running iron

Cinch-ring branding iron

Stamp iron

Stamp iron

Crop   Overslope   Underslope   Swallow fork   Steeple fork   Oversharp   Undersharp

Split, or Jingle Bob

Bit, under or over

Ear brands

Branding

Brands were registered in a brand book in each county, and there were thousands of different marks. One man might own forty to fifty different brands. In addition to the brand or brands (and sometimes a steer would have so many on his sides he'd look like a traveling brand book) the animal would be earmarked; that is, assorted crops, bits, and bobs would have been carved out of his long ears, also according to the registered pattern, so that a rider could recognize ownership of the critter either by the brand on his side or by the remnants of his ears. Perhaps the most famous of all earmarks was the Jingle Bob of John Chisum, king of the Pecos. John Chisum branded with the Long Rail, a huge bar down the entire side, from shoulder to flank, an example of the so-called barn-door brands which fell into disfavor when hides started being worth something. But it was his earmark that became the name of his herd, the ear split lengthwise so that one half stood up, the other half dangled, like the jangler on a spur, thus marking a Jingle Bob cow—a name remembered long after John Chisum had been gathered to his fathers.

Ordinarily not more than 3000 to 3500 steers would be included in a single trail herd, though there are records of a few up to 5500. The herds would be pushed hard the first few days, 25 to 30 miles a day, to get the cattle away from their old stamping grounds as rapidly as possible, and also to break them into traveling. After that, 10 to 20 miles, with an average of

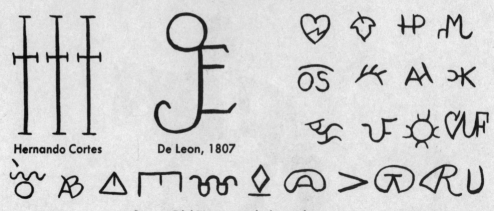

Hernando Cortes   De Leon, 1807

Some Old West cattle brands

perhaps 12, would be the usual day's travel. Typically the herd itself would develop a lead steer, if one were not provided beforehand by the drivers. This animal, day after day, would lead off the bedground of his own accord, the others following. A good lead steer would often be brought back down the trail to repeat the trip with another flock of deluded followers, and there were several such critters that became quite famous. Much like human beings, the same animals would be found in the same relative positions on the drive each day, the leaders always leaders, the drags always drags. Only when something happened to him, sickness or injury, would a steer fall back. When he recovered, if he did, back to his old position he would go.

Guiding the herd, right and left in the van, would be the point riders, then farther back on each side the swing riders, and finally, bringing up the rear in the dust, the drag riders.

A typical trail outfit would consist of a trail boss and nine to twelve men, including a cook, who drove the chuck wagon and prepared meals. If the outfit furnished the horses, which it usually did, the ordinary trail hand would get about $30 a month. If he furnished his own mounts, as sometimes happened, he might get double that. The boss would draw $100 or more, and the cook—well, it depended on how good a cookie he was.

The famed chuck wagon was an invaluable piece of trail and range equipment and is supposed to have been invented by Colonel Charles Goodnight. But I suspect that just about the first man who ever went any- where in a wagon had the general idea. Where else were you going to stand, to haul your grub out and prepare it, if not at the tailgate of your wagon? Anyhow, the chuck wagon that Goodnight devised, which had a sort of crude kitchen cabinet built on the back, plus a tailgate that let down

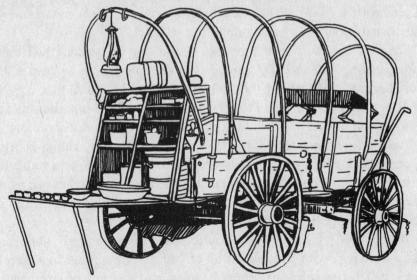

Chuck wagon

to form the cook's working table, became the general pattern for all later cow-country chuck wagons.

The very earliest cowmen had used two-wheeled *carretas*, or even packed their grub on horseback or muleback in *alforjas*, big clumsy leather bags, on an *aparejo* pack saddle. *Aparejo* just means "rigging," or "harness," and an aparejo was a clumsy, padded affair, to hitch things on. The American version of the pack saddle was the crossbuck, which had a tree with wood or iron crossbucks sticking up, like the tops of X's, at pommel and cantle, to sling your hitch ropes over. On this you might cover your plunder with a tarpaulin and then throw a diamond hitch, a very fancy way of roping the pack so that the rope made a diamond-shaped figure atop the load when you had finished.

The early chuck wagons were pretty sparsely provisioned. Flour or cornmeal or both, probably green coffee to be roasted and then ground in a little hand coffee mill (it would be just "Rio," from the source, at first, but later Arbuckle's became the well-nigh universal coffee brand of the range-land), salt, sugar (probably brown), some bacon or salt pork, soda, probably a sourdough barrel, maybe a bottle of calomel to counteract the inevitable effects of the cooking. And pinto beans, of course, a range staple. The fresh meat supply, including sirloins, T-bones, and whatnot, even tallow for emergency shortening, was hoofing right along beside you, delivering itself.

Son-of-a—well, polite folks said "gun"—stew, a cowboy favorite, was made of cubed tongue, liver, melt, and sweetbreads, rolled in meal, fried slightly, then boiled with onions, thickened with flour, and sometimes fortified also with a chunk of lean meat. Prairie or mountain oysters were an unmentionable part of a male animal.

Sourdough biscuits you'd get out of the keg that cookie had brought along, guarding it like a baby, maybe even sleeping with it to keep it warm. Before beginning the trip he'd have made a start of yeast in that keg, likely by letting some dough sour in it. Now, each day he'd put the sourdough keg in the sun or near the fire, to keep it warm and its contents fermenting. He'd take out just enough dough to "raise" his biscuits, adding flour, salt, and water both to the keg, to replace what he'd taken out, and to his batch of biscuit dough. Then he'd bake them in a dutch oven, which is just a heavy, covered iron pot. Continually replenished that way, the dough in the sourdough keg, I suppose, would go on working almost forever.

If you tired of biscuits you could easily make yourself some bread. Make a little hollow of flour on the lip of your flour sack, put in a teaspoonful of salt, 2 teaspoonfuls of baking powder, and a chunk of lard about the size of a small egg (this is a dude outfit, see, all these fancy groceries!). Add a cup of water and mix in flour until you have stiff dough. Roll in strips, wrap them around your ramrod or a peeled, green stick, and bake over the fire.

If you liked venison, antelope, buffalo, wild turkey, prairie chicken, quail, squirrel, 'possum, with your bread, the West swarmed with game in those days. You could even kill wild geese with your pistol! Yes, you could starve, too, but you had to work at it.

In the wagon, along with cookie's pots, pans, dutch ovens, and such, would be the tin plates and cups, iron forks, knives, and spoons of the mess gear. Only cowboys said chuck, not mess, or even chow. The bedrolls and war bags would be there too, the branding irons, the fire irons—these were rails to set over the fire—the pothooks (S-shaped hooks to hang the pots from), and whatever other heavy equipment the outfit carried. And a big water barrel, of course, usually slung on the side—that would come in handy lots of times along the road. Plus a cowhide stretched under the wagon bed, called a 'possum belly, or coonie (from Spanish *cuna*, cradle) into which coosie (cowboy Spanish for *cocinero*, cook) would heave every likely-looking chunk of firewood he passed. You don't have to do much traveling to appreciate the natural orneriness of nature when it comes to wood and water. All day long you'll pass millions of nice, dry chunks of wood and cool, sparkling creeks and springs. Comes time to camp, though, and there aren't any, for miles and miles and miles.

Each hand generally would have six or more horses assigned him, which he rode in rotation. Some outfits hobbled their horses at night,

Rawhide horse hobbles

which wasn't such a hot idea, because hobbles (leather cuffs, connected by a chain, fastening the front feet) sometimes chafe, and if they don't, still it's amazing how far a homesick or just plain hammerhead pony can crowhop in a night, if he takes a mind to. Most outfits, accordingly, had a horse wrangler, often a boy just starting in. In Texas the horse herd was called the "remuda," but as the cattle industry spread northward, the term "cavvy" came into use up there. Both terms are from the Spanish. A *remuda de caballos* means an extra stock, a relay supply of horses. A *caballada*, strictly speaking, is a band of saddle horses, but that was a little harder for the American cowboy to say than remuda. So he generally made it just cavvyard or cavvy.

Sometimes there would be both a day and a night horse herder, the former usually called a wrangler and the latter a nighthawk. But more often both jobs would be held by the same luckless youth, who could "ketch up on his sleep next winter," as the trail boss usually told him. Well, he could get some sleep right in the saddle, and moving, too. But if he failed to bring the remuda in, reasonably intact, at daylight, woe to the luckless wight.

Sometimes a bell mare was used to keep the remuda together, since the horses would ordinarily follow her. But not many outfits followed this custom, because the mare herself was likely to be a nuisance. The saddle horses were almost invariably geldings, stallions being too much trouble and mares causing too much. But the old Spaniards and the Mexicans after them often rode stallions and mares. While we're on the bell theme, the lead steer of the herd sometimes was belled too, and quite often would "gee" and "haw" at command; also "whoa." Cattle are a lot smarter than some folks give them credit for being.

Now the horses themselves. For my money, anyway, horses are the poetry of the outdoor world. Did you ever notice how many of the poems and songs of the West beat to the rhythm of a horse's different gaits? You can jog along in a saddle and the hoss will practically make up a song for you.

The Western cowhorse had a lineage as proud as that of any man who rode him; in fact his back trail might reach even farther. The rider might have come from no more distant place than Missouri or Kentucky or Tennessee, possibly leaving behind him on the home sheriff's books that once-famous designation: "G.T.T."—"Gone to Texas." But the forebears of the horse like as not had come from Arabia or North Africa. On his second and third voyages of discovery, Columbus brought some Spanish cavalry with him, and Cortes, landing in Mexico for his fabulous conquest, brought more. Actually they were returning the horse to his home. The horse as a species probably originated in America, vanishing in the glacial ages, but not before sending emigrants to Europe via Asia. Cortes brought sixteen stallions and mares and one colt, which was foaled on the voyage. Small enough stock, with which to sweep two giant continents off their feet. But that was what the horse was destined to do.

Almost certainly it was the horse that really won Mexico for Cortes and his tiny band, for the Spaniards afoot did not terrify the swarming myriads of Aztecs. But the Spaniard on horseback was another matter altogether. He was a superman, a god. In Tayasal the Mayans, entrusted with the care of one of Cortes's lamed horses, El Morzillo, actually made a god of the animal, starved him to death on flowers, honey, and incense (they couldn't imagine a god eating hay!), and then erected in their principal temple a huge statue of him, a horse idol, sitting quaintly on its haunches. A century later the devout Christian padres, breaking through the jungle, were horrified.

But, at that, the simple Indians were not so stupid. The horse did mean a new life to the brown and red men of America, for before him they had had no beast of burden larger than a dog. Though the Spanish tried ferociously to keep the Indians from getting horses and then, failing that, from getting saddles, the Indians stole both. And, from being humble pedestrians, they developed into some of the most skilled horsemen the world has ever known. And hoss soldiers too. Later American cavalry officers who had fought against the North American Plains Indians testified frankly that they considered their red foes just about the best irregular cavalry on earth.

The horse liked America, and the horse spread himself high, wide, and handsome. He ranged in tame herds and wild. Like the longhorn, he took on the nature of his homeland regained; he became a living symbol of freedom. He was the prime mover of the West, and he never let you forget it.

The horse that went up the old cattle trails, chivvying the dogies to ranges far away, was a combination of Spanish cowpony, mustang (which is merely the name for a strayed, gone-wild horse, the original word,

Mustang

Appaloosa

mesteno, having been corrupted into mustang), and various Anglo-American bloodlines. For some years the Texans had been bringing in Morgans, Thoroughbreds, Arabians, and, probably most of all, Quarter Horses.

The antecedents of the Spanish horse were Arabian and Barb. The Barb was the horse of the Berbers of North Africa, the Moslems who warred with the Spanish. He is a bit coarser animal than the Arab, longer coupled, and typically with a slanting rump and low-set tail, whereas the true Arab carries his tail characteristically high and has also a finely tapered head, with a sort of concave depression or dish in the face. The mustang, too often inbred and scrubby, in spite of legends to the contrary, showed some Barb or Arab characteristics, and had a special one of his own, besides his amazing stamina. He craved to wear no man's saddle and he was quite regularly the doggonedest bucker ever foaled.

The Quarter Horse, still much beloved by Westerners, came out of the original Thirteen Colonies. He was English with a mixture of Spanish— that is, of Arab and Barb. He was a short, stocky horse, a "Short Horse," in fact, as they called him in the eighteenth century, when they expected him to do no more than a fast quarter-mile. But in the nineteenth century they began to breed for more distance, still trying to retain the speed and maneuverability of the old Short Horse. Plainly this was promising cow-pony stock too, and that was just how the old Texans considered him. Cross his speed with the cowpony's endurance and you really had you something.

The Thoroughbred is an English breed brought to America in Colonial times. The Morgan (sometimes called in old horse books the Black Hawk

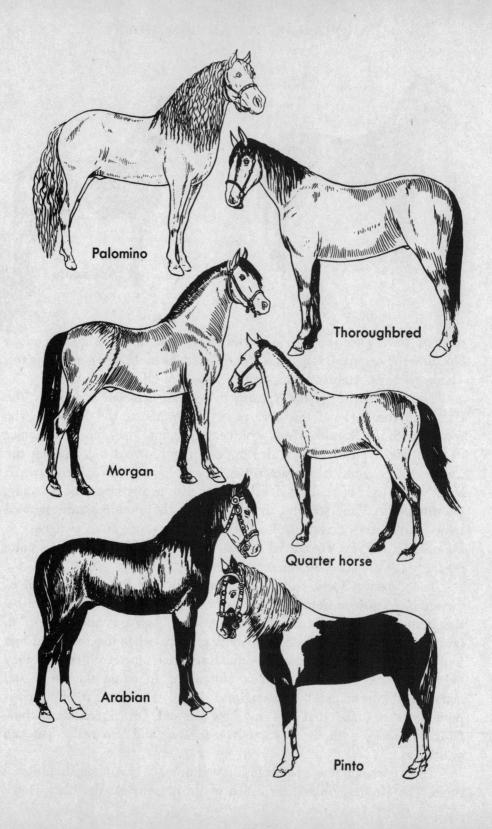

Palomino

Thoroughbred

Morgan

Quarter horse

Arabian

Pinto

after a grandson of the original stallion) is an American breed tracing back to one great horse, Justin Morgan, foaled in Vermont in 1793. It seems likely this tremendous sire was a Dutch horse, a breed of the times, though he may have had Thoroughbred and Quarter-Horse blood also. Morgans were used for light draft work, harness racing, drawing buggies and buckboards, as well as for saddle animals. The Standard Bred, or American Trotter—sometimes called Hambletonian from the great sire of that name, foaled in 1849 in New York—was primarily a trotting horse, intended for harness and road work. The American saddle horse began as a pacer (a pacing horse moves both legs on the same side simultaneously, thus ambling or rocking along, while a trotter will bounce from one diagonal stance, right front, left rear leg, for example, to the other). And there are a lot more breeds, strains, types—enough to fill several books.

When you're distinguishing among horses, you have to remember that the different kinds are a lot like different human families, the Smiths and the Browns and the Joneses. There may be some Joneses that look exactly like Smiths, and even act like 'em, but they're still Joneses. What makes them Joneses is their pedigree, their bloodlines. So, too, are horses classified by their family trees, and also, like people, by their colors.

A pinto or paint horse was one variously spotted or splotched, bay, chestnut, red, or brown on gray or white. Old-timers generally mistrusted loudly splotched pintos, I don't know why. Lots of paint horses are A No.-1 performers, as well as pretty. Injuns loved 'em anyway. Appaloosas, Indian horses from the Nez Percé country, had leopard-like spots on the rump. Palominos are gold-colored horses, light tan or cream, with white manes— a color variant, not a breed. The Indian pony, by the way, actually the old Spanish horse with a dash of wild in his blood, as if he needed it, was still called a Chickasaw horse in the old Indian Territory where I was born. "Cayuse" is a northern term for horse, deriving from the Cayuse Indian tribe of the Oregon country. "Broncho," shortened to "bronc," is from the Spanish and means "rough one."

Now let's look at the saddles and bridles. Just as about horses and boots and bandannas and such, horsemen have been arguing about bridles and saddles since the year when, because they have a history, too, that reads like a logbook of adventure itself. Like the cattle he drove and the horse he rode, the old trail driver's saddle was a combination, part Anglo-American but more Spanish-Mexican. When the first Spaniards came to America they brought with them two kinds of saddles and two ways of riding, as, for that matter, the English colonists did. The two ways of riding have already been discussed in Chapter III. The first type of saddle was the war saddle, very stout and heavy, often with metal plates at pommel and cantle, additional armor that protected the already armored legs of the rider, and, incidentally, sometimes curved out like the cow country's swell fork and so perhaps helped keep him in the saddle. For this type of saddle the stirrup leathers were very long, and the rider rode a la brida, with his legs all but straight. The other type of saddle like the second style of riding was brought into Europe by the Moslems, and is the ancestor of the racing saddle and the English saddle. The stirrup leathers are very short, bringing the knees up and the thighs almost horizontal. For monkey-shining in the saddle, for racing or jumping, this type of saddle and seat are fine, despite the sneers of the war-saddle advocates.

But fine as it may be for doing something, the long seat isn't so hot when something is being done to you. Suppose the horse decides to balk, or, worse yet, buck, just when you're expecting him to sail right over the ditch? Or suppose a rough, tough cow on the end of your rope tries yanking you right smack off there? Or, most prosaic of all, suppose you have to ride forty miles cross-country, bouncing up and down on your knee joints every last step of the way? That is when you really crave a good, big, heavy, comfortable stock saddle.

If you had to live in that saddle, go over all sorts of country, hitch onto various brutes that could yank the bejabbers out of an Army tank and love to, you probably would do just what the old Spaniards and Mexicans did—devise a saddle that was a combination of the old war hull and the light racing pad, doing your best to keep the advantages of both. That was what the Mexican stock saddle was, the rig the Anglo-American cowmen found on the job when they moved in.

It was stout and heavy, with a slick fork, low cantle, so you could get on and off in a hurry; Spanish or center-fire rig (they're not the same, as we'll see); and a big, low, flat horn that looked like half a grapefruit set on a short forward-slanting stem.

The slick fork means that the forebow curved smoothly up to the horn, more or less following the contour of the horse, with no bulges or swells on the sides to hook your knees under and so hold yourself aboard. In this, and in the fact that the front was higher than the back, it was like the old jineta saddle. But in its bulk and weight it was the war saddle, built to take it! Spanish rig means that the rigging rings that caught the girth or cinch that held the saddle on were located on the front of the saddle, right and left, directly below the horn. Center-fire means the rings were placed at the middle of the sides of the tree, a style so much preferred by Californians that it also was known as the California rig. If you located the rings about

Fork seat—*a la brida*   Long seat—*a la jineta*

three-quarters of the way to the front, it was a three-fourths rig, or even a five-eighths or seven-eighths if you kept moving the rings. These were mostly later innovations. They are all alike in having just one cinch, one band under the horse's belly.

On the Mexican saddles, the rigging straps were exposed, coming down from the fork, or wrapped around the horn, and braced by another rigging strap that came from behind the cantle. The tree of the Mexican saddle was pretty much Army saddle stuff, with a slot down the middle, covered with shrunk-on rawhide like the later McClellan. But the Mexican vaquero wasn't dumb enough to ride on rawhide and nothing else, not him! He had a big leather cover or housing, called a *mochila*, which went over this rawhide saddle much like the shabracks or overhousings we noticed on Civil War Army saddles. Sometimes, for fiestas and such, his was even fancier. Finally, his narrow stirrup leathers held the wooden or all-leather stirrups at just a nice compromise between the extreme bent-knee and the straight styles. Those stirrups were usually hooded, once again like the Army style, though the vaqueros called the hoods tapaderos.

The Anglo-Americans, coming into the area, brought with them various military-type saddles, and lighter riding, racing saddles of the English pad style. But they soon switched to the Mexican stock saddle. They improved it, first by stitching on the housing or mochila so it wouldn't come off, then by doubling the rigging. The saddle with two cinches was called a double-rigged or rim-fire saddle, and it came to be the Texas

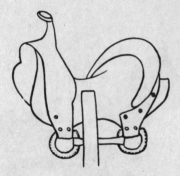

Double rig, or rim-fire hull

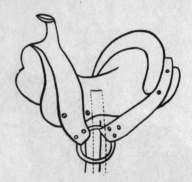

Three-quarter single rig, or Montana rig

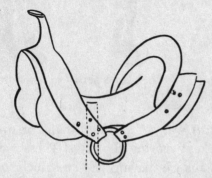

Center-fire single rig, or California rig

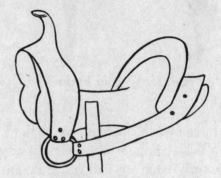

Spanish single rig

favorite. It was made up to order for these strange new customers, by the Texian saddlemakers and the Mexican *talabateros*. The Americans called the result a Mother Hubbard, because of its long skirts, or sometimes an Apple Horn, because of that feature's resemblance to half an apple. They'd reduced the diameter of the horn too, not caring much for a dinner plate in their middles. And usually the stirrup leathers carried a wide leather sweat guard called a fender, *sudadero*, or *rosadero*.

The stirrups themselves were now sometimes wooden box stirrups, very wide and squared, or ox-bow, narrow and rounded, usually with leather-bound treads, or, sometimes, all heavy leather. Typically the Texan stirrup was hooded. The Texan called the tapaderos "taps," and sometimes had them built into very fancy deals indeed, stamped, carved, and decorated with conchas and the like. For cold-weather use there were tapaderos that were practically overshoes, closed at the bottom and fleece-lined. For fiesta or parade there were eagle-billed taps, with a snout like an eagle's in front and wide, down-sweeping wings that sometimes all but scraped the ground.

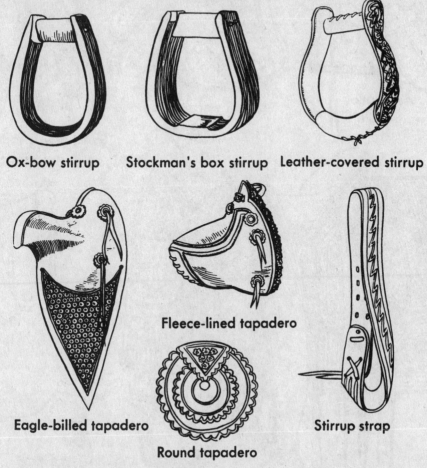

Ox-bow stirrup   Stockman's box stirrup   Leather-covered stirrup

Fleece-lined tapadero

Eagle-billed tapadero   Stirrup strap

Round tapadero

The Mother Hubbard or Apple Horn was the main saddle of the early trail drivers, and you saw it all the way from the Bravo to the Big Horn, clear up into the nineties. But meantime, out in California, another type had evolved, as we've already noted, the center-fire or California stock saddle. Along with its single cinch, this one had double, rounded skirts, a very noticeably higher, deep-dished cantle and slimmer, higher horn than the Texas hull, and very long tapaderos. No matter what Texans said, this was a very fine saddle, preferred on the Coast and much liked in the Northwest also.

Horse styles don't change quite as rapidly as women's fashions do, but they change, nevertheless. And nobody has ever figured out an entirely satisfactory saddle tree, the framework that fits the horse's back and gives the saddle form. If the tree fits when the horse is fat, it galls when he loses flesh, as he will under hard work. And vice versa. So there were lots of different kinds of trees, tried a while and liked or discarded, and back in

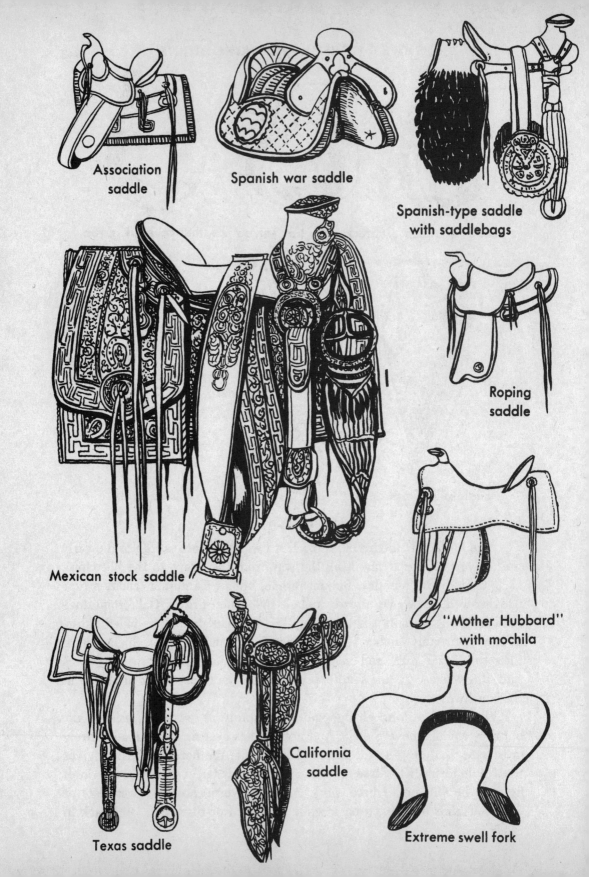

Association saddle

Spanish war saddle

Spanish-type saddle with saddlebags

Mexican stock saddle

Roping saddle

"Mother Hubbard" with mochila

Texas saddle

California saddle

Extreme swell fork

the early days you'd most likely just say you had you a stock saddle, "on a Morgan tree," or a Frazier, Ellenburg, or whatever.

The next general style to come along must have been the Cheyenne, which seems to have originated up on the Northern ranges, a sort of modernization of the old Mother Hubbard. Or maybe you could say it was old Mother Hubbard sorta married off to that slick California rig, because it was double-rigged, like the Texas saddle, but had double skirts, like the Californian—only the skirts were squared off, again like Texas. The rigging straps were generally exposed where they went around the horn, and there was an extra piece of leather over the seat, and—the truly distinctive feature —there was a sort of crash pad along the rim of the cantle, behind your back. This was called the Cheyenne roll, and if you ever got popped off right at the kidneys by some fool hammerhead hoss, who decided to depart sudden while you were all set on staying, you'd appreciate the roll.

The next in line, which I've been told appeared in the late seventies, was a mountain hull, a regular old war saddle, made up in Colorado. It came to be known as the Pueblo, since two saddlemakers of that town, Gallup and Frazier, were especially noted for their saddles. The horn on this was small, usually nickeled, the fork stuck way up, with the beginnings, at least, of the swell fork that was to come later; and the cantle was about 5 inches high, with maybe a 2-inch dish. It was what the old armored knights' war saddles had been, a form fitter, and that was what the cowboys eventually called it. They fitted you in with a shoehorn and the horse that got you out of it had to use a screwdriver, and maybe a pinchbar as well. For ropers, always in and out of their saddles, tying calves and such, it wasn't too good. But for rough country or for topping rough horses it was a dandy.

These were about all the important Western saddle styles until some-time in the nineties, when the swell fork put in its appearance. This was

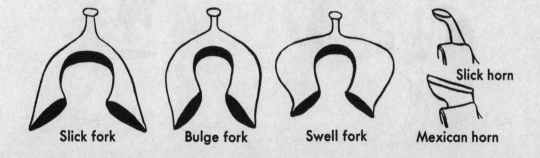

Slick fork   Bulge fork   Swell fork   Slick horn

Mexican horn

supposed to be startlingly new, though, as we've seen, the old knight's war saddle had a similar feature centuries before, and even some of the light hunting saddles had been equipped with something very like the Western bronc peeler's bucking roll. This, we'd better explain, was the forerunner of the swell fork, consisting of simply a tight-rolled blanket, or slicker, or sometimes a stick, strapped across the fork, to brace the knees under when riding a bucker. The swell fork built this idea into the saddle itself; and presently, from having built-up shoulders 15 or 16 inches across, the darn things looked like football players, with 20- and 22-inch swells, undercut and curving back over the legs as well, so you could practically hide under them. The swell fork was the thing up to World War I. Then the slick forks started coming back strong and now you see more of them than you do swell forks, in most cow country. For general chores and especially roping the boys ride a low-horn, low-cantle saddle, loosely called some kind of roper. In 1920 the rodeos banned the swell forks and adopted a hull called the Association saddle, usually supplied by the rodeo.

And speaking of rodeos (*ro'-dee-oh*, as they call it in the Midwest and West, not *ro-day'-oh*) the famous old 101 Ranch of Oklahoma has about as good a claim as any to having started the now nation-wide spectacle sport. Colonel George W. Miller, founder of the 101 in 1878 (it was supposed to have taken its brand from a real rough, tough honky-tonk in old San Antone, where the boys had some trouble), is said to have staged a more or less impromptu cowboy show for Winfield, Kansas, in 1882, though it was about 1905 or 1906 before the 101 got into the Wild West

show business on a touring professional basis. Prescott, Arizona, staged its first contest rodeo in 1883 and Cheyenne, Wyoming, had one in 1896. Madison Square Garden in New York added some Western riders and ropers to its "horse fair" in 1905. The immortal Will Rogers, with his rope tricks, was in the first 101 bunch to show at the Garden. So were Tom Mix, later a star of the silent movies, and Bill Pickett, a South Texas Negro and

Buffalo Bill

the greatest bulldogger bar none, ever to sweep out of the saddle onto the horns of a steer. Bulldogging, by the bye, throwing a steer by twisting his head down, succeeded an even rougher vaquero sport, bull tailing. In this you sailed by your steer, grabbed his tail, dallied it around your saddle horn, cut away sharply, and just upended that steer, probably busting his neck, too, in the process, so as cattle grew valuable it was frowned upon. The Mexicans called this process *colear*, literally, "wagging the tail."

Cowboy displays started as professional shows with hired performers, and then developed into the freelance exhibitions, the contests for prizes, which they are today; this is just the reverse of a sport's usual history. Colonel William F. Cody, Buffalo Bill, organized his Wild West Rocky Mountain and Prairie Exhibition show in North Platte, Nebraska, in 1883 and Major Gordon W. Lillie, Pawnee Bill, was one of his employees, brought up from the Indian Territory to act as Indian interpreter. Later Lillie formed his own Pawnee Bill's Historic Wild West show, and these, plus many imitators, were very hot entertainment in the eighties, the nineties, and the early years of this century. They toured like circuses, generally playing in open-air canvas walled arenas. The Cody or "Bill Show," as it came to be called, had its first tryout in, of all places, Brooklyn! On the other hand, the Rodeo Association of America, which controls the big free-lance contests of today, was not organized until 1929. In the real Old West, of the seventies or thereabouts, "rodeo," if anybody used the term at all, had the Mexican connotation of roundup, and not of a show, amateur or professional.

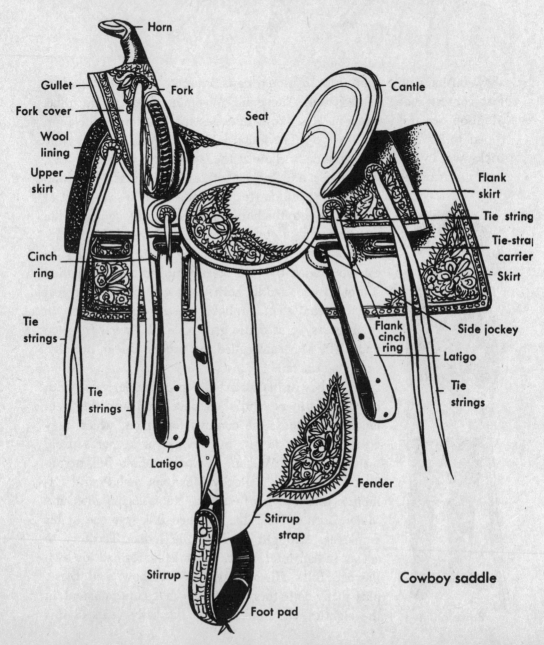

Cowboy saddle

Now let's get the trimmings on the saddles and we can go on to the bridles. Fastening around the horn, or through the fork, usually on the right side, there'd be a rope strap, to hold the coiled rope or lariat. On

Mexican fiesta saddle and spurs

both sides, under the pommel in front and the cantle in the rear would be saddle strings or straps. These would be long doubled leather thongs, about ½ inch wide, to tie on your slicker, bedroll, or what have you. Where the cinches connected with the saddle via the cinch rings, on the off (right) side there'd ordinarily be a billet to buckle into the ring on the cinch, since you didn't often touch this side. But on the near or left side there'd be heavy leather straps called latigos, or tie straps, and these you wove through rigging and cinch rings, then cinched (tightened) up and tied, to make connections of saddle and hoss. Usually you tied the latigo the way you would a four-in-hand necktie. You saddled and unsaddled, of course, from the near side.

That's about all the major dope on saddles, and it skips the real fancy details, most of them thought up by the Mexicans, the Californians, and the New Mexicans, all of whom had their own peculiar ideas about the last words in hoss millinery. Dressed up in his go-to-meeting fiesta saddle, a cayuse from any of those three great areas in the old days was really something gorgeous.

There wasn't any of that fofurraw, as the Mountain Men termed all fripperies (the word comes from the Spanish *fanfarrón,* maybe by way of the French *fanfaron*), on a working saddle on the old trails, you may be very sure. But by a hundred and one small details you could be pretty sure where a man was from. The very way he handled his rope, for instance, marked one great difference between the Texan and the Californian. The Texan was a tie-fast man; that is, he tied the end of his rope to his saddle horn, hard and fast, and let her rip. The Californian, on the contrary, and many of the Northwestern cowmen as well, were dally men, the word coming from the Spanish *dar la vuelta*—"to give it a turn." It means, of course, turning the rope around the horn of the saddle, using the horn as a snubbing post. Tie-fast advocates generally carried short ropes, not over 30 to 40 feet, and got right up on their prey before spilling a loop. This makes sense in brush country. Dally men, on the other hand, customarily worked in more open ranges, ran to long ropes, as long as 100 feet, and quite often made catches at fantastic distances. The debate over which is the better system is another eternal argument of the West.

The first *reatas* or ropes (the word lariat is simply a corruption of *la reata*) were braided rawhide, with from four to eight strands. The working reata was generally a four-strand job and about ⅜ inch in diameter. Braiding such a rope was a fine art, and a good *reatero* was a real artist, just as a vaquero who could handle such a rope properly was a master of his trade. But, as you can imagine, such a reata cost a lot more than a grass rope, as the Anglo-American cowboy called one made of Manila hemp, Mexican maguey, sisal, or cotton. It required more care and it could not take the pop-your-head-off strain that a grass rope would, and that all lariats get, sooner or later, in stopping husky cattle. So presently the Texas-style cowboy, tying fast, would be using a grass rope, which he called a rope or lariat, and if he took the trouble to say *reata* properly he was probably distinguishing a rawhide rope. But if your roper was a Californian he probably wouldn't say lariat at all, he'd say lasso. This is also Mexican, possibly from the Spanish *lazada*, a running knot, a bowline, or from *lazo*, snare. At any rate the lasso, lariat, reata, or just plain rope, cowboy speaking, is a snare and at the end is a bowline, slip knot, or *honda*, a little eye through which the rope passes to make the big loop.

Sometimes this honda is just an eye in the rope, maybe bound with rawhide, maybe not. Sometimes it is an iron or brass eyelet. Or it may be a little U-shaped reinforcement that fits in the top of the eye and is held there by prongs. Or again (though they didn't have this in the old days) quite often you'll see now an ingenious "breakaway" honda, that's got a trigger in it so that you can release the rope instantly if your catch is strangling or killing itself struggling.

There are a lot of things an expert can do with a rope and they all have names. The simplest is busting an animal. You catch him from behind, over the horns or over the head. Then you flip the rope to one side of his body and cut your horse sharply away to the other, thus making the rope slash his hind legs from under him. The steer turns a flip, you've busted him proper, your pony holds the rope taut while you light down with your piggin strings and hogtie the animal's legs.

A *peal*, which takes its name from the Spanish word meaning "sock," is a throw which literally does sock the captured animal, catching each of the hind feet, amazingly, in each loop of a figure 8. A *mangana* is an under-hand throw, usually made in the corral to catch horses, which forefoots the animal, that is, catches the front feet. A Blocker loop, named for a famous Texas cattleman and trail driver, is a very large loop that, originally anyhow, went over the steer's shoulders to pick up the front feet. Nowadays some hands call any extra-large loop a Blocker.

And here's where I get off. I'm just telling you what I've seen and been told. I'm no cowboy. Top hands, and particularly expert ropers, are, in my experience, hair-trigger touchy and temperamental artists, and it pays to let them settle the fine points among themselves.

One thing we might add, though. A horsehair rope won't stop a rattle-snake. Practically everybody in the old days thought it would, and lots of riders carried a horsehair rope to coil around their beds at night. But I can remember, 'way back when I was a kid, seeing it tried out, a horsehair loop tossed around a genuine live rattler. After he got tired waving his ugly head at us scientists, he just unraveled and went over that rope like it wasn't there.

Before we get to regular bridles, there was the hackamore, which is just a kind of halter, with a bosal, noseband, plus a couple of cheek straps that maybe just tied behind the ears to hold the thing on or maybe had some simple kind of headstall, a split in the strap, say, to stick an ear through, or two splits, for both ears. A halter hasn't any bit to go in the horse's mouth.

Since the hackamore is the prime tool of the horsebreaker who tames and trains colts, sometimes there will be a blinder on it, a wide strip of leather which slides up and down to cover the eyes while the breaker is saddling up or mounting. He can lean forward and pull it up on the colt's forehead to let him see again. Attaching to the bosal is the mecate, or, as the Texans soon corrupted it, the McCarty, usually a hair rope about 20 feet long, and with a tassel on one end. Horsehair ropes, by the way, are too light for lariats, catch ropes, but they're pretty, so a lot of them were used this way, and range slang might make just any old hair rope a McCarty. To use it on your hackamore you just tie it on each side of the noseband. Then when you get on, you have reins, and when you get off there's a trailing rope you can maybe grab and stop your pony if he tries to get away. Or you use it to tie him up with while you're taking time out.

Hackamore bits are sometimes used, looking much like ordinary curb bits, complete with curb chain under the jaw, except that the hackamore bit has an attached noseband, usually braided or padded, just as in the regular bosal, and there is nothing in the horse's mouth. And sometimes there'll be a *fiador,* or Theodore as the Texans pronounce it, on the hackamore. This is a knotted rope under the jaw, fastening to the bosal, tying again at the throat, then going around the neck, like a throatlatch. Its big advantage is that it makes the hackamore a real hard-to-get-out-of halter, and you don't have to tie a rope around your colt's neck, just to be sure, when you get off. A lively horse can sometimes yank himself out of a hackamore without that Theodore.

Now the bridles. Except for being a lot fancier, at least on occasion, they weren't much different from the military bridles described in Chapter III. You can describe any of them as consisting of a noseband, cheek pieces, some kind of headstall—that is, a strap that goes over the head

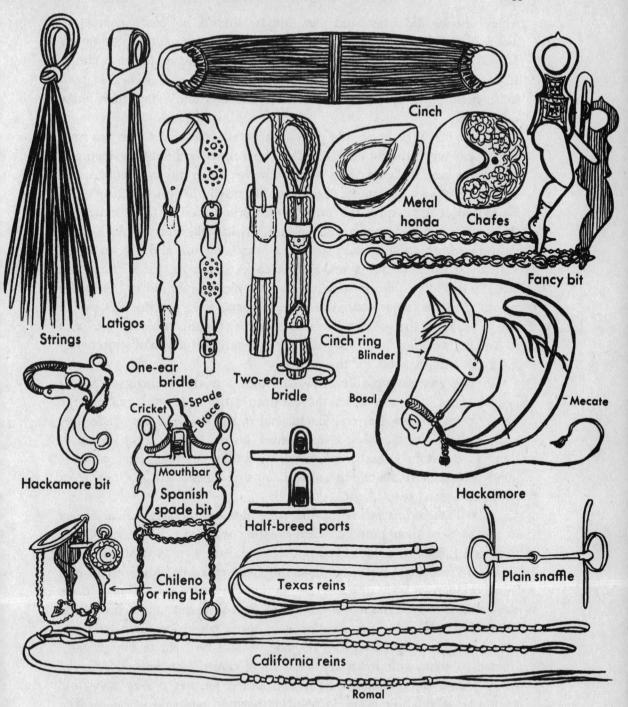

Strings

Latigos

Cinch

Metal honda

Chafes

Fancy bit

One-ear bridle

Two-ear bridle

Cinch ring

Blinder

Hackamore bit

Cricket Spade
Brace
Mouthbar
Spanish spade bit

Half-breed ports

Bosal

Mecate

Hackamore

Chileno or ring bit

Texas reins

Plain snaffle

California reins

Romal

behind the ears and another across the forehead above the eyes—plus a
throatlatch, a strap that goes down under the throat from the points

where cheeks and browband join. Maybe there'd be conchas, rosettes, nickel nailheads, *najas,* fancy stitching, tassels, or whatnot as decoration. Maybe the bridle would be braided, instead of having just flat straps. It could even be horsehair or something. It was still a bridle, with those basic parts. But when it came to the bits and reins, there were differences.

In the Old West you could pretty nearly tell what area a man was from just by looking at the bit on his bridle. The Texans, and most cowmen east of the Rockies, deriving their gear from the Texas riders, would use a curb bit, maybe with fancier cheeks but essentially like the military curbs we looked at in Chapter III. But the Californians and cattlemen west of the Rockies would be apt to use a Spanish spade bit, which looks like the most ghastly thing you could stick in a horse's mouth, and I guess it is— unless you can ride like a real Californio. A spade bit has a thing that actually looks like a spade sticking out from the straight bar in the horse's mouth. This spade has curved braces coming in from the sidebars, and if you're heavy on the reins you can cut a horse's mouth to bloody bits with it. But, on the other hand, they say it's a splendid bit if you're a top horse-man. Let's call it a bit for the expert.

In one way it's typically Latin, and that part always intrigued me. It can be cruel, yes. But, as in the Mexican attitude toward gelding, the horse's point of view was considered, and in the shank of the spade they put a little roller, or cricket, a little wheel, mainly to give the pony something to entertain himself with when he hasn't anything else to do. A horse will stand at a hitching rail and roll that wheel with his tongue for hours, so I guess they like it.

The Texas riders picked up the same idea too, putting similar rollers in the ports of their port bits, thus creating what is called a half-breed port, and the Texas ponies liked crickets too. But, as a general thing, the Texas bits were much plainer than the California bits in all ways. And Texas bridle reins were different, too, in that they were split. That is, there were two of them, fastened to the bit on each side, but unattached at the rider's end. The rider, dismounting in a hurry, could just drop his reins, they'd hang straight down, and the pony would be "tied to the ground," trained to stand still when the reins hung down that way. Usually he would stand. But sometimes he didn't, and if he was a very savvy old cayuse he might even learn to hold his head to one side as he sneaked off, so as not to step on his own reins. A horse has lots of sense when it's to his own advantage.

California bridles were typically narrower in cheeks and headstalls than Texas bridles, and their bit shanks or cheeks were usually heavier and wider. California reins also were closed at the rider's end, usually extending into a *romal*, or extra length made with a cracker, for use as a quirt. When the Californian dismounted, his reins, of course, stayed up on the saddle, and he hitched his horse with the mecate, which he kept looped on the side of the saddle, or maybe tied fancily around the horse's neck. Still another kind of bit, which was not much used though you saw it sometimes, was the chileno, or ring bit, the cowboy version of the Army's horsebreaker we have described already. It was primarily a Mexican bit, with a large metal ring attached to the center of the port, or spade, to go under the horse's jaw and act as a severe curb. Usually this ring was also attached by chains to the bottoms of the shanks.

A bar bit was one with a straight or slightly curved bar for a mouthpiece, used on gentle horses or harness animals, where you didn't need too severe control. A snaffle bit is much the same thing, except that the mouthpiece is jointed in the middle. Both usually have simple rings at the cheeks. As we noted in Chapter III, any kind of curb bit requires a curb chain, or strap, around the horse's lower jaw, so that leverage can be applied to the horse's mouth; and to get this as it should be, the curb chain or strap must be adjusted just right, neither too tight nor too loose.

Well, that about fixes our riders up so far as saddles and bridles are concerned. But did I think to put anything under those saddles, except the horse? Through the centuries horsemen have tried all sorts of things under there, fleece linings, sweat pads, underhousings, whatnot. They discovered that usually the fancier the pad the more certain it was to make the horse's back sore. So at last nearly all of them settled for just folded blankets, which you could refold, turn, rearrange, and thus take care of the peculiarities of your pony's back. The blanket practically always was, and is, wool.

The Army used the regular Army blanket. The old Californians liked *tirutas*, a heavy white and black blanket woven by the Indian women in Sonora. New Mexicans and, as soon as they could get them, Texans also preferred Navajo saddle blankets, woven in the Navajo hogans and often with big tassels on the corners. A few cowhands would use felt or hair saddle pads, bought in the saddlery shops. Double-rig riders usually folded the blanket large so that lots of it showed; center-fire riders followed the old California style and folded it close, so that little, if any, of the blanket showed under the rounded California skirts.

A good stock saddle would weigh around 40 pounds, sometimes more, almost never less than about 30, and would cost from $25 up, mostly up. About $50 would be average. If you went in for jewelry—stamped, carved leathers, silver mountings, and such—you could pay practically anything, clear up into the thousands. But generally the working saddle was pretty plain.

It had to be heavy, to stand the terrific strains. When you go to joining some 900 pounds of horse and 1000 pounds of agitated steer with just one rope, hitched to one point on one saddle, you better have you a rough, tough saddle. Though, while I'm on this, the South American cowboy solved this little problem by tying his lazo to a ring on a cincha or surcingle buckled around the saddle, and the old Spaniard just hitched his reata to the horse's tail. I wonder what the horse thought about that.

Cinches or *cinchas*, the bellybands or girths that go under the horse, were generally of mohair, which is Angora goat hair, usually the best cinch you can buy. Others were made of horsehair, fishcord, various woolen and cotton materials, and sometimes just plain leather. There'd be a cinch ring at each end, sometimes with a tongue also, to make the ring a buckle. Sometimes these rings carried leather *safes*, or chafes, that is, rub pads. For a center-fire rig, the single cinch would usually be wide, say 6 inches. For a double rig, the front cinch would likely be, say, 4 inches and the rear or flank cinch might be a leather strap, say 2 inches or so. Quite often there'd be a little connecting belly strap linking this flank cinch with the front cinch, to keep the rear one from crawling. Sometimes the flank cinch would just buckle, instead of connecting with latigo tie straps. Most horses hate that flank cinch. They don't like the front one either, for that matter, and a smart hoss will take a deep breath and try to bloat himself plenty as you saddle up.

A good cowhorse weighs somewhere around 1000 pounds, give or take 200 pounds either way, and stands about 14 to 15 hands high. A hand is 4 inches, presumably the width of a human hand across the palm, and a horse's height is measured from the ground up to the top of his withers, the ridge between his shoulder blades.

Say, did we get those cowboy bedrolls? In the sixties and early seventies, a cowboy's bedroll was apt to be pretty impromptu, just some *sougans* (homemade comforts), a blanket or two, and maybe a tarpaulin. But as they sold those longhorns and got money, the cowboys developed their bedroll into a waterproof tarp, up to about 10 by 20 feet, usually heavy white ducking with tie strings or snaps along the edges, so it could be made into a sleeping bag. Inside would be a couple of sougans to serve as mattress, two blankets, and the rider's war bag, which we have investigated already. He used the war bag or his saddle for a pillow.

Bedding down for the night, the cowboy always took care he wasn't in a hollow where he might wake up in a small lake if it rained during the night. Next morning he rolled and roped his own bedroll, if he craved to keep it. If he didn't get it on the wagon himself, cookie was liable to leave it right there. In a real downpour it wasn't any trick at all to improvise a small head tent from the long tarp. In the rain, or on cold mornings, the cowboy dressed under his blankets, that is, if he had undressed any the night before. Usually getting ready for bed just consisted of taking off one's hat, boots, and gunbelt, if one were packing a gun. It was a right simple way of life.

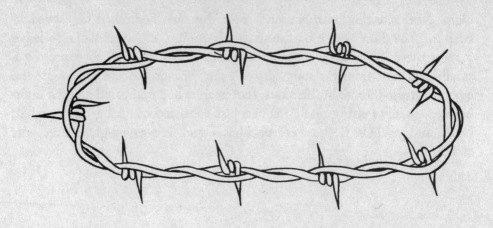

IX

FREE GRASS AND BARBED WIRE

WHEN I was very young an old cowman used to come occasionally to our table. He was a fierce, white-bearded old man, an ex-Confederate who had ridden with Nathan Bedford Forrest. As our elder, he was always asked to say grace. And I remember one thing he always included: "God bless the grass."

It took me quite a while to understand that he was entirely right in his prayer. For, while the Lord had prepared a table before us, He also had not neglected to spread one outside for His other creatures: He had given them the grass. At one step removed it was our food too, our living.

Wheat is a form of grass, do you not forget, and corn, and oats, and rye, and rice, and even sugar cane! But what the old cattleman was thinking about, I know, were the prairie grasses, buffalo, and grama, and bluestem, and their kin. And I do not think anyone who remembers the Old West can close his eyes without seeing immediately the grass, mile on mile of it, changing color, flowing like the sea, talking to the wind.

Buffalo grass just doesn't take to white civilization. It's like the buffalo it once fed. You plow it under and it's gone; you can't replant next year and have it back good as ever. Some of the other grasses are not quite so choosy, such as the Easterner, educated grasses, brought in to show the natives how. Timothy, or herd's-grass, for instance—one name comes from Timothy Hanson, who introduced it into the Carolinas; the other from

John Herd, who grew it in New Hampshire. It makes fine hay. Or Bermuda, which the slaves are believed to have brought in from Africa in their bedding. Or clover or alfalfa, which aren't true grasses at all but legumes, originally from Asia Minor. But the principal native grasses of the Old West were buffalo, grama, and their tall partner bluestem or bluejoint, and these you surely want to be able to recognize.

Buffalo grass is a short grass, seldom growing more than 5 or 6 inches high. It grows in patches, spreads by surface runners, and forms a fine turf. It's a kind of gray-green, and in winter a straw color, yellow and brown and rose, and in the wind it seems to turn color like changeable silk. This was the grass on which the buffalo and the longhorns thrived, and, what with all the plowing and sodbusting, it seemed on its way out, like the buffalo, in the early years of this century. Its seed comes in a tough bur, mighty hard to process. But smart ranchers and farmers are trying to encourage it nowadays.

Grama grass grows taller than buffalo grass, about 12 to 18 inches for blue grama, and up to 3 feet for side-oats grama. It generally grows in bunches or patches, with little bluish spikes on the stems, and it cures well. Stock love it.

Bluestem or bluejoint, of which there are two main kinds, big bluestem and little bluestem, is another extra-nutritious bunch grass, getting its name from its bluish-green color, which turns reddish-brown in the fall. Out on

GRASSES

Buffalo grass   Grama   Gietta   Bluestem

the prairies where there's little moisture is where you generally find the little bluestem, which seldom gets more than about 2 feet tall. But in the bottoms, or well-watered areas, big bluestem will reach 6 feet. Both kinds grow in the Osage hills in my land, Oklahoma, some of the finest rangeland in the world, and you ought to see the old cows when they get shipped in there from some rockpile, dustbowl pasture in West Texas or New Mexico. They just say, "Lawd, I'm home!" and lie down and roll.

There are hundreds of other Western grasses, sometimes with different names in different areas, galleta, mesquite grass, wild oats; a flock of different kinds of reeds and weeds, bluegrass (there are sixty-five kinds of American bluegrass alone, ranging from Canada bluegrass to Texas bluegrass), lovegrass, switchgrass, Indian grass, gietta—you could go on forever. And another point about the good Western grasses is that they don't just decay, they *cure;* that is, they preserve themselves on the ground when the frosts come in the fall, and cattlemen often claim they're better for stock in the dead, cured state than when they're still green and growing. Anyway, they're good food all winter, and the cow can do her own harvesting, which is something! (Ever pitch any hay?)

There are many kinds of poison plants, too, which kill about 4 per cent of the stock a year. The most famous of the lethal stuff is undoubtedly loco, or crazy weed. While horses usually won't eat it, they sometimes will, especially when grazing is scarce. And once they get the habit, they'll look for

POISONOUS PLANTS

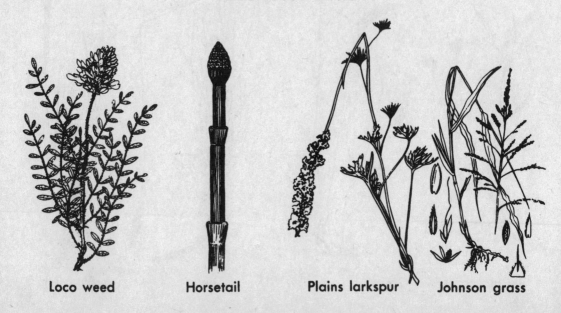

Loco weed   Horsetail   Plains larkspur   Johnson grass

it, just like dope fiends. Loco grows all over the West, and a locoed horse is easy to spot. He's crazy, which is what loco means in Spanish. The stuff affects his eyesight, and he stumbles and staggers, he'll rear and shy at nothing—maybe he's seeing pink elephants or snakes—and his mane and tail often grow long, wild, and shaggy. He'll kill his fool self, going without food or even water, looking for loco, unless you pen him up and get a vet to treat him. But if he isn't too far gone, he'll usually get over it in time, if you keep him strictly off the habit. Cattle eat the stuff, too, but since you don't ride steers the effect isn't so noticeable or so dangerous as it is with horses.

Larkspur grows wild on Western ranges, and some varieties of it are poison to cattle, paralyzing them so that they fall down, can't get up, and, if they've eaten enough of the stuff, die from suffocation because their lung muscles are immobilized. White snakeroot is another plant that sometimes poisons cattle, giving them the shakes, and, if the critter is a milk cow, poisoning the milk too; if you drink it you can get seriously ill. Horsetail is another poison growth, and so are bitterweed, poison vetch, and death camass. And finally, not to make a dictionary out of this, a number of other plants, when they're young and, as you'd suppose, tender, or are making a rapid second growth, have a bad habit of producing cyanide, as Sudan grass and Johnson grass will do on occasion, and sorghum. Sudan grass, by the way, is another newcomer, not found in the Old West.

But all these, plus the hazards of Indians and wolves and blizzards and rustlers and whatnot, were just part of the risks the Old West cowman took in stride. When he trailed north or west he was after free grass, free range, and he was willing to take his chances with trouble. His idea of property was primarily ownership of living creatures—cattle or horses—rather than land. He might one way or another contrive to own the land his ranch house and corrals were on. But as for his range, his attitude toward that was more like the Indian's, it was his the way a man's country is his. A free country, but just try and take it away from him!

This was the exact opposite of the sodbuster's thesis that a man should own the land he tills, either claiming it from the government as a homestead, or buying it from a railroad, land company, or other owner.

Under the Federal Homestead Act, which went into effect January 1, 1863, any person who was twenty-one or older, or head of a family, a United States citizen or in the process of becoming one, and had never borne arms against the U. S. government or given aid and comfort to its enemies (which meant, of course, that no Confederates or Confederate sympathizers need apply) could file on any open 160 acres of government land in some sections, or on 80 acres in some more favored areas. For this homestead, as it was called, you paid a $10 filing fee, plus registers' charges. The total cost was something under $20. Within six months after filing on a homestead you must be living on it and making improvements. After you had lived on it continuously five years and produced evidence that you had complied with all requirements, it was yours. You had proved up, and you received a patent to the land.

By a later amendment, soldiers who had served at least nine months could deduct their service time from the residence time required, and there were other minor changes. But this, essentially, was the law that settled the West.

Prior to the Homestead Act there had been other land laws. Pre-emption laws had existed in various forms since 1830, in general permitting a would-be settler to pre-empt up to 160 acres of the public domain, on which he was supposed to settle, erect a dwelling house, and, on proof of this, be allowed to buy the land at a minimum price of $1.25 an acre. Which is certainly dirt cheap, but not free land. All sorts of frauds were perpetrated under these laws. For example, a settler would solemnly swear to the land office that he had erected a "12 by 14" house, not adding that he meant a structure 12 by 14 inches, a doll's house, and not, as you'd suppose, a 12-by-14-foot human residence. Or you could rent a cabin on wheels, a sort of pioneer trailer house, which you could keep on your claim until you had sworn you had a residence, after which you trundled it back to its owner. So the law got a bad name. Nevertheless, when the Homestead Act was passed in 1862, the pre-emption law was not repealed and accordingly a man could homestead one quarter section, 160 acres, and then pre-empt another, paying for it. Or he could change his homestead into a pre-emption after six months' residence, and buy it at $1.25 an acre. As you can gather, there were a lot of opportunities for chicanery and fraud in those land laws.

There was another way you could acquire land, even though you might not be able to qualify as a homesteader. A citizen, an alien, even an ex-rebel, wholly unreconstructed, could buy from the railroads or land companies who had actually millions of acres to sell. And just how they had acquired these small empires is yet another fascinating story.

To encourage railroad building, especially westward across what everybody then considered the worthless American Desert, Congress granted land to various railway companies. For example, the Union Pacific and the Central Pacific, in 1864, had been promised every odd-numbered section, valuable mineral lands alone excepted, for 10 miles on each side of the right-of-way. (A section is 640 acres, in case you've forgotten.) The Northern Pacific got all the odd-numbered sections for 20 miles on each side of its tracks in the states and for 40 miles in the territories! The Santa Fe got something like 3 million acres. These companies, known as land-grant railroads, were in the business of hauling stuff, not ranching or farming, so, as rapidly as they could, they began to unload their land holdings, seeking settlers and buyers far and wide, advertising not only in this country but abroad as well, bringing in trainload after trainload of immigrants, who often spoke no English.

Generally the railroads held their lands for higher prices than the government pre-emption laws demanded, selling at around $3 to $5 an acre. But they also offered ten-year terms and low interest rates, required payments on principal only after three or four years, gave liberal discounts for cash, and financed free exploration trips if you bought your land. They went after the business. Since the railroad lines ran mainly east and west, right across the north-south routes of the trail drivers, the sodbusters who bought from them settled right smack across the trails, and the big struggle was on. The panic of 1873 put only a temporary check to this activity. By the early eighties the free grass of the north and west was just about gone along with the Mountain Men and the buffalo, and the cowmen, who had run off the buffalo and the Injuns, were now fighting for their lives against the boys with plows and barbed wire who aimed to bust up that-there grass and grow corn, or mebbe wheat, some of that Turkey Red wheat perhaps, that the German Mennonites, fine farmers, had fetched in with them from Russia. The Santa Fe had brought in the Mennonites in 1874, and their Crimea-raised wheat was darn good and surprisingly adapted to the West.

Let's go back for a moment now and pick up some pieces. In 1865 there were in the West, from Mexico to Canada, nobody knows how many buffalo exercising their sovereign and hereditary privileges of eating the grass and muddying the water. Estimates run to more than 100 million. Probably there were over 10 million in the so-called Southern Herd and a somewhat smaller number in the Northern Herd (the north-south division extended even to buffalo!). Apropos of this, one of my own pet theories is that there were no separate northern and southern herds in the very old days. I think that the westward trails, first the wagons and then the railroads, cut the continuous belt of buffalo into separate parts. I suspect the buffalo, for the most part, were much like range cattle, moving back and forth, covering maybe a 30- or 40-mile range, but not drifting much farther away from home stamping grounds, except in very unusual times, such as great droughts, or blizzards like that of 1886, when steers from ranges 500 miles north were found in Texas. Now you cut tracks across a continuous herd like that, with

meat hunters killing off the animals for maybe 10 to 20 miles on each side of the trail, and pretty soon you've got the animals split into a "Northern" and a "Southern" herd. Let more hunters chivvy the survivors mercilessly and they'll try to migrate too. But not because all this was their natural custom.

No matter; during the Civil War there were Northern and Southern buffalo herds, and even before the cannon stopped booming at Appomattox, the buffalo rifles were roaring out on the Western plains. Whatever the buffalo numbered in 1865, ten years later all but a remnant of the Southern Herd was gone, and by 1880 even the Northern Herd was melting like snow in a chinook. In 1883 the lines of the Northern Pacific, building simultaneously west and east, met at Gold Creek, Montana, and that was track's end for the buffalo. The next year less than 500 buffalo hides were shipped east over the line. Five years later, in 1889, Dr. William T. Hornaday, the famous American zoologist, reported that there were about a thousand American bison left alive. The last of the hundred million!

How did this happen? Of course, both whites and Indians had hunted buffalo from the very first. But the release of thousands of professional killers at the close of the war, men on both sides who had spent four long years practicing the trade of violent death, and who now found it difficult, if not sometimes downright impossible, to settle down—this really spelled the doom of the buffalo.

After the sixties, the buffalo hunters were much like the Mountain Men before the war. Among them, as among the Mountain Men, were many good citizens, educated and intelligent. But all too many were Ishmaels, outcasts, outlaws, guerrillas, the riders under the black flag, the deserters, renegades, and pariahs from both sides.

Usually the hunters worked in small parties, especially when Indians were not troublesome. And even when they were, more often than not the hunters depended on the casual association of men happening to be in the area, rather than on any formal protective organization. Typically there would be one or two hunters and perhaps two or three skinners for each hunter in a party, with two or three wagons to carry out supplies and freight the hides back. The wagons ordinarily were drawn by four-mule teams.

The actual killing was done with large-caliber rifles, some of them muzzle-loaders at first, some needle guns, the latter a European development enormously publicized by the Franco-Prussian War of 1870-71, in which such guns were widely used. The name comes from the firing pin, which is very long and slender, like a needle, to pierce clear through the paper-encased cartridge to strike the primer, placed inside, at the base of the bullet, usually in a papier-mâché *sabot* or cup. The Prussian needle gun was the Dreyse, .51 caliber, the father of all modern bolt-action rifles, and some of these found their way into buffalo country. And a few needle guns were American-made, Klein Patent rifles. But needle guns spat too much smoke and flame at the breech, so they were soon displaced by metallic-cartridge weapons, foremost among them the big Sharps.

This famous weapon we have noted already as serving in the Civil War. After the war it was converted into a metallic-cartridge gun. The metal-

Sharps buffalo rifle

cartridge Sharps—all single-shot, since no one ever figured out any prac-
ticable way to adapt the action to magazine loading—were made in many
models and calibers, from .40 to .54. A .54-caliber rim-fire, the Model 1866,
was produced briefly in that year. The most favored buffalo rifle, however,
was the "Big Fifty" Sharps, which, according to some authorities at least,
was sometimes chambered for a monster shell carrying 170 grains of powder
and 700 grains of lead (compare that with the Army 450-grain slugs!)
and a shellcase 3¼ inches long. The more common size, however, was the
.50-90 Sharps Special, with a 473-grain bullet and 90 grains of powder,
which seems big enough.

Prices on these guns are hard to give. At first, naturally, they were high,
but after the panic of 1873 all prices dropped and the buffalo were vanishing rapidly anyway. So a rifle that cost, say, $50 to $75 in the early seventies would be $20 by the eighties. In addition, just where you bought your
rifle affected prices materially. In town, especially back in civilization, a
Sharps Fifty might cost you $35 to $40; out on the frontier the cost might
be doubled. For example, at Adobe Walls, buffalo-hunter outpost in the
Texas Panhandle, in June 1874, the famous Army scout, Billy Dixon, one
of the better type of hunters and later a Congressional Medal winner, was
very happy to be able to buy a .44 Sharps for $80, to replace the Big Fifty
he had lost. And well he did. Next morning 700 Injuns under Quanah
Parker, Lone Wolf, and Stone Calf attacked the little town and there was
quite a shootin' scrape. The story is told in *The Life of Billy Dixon*[1] by his
wife, Olive K. Dixon, which is a classic of the old buffalo days.

Some Remington, Ballard, Whitney, Phoenix, and other makes of
rifles were used in buffalo hunting, all single-shot and usually .45 or .50
caliber, since it took a real jolt to down a buffalo. The repeating rifles,
principally rim-fire Spencers in the very early stages, and then Winches-
ters, did not have a sufficiently strong breech mechanism to stand the very
heavy charges necessary and hence were not much used by buffalo hunters.
Winchester did something about this, but by then the buffalo were mostly
gone.

Killing buffalo, as the professional hunters did it, was a cold-blooded
business, not a sport. Having spotted a bunch of the animals, the hunter
would try to creep up and make a stand, that is, start firing deliberately,
ordinarily from a prone position, until the bunch stampeded or were all
killed.

The buffalo were stubborn beasties and slow to learn. They knew
Indians were their enemies and would run from their scent. But they did

1. Dallas, Texas: P. L. Turner, 1927.

not learn to stampede at the scent of white men, or so it is said, until they were on the very brink of extermination, nor did they even associate the distant boom of the big guns with danger until it was too late. A hunter using the "approach" system, creeping up and being careful to keep the buffalo from seeing him, could shoot down animal after animal, needing only to watch the survivors and shoot next any beast showing signs of catching the blood scent. This until he had killed all or nearly all of the group!

With the heavy-barreled Sharps (some of them weighed as much as 18 pounds) the hunter often used a support for the muzzle, a shooting stick. Or the piece was fired in what was called the back position, or the Texas grip, the rifleman lying on his back, feet to the target, shooting past or over his own toes. You could ruin one of the big barrels by too rapid shooting, and the black powder fouled horribly, so every two or three shots you ran a moistened cleaning patch through the bore, or a Fisher brush, a combination of rubber washers and bristles, first wetting the brush if you could. Or even breathing through the barrel might help, by moistening the powder cake with the moisture in the breath. As you'll notice, this doesn't sound like terribly rapid firing.

After the hunter had shot out his stand (and, by the bye, he tried to shoot the doomed beasts through the lungs, the "lights," as he said, knowing that with such a shot they'd go a step or two and drop, whereas a heart-shot buffalo might run several hundred yards), his skinners took over. Sometimes these worthies were hired by the month, $50 to $75 and keep; sometimes they were paid by the animal, 10 to 25 cents, and they could strip off the hide in an amazingly short time. A good skinner could handle 40 to 50 buffalo a day, or even more. He carried his own tools, an assortment of straight-bladed ripping knives, and curved skinning knives, both honed razor-sharp. First he ripped the hide down the belly from throat to tail, then he slashed down each leg, and again around the head, up to the ears. The rest of the head was not skinned out. The hide was rolled back for a starter and then a rope was drawn tight about the neck flap. A team was hitched to the other end, and the skin was shucked off by brute force.

The green hide, as it was termed, was then hauled back to camp, where it was pegged out on the ground, flesh side up, to dry. A green hide would weigh from 60 to over 100 pounds. Depending on the weather it would take three to five days to dry. Then it was turned over and the hair side dried out; after which, to cure the hide completely, you probably had to turn it some more, subjecting it to sunning until at last it was a flint hide, a pretty darn descriptive name, too. After that you stacked the hides flat on the wagon, or possibly folded or rolled them, by main force, and piled them on. Dried, they weighed less than half their green weight. Then you freighted them into town for the hide buyers.

The long curly hair on the big heads was sometimes taken for cushion or mattress stuffing, and some casual efforts were made, here and there, to do something about the meat. For example, one firm tried curing and marketing buffalo hams, with indifferent results. But for the most part, the huge carcasses were simply left to rot, a ghastly waste that infuriated the Indians to blood madness, and scant wonder!

Hides, at first, brought only $1 to $2, since buffalo skin is too spongy for sole leather. But as other uses were developd—lap robes for the open vehicles of the time, coats, buff leather for belts, saddle coverings, and the like—the market expanded and prices rose, to $2 and up for cow hides, $4 for bull hides. The panic of 1873 brought thousands of jobless men out to the prairies, to share in this bloody bonanza. And that was the end of the buffalo herds.

In 1876, the year General Custer and the Seventh went on to immortality on the Little Big Horn, the Osage Indians came home from their last great buffalo hunt; and it had been an utter failure. That fall and winter the Cheyennes and Arapahoes, on their last hunt, found only 219 hides to bring home. A way of life was gone forever.

Only the millions of tons of whitening bones remained, to be picked up by the bone pickers and shipped east to fertilizer factories; those and the buffalo grass, the buffalo gnats, and the buffalo wallows.

The grass we've looked at. The buffalo gnats we have with us yet, millions on millions of pesky little bugs, so small they can come through a screen, dancing in clouds, but, thank God, usually here today, gone tomorrow. The buffalo wallows are now mostly gone too, filled up and plowed over. They were the pits where the great beasts wallowed in the dust, saucer-shaped depressions seldom more than 6 feet deep but from 10 to 50 feet across. You used to find them all over the western plains.

Rarest of buffalo were the albinos, the white buffalo, which the Indians held in superstitious awe. They were not always white. In fact, like a "white" elephant, they were more often grayish, or merely a noticeably lighter shade than their fellows. But they were big medicine, and their hides rare and valuable prizes.

The habits of the buffalo would make a book. We might notice in passing that when he got up from lying down, he got up front feet first, like a horse and unlike a cow. He preferred to pass in front of rather than behind a moving object, a wagon train, say; so if you met a moving herd, you usually stopped until it went by. He was a fighter, hard to kill. The best meat on him was the tongue, usually cut out through the lower jawbone; the hump, over the shoulders; the depouille, or back fat, sometimes called Indian bread, since that was how the Indians used it; and the boudin, or intestines, eaten with the partly digested food, the chyme, still inside! Or, if you stomach that, the liver, eaten raw and with a little gall from the gall bladder sprinkled on it for sauce—I told you the old-timers were tough customers!

Dried meat, called jerky, you could make in hot, dry weather, especially in the Southwest, simply by slicing the meat into thin, long strips and hanging it up in the sun. If the weather was hot and dry enough, the meat might dry in a day. Farther north, or in damp or cool weather, you built a scaffold over a bed of coals, dipped your meat into boiling brine, then draped it over the scaffold to cure. The smoke imparted its own flavor and also kept off insects which might spoil the meat. Once properly cured, jerky kept indefinitely, and was quite as palatable as an old boot.

Whites and Indians had different methods of tanning the hides. White frontiersmen typically tanned hides by felling an oak tree, hollowing it out, tossing the chips and bark back into the trough and adding water, thus forming a tanning solution for soaking the hide. Indian tanned hides were prepared by patient fleshing and scraping by the women, who dressed the hide with the brains and liver of the animal, soaked it in water, and sometimes then smoked it over a slow fire, so that the odor of woodsmoke seems always with Indian leather. Tanned deer and antelope hides, as well as those of buffalo and cattle, were used instead of cloth by the Indians until the white traders came. Buffalo hides to be used for teepees were first put in water like the others, but were left soaking until the hair fell out. Then they were pegged out tight, fleshed with elkhorn scrapers, and softened. Only the much thicker buffalo bull hides were used for lodge coverings, and it usually took from ten to twenty of them, thonged together, for each lodge.

Fifteen to twenty-five poles, about 20 feet long, were tied together in a big cone, with several feet of the tops of the poles sticking out above the apex, and then the hide cover was drawn around and fastened with sharp skewers or sticks. The door was a round hole, usually covered with a flap, which was a skin drawn over a loop made from a limb. And up at the top were two flaps, with poles stuck in their corners, to handle the smoke. The fire inside, for warmth, needed a vent at the top for the smoke to get out or it would soon drive the inmates out. So the old Indian women managed those smoke flaps much like a modern ventilator, keeping the opening always turned downwind, so the smoke would be drawn out and not blown back inside. Those old squaws would get so expert at gauging the gusts that they'd dash outside and change the smoke flaps practically on the change of wind. But even so, living in a teepee was pretty rugged.

The Indians had a lot of skills. They made their own saddles, even made boats out of buffalo hides, packed their stuff on travois. They had a wonderful sign language they could use to talk to other Indians of practically any tribe, even if the spoken language was entirely different; yes, and they could use it for deaf people, too, and South Europeans, folks who'd never seen an Indian before and didn't know any more Indian words than the Indian knew English! Sort of a universal language.

But let's get back to those trail drivers and keep traveling. What were they looking for, besides free grass? Well, the cowman, and the sodbuster too, also had to look for water and fuel. Buffalo and cow chips might make you a good enough fire en route, but, once the home place was staked, you preferred more substantial fuel, particularly up in Nebraska, the Dakotas, or Wyoming, where on occasion it has been known to get a mite chilly. So the first settlers lit near streams and springs, where they naturally found timber too. But, as all these better spots were taken up and late arrivals had to spill out on the bare prairies, there was trouble.

You could burn grass or hay. There actually were hay-burning stoves, with spring-backed cylinders which you filled with hay and then inserted in slots in the front of the stove, something like shells in a double-barreled shotgun. The springs pushed the hay into the fire until the cylinder magazine was empty, at which time you'd better have the other magazine filled and ready. And the Mennonite farmers from Russia brought with them the idea of a Russian stove, practically a furnace, 6 feet high and 2 or 3 wide,

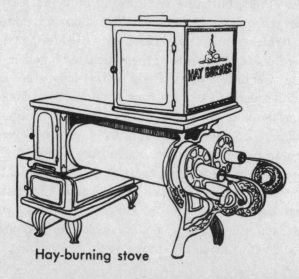

Hay-burning stove

made of brick and built into, or against, the house wall. It would burn anything, even weeds, and it was so big you didn't have to stoke it more than two or three times a day. But they were hard to build and never popular.

There were drum-type hay burners, in which you pulled out the bottom part, the firebox and enclosure, and substituted a fresh-loaded drum when the hay burned out. I don't know what you did about the smoke that doubtless came right out with it. There was still another type where you upended your drum of hay, grass, weeds, and whatever over the top of the stove. And imagine going out and gathering all that stuff! Or, of course, you could just build a pioneer fireplace and try frying your face while you froze your behind, or vice versa. But the heating problem of the plains never was really solved until the railroads began to supply first coal and then oil.

Settlers, cowmen and nestors alike, would go as far as 20 and 30 miles for wood, desperately stripping the railroad grants, grubbing up stumps, carrying away abandoned sheds and dwellings, doing 'most anything to get something to burn! It was a mess.

So was the water supply. After the natural living water, the springs and creeks, had been claimed, the settlers turned next to dug wells. Typically a dowser, or water witcher, was called in first. There was one in almost every frontier neighborhood in the old days, nor is his very ancient art extinct today. In fact, quite a few of his descendants work the oil fields now, solemnly "locating" oil much as their forebears did water, with the forked stick. Or they use the mysterious little ball, or cone, on the thong, the same device that will also—allegedly anyhow—tell you the sex of the unhatched chick.

Once the frontier dowser had located water for his customer, it was necessary to dig down to it, by hand, with pick and shovel. And in the Northwest particularly, in Nebraska and the Dakotas, some perfectly astounding feats of digging by hand were performed, wells as deep as 300 feet. A windlass and rope, of course, were needed for elevating machinery and the old iron-bound buckets brought up the soil and rock and, later, the water if you struck it. Cave-ins, black damp which smothered the digger, and fire damp, which could and sometimes did explode and blow him up, were some of the dangers, as was the risk of accidentally falling into an abandoned well on some droughted-out, deserted ranch or claim.

Sometimes, instead of digging the well, the settler would use a patent

Drive-well point

Pump

drive pipe, with a sharp point on the bottom. You simply pounded this into the ground, adding pipe as it went down. You couldn't go very deep with this method, of course, and you had to have a pump, or a long slim bailer, to get the water up, if you did strike pay.

Or maybe you could auger a well—that is, bore it out with a posthole auger, adding to the handle as the hole sank. Or, finally, you might drill a well.

There were several ways to manage this last. The easiest and most costly was to hire a water-well driller, another important personage to be found all over the West, as soon as settlement really got started. Often he'd be from Pennsylvania or West Virginia, where oil-well drilling had begun even before the Civil War. He'd have a drilling machine, a little steam engine and a boiler, to work a walking beam, which lifted and dropped the cable-supported bit assembly, or tools as they were called, in the hole. In the oil fields this system was called the percussion, or, later, the standard drilling system. And he'd charge you maybe a dollar a foot or so, huge money in the seventies.

But you could also drill your own well, with a spring pole. To rig this you found yourself a long, stout, limber sapling, which you anchored at one end so that it slanted over a fulcrum, with the free end above the spot where you wanted to drill your hole. Then you swung your tools from this free end, and added another cable, with a stirrup or loop in the bottom. If you stepped into this stirrup, threw your added weight on the spring pole, it would bend and let the bit hit the ground. So all you had to do was "walk" or "jig" the well down.

As the hole deepened and the added weight of cable and tools kept the sapling from springing back, you simply adjusted the fulcrum. Sometimes you'd have two or three men jigging in the stirrups, to get enough weight. You'd guide the bit until it hit solid bedrock by using a hollow log or a wooden tube for a conductor, or, as they'd say when iron casing became available, a surface pipe or drive pipe. Cuttings you got out with a sand pump, which was a kind of bailer with a suction-valve arrangement on the bottom that sucked the cuttings in. Sometimes a hinged platform was substituted for the stirrup and on this you could really get somewhere by throwing your weight around. It sounds primitive, and of course you couldn't drill very far. But plenty of wells, even oil wells, were drilled by this method.

Of course if you were a cattleman, or even a stock farmer, you needed lots of water, probably much more than you could haul up in a bucket, or pump by hand from a well. You would first try for living water, of course. Failing that, finding some place where you could make a "tank" would be one of your first thoughts. Tank is cow country for a small pond, made by damming a ravine or fixing a hollow to catch and hold rain water, and if you were going in for any sizable operation you'd doubtless need several tanks.

A range steer will drink as much as 30 gallons a day if he can get it. While you hear lots of yarns about old steers that must have been part camel, ranging 25 to 30 miles from water and maybe coming in only once or twice a week, or even just living on dew or cactus juice, I bet a lot of those boogers were the ones with the 13-foot hornspreads, too. Cattle nowadays will graze out not more than 3 or 4 miles from water, and the ranchers don't even like that, since they're breeding beef, and not racing stock, in these effete times.

So you'd want your water plentiful and, say, within a mile or two of your pastures. If you could, you would avoid pumping it by hand and haul-

Fifty years of windmill-blade arrangements

HALLADAY STANDARD
BATAVIA, ILL.
1860s
PERKINS
1880s
1870s
1890s
1850s

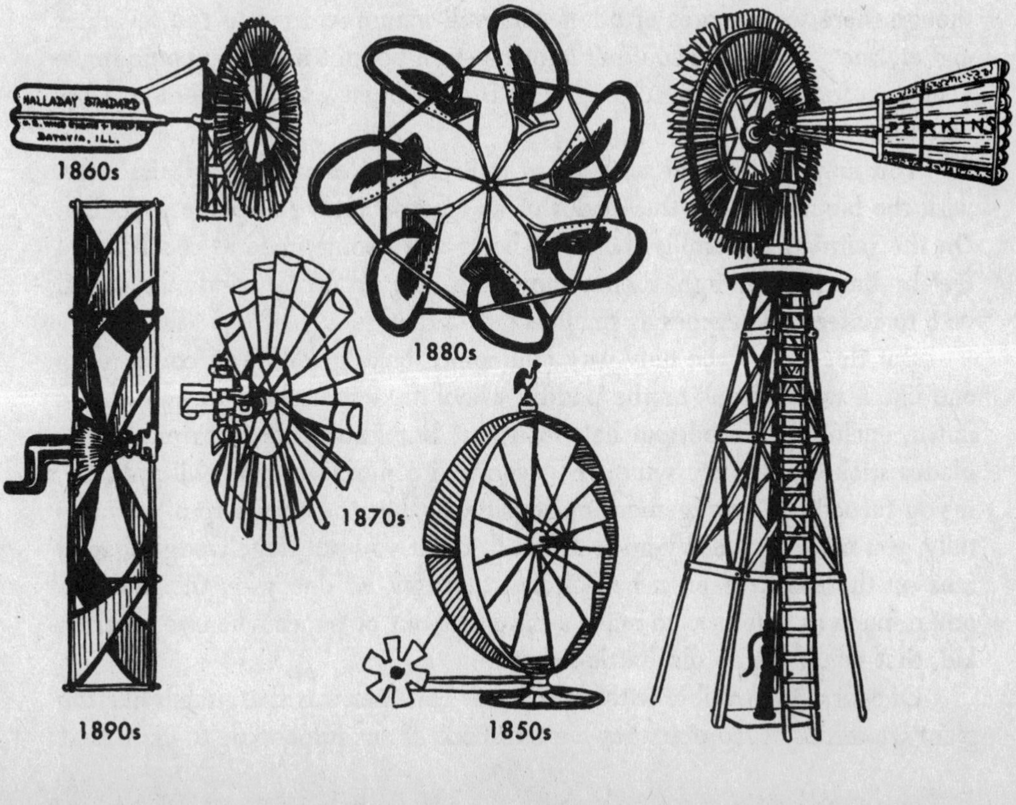

ing it where you needed it, or depending entirely on rainfall and surface water. So even back in the sixties you'd probably think of buying or making a windmill, to let that eternal prairie wind do some good. If the notion hadn't come to you from the windmills back in the Old Countries, in Holland and Belgium, you could have picked it up from the railroads, which even then were using windmills along the rights-of-way, to pump water for the engines.

Differing from the European mill, the American version was generally much smaller, and arranged so that the wheel, rather than the whole mill, turned to face the wind. That is, it did unless you had the mill cut off, with the fan wheel pulled flat against the vane, the big sail which, like the feathers on an arrow, kept the wheel pointed to the breeze. In the American mill, there also would often be some kind of mechanism to feather the blades, or do something to keep the wheel from blowing itself to pieces while operating in high winds. Daniel Halladay, of Ellington, Connecticut, is generally credited with being the father of the American-style mill, back in the 1830s. The United States Wind Engine and Pump Company, which bought out the Halladay company in 1862 and established a factory at Batavia, Illinois, and Fairbanks, Morse & Co., which began manufacture of their famous Eclipse windmill in 1876, doubtless were the real pioneers, though there were scores of other windmill manufacturers in the seventies and eighties. But if you couldn't afford a store-bought mill, you could make your own for practically nothing. The frontiersman was an ingenious soul, when put to it.

You may be familiar with these mills I am describing, turbine mills, with the blades set like the blades of an electric fan or airplane propeller. On the railroad windmills the fan wheels were sometimes as much as 30 feet in diameter, though, then as now, the fans on ranch windmills would be 8 to 10 feet, sometimes as small as 3 or 4 feet.

But this wasn't the only way you could make a mill. You could make one like a waterwheel, or the paddle wheel on a steamboat turned upside down, enclosing the bottom half in a box, but letting the tops of the flat blades stick up into the wind; then you had a jumbo or go-devil mill. Or, if you turned the arrangement on its side so that the wheel spun horizontally, you made it a merry-go-round mill. Or, if you put huge wedge-shaped fans on the shaft, or even half-circles, one twisted one way, the next the other, much as you used to make a pinwheel out of paper when you were a kid, that would be an old battle-ax mill.

Of course the trouble with these latter varieties was that, much like the giant windmills of Europe, they were difficult if not impossible to fix so that they'd turn into the wind, or turn out of it, or turn themselves off, should the velocities get so high as to be dangerous. If you had a prevailing wind, north wind half the year, south wind the other half, which is just about the way it blows in some parts of the West, you'd be all right. You could just fix your mill to run north and south. But suppose the wind blows from every which way?

That's where the windmill manufacturers had 'em beat. The wheel and the vane mills would face around. The European mills either didn't rotate at all, or the top of the tower or the entire tower rotated, and that was clumsy. But the American windmill was like the American longhorn or the American horse; it could pretty well take care of itself, except for an occasional greasing and oiling; and even that, in time, was provided for with self-oiling mechanisms that required a minimum of attention.

Windmill towers, of course, were wooden at first. And you not only

climbed the tower to grease the gearbox; you could go up for a view of what was coming, and so you used it as a sort of watchtower. Or maybe, if you got lost, a windmill tower poking up over the horizon like the mast of a ship would be your saving beacon. The darn things always creaked and groaned as they pumped, and even remembering that lonely sound in the night can make a country boy right homesick.

Fences, now, and a shed. And I hope you won't mind living in the wagon until we get the stock taken care of. The first enclosure, particularly in the early days, would probably be a pole corral, a pen fenced with whatever kind of poles or posts there were at hand, but preferably cedar if you could get them. Sometimes these poles would be set vertically in the ground, like a stockade, maybe tied together with rawhide. Or holes would be augered or chiseled in heavier posts that were set vertically, and then the ends of horizontal rails would be inserted in the holes, thus making a kind of rail fence. Or you could tie or nail the rails on the posts. Or you could raise a rock fence, as many settlers in rocky areas did, especially the new arrivals from Germany. I remember one time when I was living in an area where there were miles and miles of rock fences that had taken those old-timers millions of man-hours to build, somebody found a pot of gold buried in one of those old fences. By golly, in the next few weeks more rock fences went down in that county than had gone up in the preceding fifty years!

Or you could make your fence of adobe or sod. We'll talk about the sod construction when we get to the house. As for adobe, there are two ways you can handle it. Adobe, as you likely know, is simply sticky clay, the kind you'll find on the bottom of a dried-out desert lake. You can work it tapia-style, which means you make up the mud and pat the wall up with your hands, or maybe use some kind of form so you can pour it, like concrete. That was the way the old Indians, the Navajos, and the cliff dwellers before them, did it. Or you can do what the Mexicans did, make big, flat, sun-dried bricks first and then build with them. With bricks you'd need mortar, which would be just some more liquid 'dobe mud. Adobe walls, properly constructed and dried, will stand up a long, long time, especially in the dry Southwest.

But, as some of the early Texas settlers discovered, an ingenious Injun or white rustler can take a rawhide rope with knots in it and saw a hole in that adobe corral wall, maybe right while you're watching the gate. Or it may just plain dissolve in a heavy rain. So, except in the dry areas, you don't see much adobe. That corral would probably be poles instead, or horizontal rails, five or six rails high. For a gate you'd make a frame, two gateposts, a connecting beam overhead, then the gate itself, swung down on rawhide

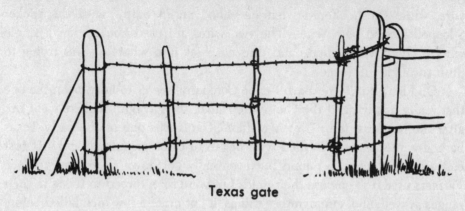

Texas gate

hinges. Or, especially in the South, you might have a Texas gate: three or four strands of rawhide, rope, or wire fastened to one gatepost and ending at the other side in a stout stick. Fastened to the other gatepost were a couple of loops to go over the top and bottom of this stretcher, when you wanted to close the gate. You'll still see this style in lots of barbed-wire fences in the West. But before we come to that sticky subject, let's build a shed or two and have done with the corrals.

You built sheds of poles, logs, rock, sod, or whatever, roofing them with more poles and brush, or sod, or shakes (which you made by whipsawing a log into about a 30-inch block and then splitting off thin boards to be used like shingles). Sometimes the sheds were simple lean-tos, sometimes more elaborate. But usually they'd be open to the south, providing merely a windbreak and shelter from the rain. There'd be a feed trough, rack, or manger inside. And, of course, the farther north you got the more substantial and enclosed the sheds would be, since your saddle horses would need protection, no matter how hardy your longhorns might be.

Now that barbed wire. It was a great day for the sodbusters and great disaster for the free-grass cowmen when that stuff arrived! It was invented, or at least perfected, by one or more farmers living in De Kalb County, Illinois. Just who was the first has long since been lost under tons of lawsuits and legal documents. But in 1875 Joseph Glidden of De Kalb applied for a patent on a barbed wire; in the same year Jacob Haish and I. Ellwood, also of De Kalb, applied for patents, and the war waged merrily thereafter, in the courts as well as on the plains. Glidden (who eventually emerged the victor) and Haish were both in the barbed-wire-manufacturing business, the principal difference between their products appearing from this distance to be that Glidden wound his short barbs around just one of the two wires which, twisted together, form a barbed-wire strand, and braced it with the other wire, while Haish offered what he called an "S barb," with the sticker S-looped around both wires. The two wires are used because on a single wire the barb would rotate and thus not stick into whatever was trying to push through the fence.

Glidden's outfit, the Barb Fence Company, seems to have been the one that really popularized the "bob-wire" label, though both makers went out after the business. John "Bet A Million" Gates was one of the early Texas barbed-wire salesmen. Barbed wire began to catch on immediately. It first cost around 20 cents a pound but eventually got down to around 2 cents. Farmers used it to enclose their fields but were soon forced to fence in their ranges as well; and, among other things, it got quite a few men killed before the fracas was all over.

The small cattlemen, homesteaders, and nestors who found themselves fenced inside greater neighbors' holdings, or fenced away from water and grass, got out their wire clippers, slipped their bandannas over their noses, and proceeded to cut those newfangled bob-wire fences, thus starting fence-cutters' wars all over the West.

This was mainly in the eighties, when the wire had spread like weeds and was threatening to strangle the whole Western country. People were fencing up the grass, the water—whether they owned the land or not—closing public roads, surrounding small settlers, blocking off old trails. Eventually the wars shook down in legislatures and courts, and both fence cutters and barbed-wire range hogs were restrained.

Arrah, let's build us a house! First a dugout, or maybe a sod house, which we'd likely have to start with, and then a real pioneer ranch house or farmhouse.

To build a dugout you really need a cutbank, or at least a sloping hillside. You *can* build one right out on a flat, bald prairie, and both the early settlers and the Plains Indians before them sometimes used such habitations; pit houses, as the Indian type was called. But in those you're liable to wake up in a covered cistern, if there's a big rain. It's almost impossible to keep the water out, once the earth is soaked. On a slope, you can keep most of it from ever getting in, or drain it out if it does.

Almost nowhere, not even on the Staked Plains of West Texas, is the earth truly billiard-table flat. You can almost always find a little slope, a little rise or bank somewhere. Into it you dig what amounts to a storm cellar, and indeed many a pioneer dugout was and still is used for just that, even though a more pretentious house has long since risen on the surface. You can make it almost any size you want to, by digging additional pits or caves for extra rooms, connecting them with the original room by passages.

Dugout

But, for obvious reasons, the original dugout room itself had to be small, not much over 10 by 12 feet. After all, you had to hold the roof up.

Sometimes the dugout was a true cave dug into the bank, with only a rude pole door frame to hold the door, or maybe not even a door—just a buffalo hide or piece of canvas. And you'd probably need a few supports inside for the roof. But more often the dugout would start with an open shelf or niche cut into the slope, then a sod-brick wall would be built for a front with room for a door and maybe even a window. The roof, made of poles or logs, was covered with a layer of brush, then a layer of grass, and finally a top layer of spade-tamped earth. You gave this roof a reversed slope toward the hill, and you made ditches on both sides of your dugout and back up the hill too, so that water pouring downhill wouldn't waterfall right over your eaves into your front door.

But no matter how well you did it, that roof was still a pain in the neck and muddy water in the soup, because, short of shingling it, you couldn't make the darn thing really leakproof in a heavy rain. It dripped muddy water all over everything. If somebody was sick you might have to hold an umbrella over the bed, or bring in the wagon sheet. It was forever spilling grass roots, clods, bits of bark, or maybe even worms, mice, centipedes, and scorpions into anything and everything below. The womenfolk hated it with a passion.

But a dugout was cool in summer and warm in winter—that much you could say. Heating was easy, too. All you had to do was dig a fireplace and up on top add a mud-daubed barrel, or a cylinder of mud-plastered sticks, for a chimney. But if you made your dugout fairly tight, you might also suffocate with smoke or deadlier carbon monoxide; if you made it flimsy and a cow or horse came strolling down the hill, you might end up with the beastie in bed with you. It was generally wet, always dirty—so, as you can imagine, the pioneer, real soon if he had women, pretty soon regardless, promoted himself out of that hole into a half-dugout, a sod house, or a real house.

A half-dugout was a sort of basement apartment, a pit about waist- or shoulder-deep, with sod walls on four sides. This, with the same kind of leaky sod roof, would be practically as objectionable as the full dugout. But you could have more windows, or at least openings for ventilation, which you fitted with glass if you had it, or oiled paper, or a hide, or canvas, or wooden cover if glass and paper were beyond your range.

Next came the sod house. To build one of these you needed from one-half to one acre of heavy grass sod. You could handle this with just a spade, if you had to, but that was doing it the hard way. Usually a turning plow or sodbuster would be available, and you'd turn the sod, taking pains to keep the furrows even and the same depth. Then, with a spade, you'd cut big slabs, about 2 by 3 feet, or maybe square, 3 by 3, and these you'd haul to your house site in the wagon or on a sledge, which was called a go-devil by some folks.

You'd have laid out your ground plan more or less carefully before you started. Since the days of the Pyramids, men for some strange reason have preferred that their buildings sit four-square to the points of the compass,

Sod house

and the Westerners were no exception. Even if they didn't have any compass, or surveying instruments, or other scientific tools for determining exact directions, they could find them just the same. At a point where they wanted one corner of the house to be they'd set a stake with a cord or rope tied to it; then that night, very carefully they'd line the cord up with the pole-star and stake it down. There was true north and south, one side of home. Then, to make the corners square, they'd do something even older than the Pyramids. They'd take a rope and measure off three units on it and tie a knot; it didn't matter what unit—the length of your forearm or whatever. From this knot, they'd measure off four more of the same units and tie another knot; then five units and then a final knot or cut the rope off. Now they had the makings of a magic triangle, or try square, which the Babylonians used.

If you peg that rope down as a triangle, with stakes at the knots, the angle at the stake between the two shorter sides will always be a true right angle, 90 degrees. You can get your corners square and your house foursquare as easy as that.

Next, usually with a rope or cord for a guideline, you laid a foundation course of sod bricks, leaving openings for doors. And here you could use another pioneer trick, which probably came from the time of the Pyramids, too. You could get the floor of your house absolutely level without any instruments at all except a spade and a bucket. You did it by putting mud mortar between your sod bricks, which you'd do anyhow, then making a temporary mud dam across the doors or other openings. Then you filled the inside of the house-to-be with water. You didn't need much water, just enough to fill the low spots and expose the high ones. The surface of that little pond was true level, of course, as true as any engineer could devise, and you could lay the dirt floor, or mark the wood one if you were putting one in, accordingly. Then you'd run the water out and go on with your building.

Laying the walls, you'd use the sod bricks much as you would regular bricks, breaking the joints, using mud for mortar, laying about every third layer crosswise to tie the wall together. You'd set the door and window frames in the walls, just as in a regular, board house, and run the walls up to the roof level. Here you'd need some timbers. If you could find a couple of stout young trees forked at about the right height, you cut them down for supports for the ridgepole. You set these posts inside the house, vertically in the ground at the middle of each end, either in the sod wall if you were doing an extra-neat job, or just against it. Then you hunted up another stout timber for a ridgepole, to extend horizontally between the forks.

Now the roof. Usually, front and back, you ran the sod walls up to the ridgepole, so that your gables were also sod. But if you had boards enough, you boarded the gables in. And to make a good roof, you boarded it over too, first setting poles for rafters as on a sod roof, then nailing boards to the poles, then tar paper if you could get it, then over that thin slabs of sod. If you wanted a real slick job, you laid the sod grass-side down and finished up with a coating of ashes and clay, which you could also use to plaster the house inside. It didn't make a bad-looking wall.

Most likely it would have only one or two rooms, this little old sod shanty on your claim. But it was a darn sight better than a dugout. It was a home. A woman, if you were lucky enough to have one, might paper the walls with old newspapers, seal in the ceilings with cheesecloth, make you do something about those dirt floors. You could make a puncheon floor by splitting logs and smoothing—if you want to call it that—the floor side with a broadax, or maybe you could find some whipsawed lumber. Logs you split with a froe, by the way, which is a sort of T-shaped chisel, with the cutting edge along the top bar of the T. You could use it to rive shakes or clapboards, or even to make long splits for doors. You pegged or nailed the splits together to get a big enough piece for the door, and you hung it on rawhide or wooden hinges, wood pins through augered holes—you didn't need any nails at all! Or any locks, either. A horizontal pivoted bar, dropping into a slot on the other side of the door frame, was what you used to keep the door closed. Above the bar you bored a hole through the door, fastened a rawhide string to the bar, thrust its end through the hole, and thus you could unbar the door from the outside, or pull the string in and "lock" it from the inside. "The latchstring's out" had real meaning on the frontier.

The fireplace you usually set at one end of the house, building it of stone if you could get any. The exact set of the throat, so it would draw well and not smoke, was quite an art. Very often, especially where stone was hard to get, the upper part of the fireplace and chimney would be split sticks, thickly plastered with mud—"cat-and-clay" chimneys some called them—or maybe just some more sod bricks, covered thick with mud. In time they would bake iron hard.

Firing that hearth, you ordinarily put a big green backlog in first, both to protect the back of the fireplace and to throw out the heat. You would need andirons, which you could improvise if you had none. Pothooks and cranes, to hold your cooking vessels, you might very well build into your fireplace, as well as a ledge along one side for the same purpose. And, as we've noted, if you had to, you could burn buffalo or cow chips, or weeds,

Texas house

or hay, or, after you'd started a crop, corncobs or cornstalks, or even corn. Corn is oily and makes a quick, hot fire. You'd use the fireplace both for heating and cooking at first. Up north and along the railroads the settlers usually got iron stoves, much more satisfactory than the fireplaces, but down south, in Texas and the Nations, lots of folks were still using the old fireplaces even when I was a kid.

Now let's look at the typical ranch house, which was the final type of pioneer Western dwelling. From Texas to Wyoming, it was characteristic, and they still call it a Texas house. It is really two houses, or anyway, two rooms or sets of rooms, semi-annexed to each other by a connecting roof over a long hall open on both sides. In Texas they'd call this a dog-trot, which doesn't sound as poetic as a modern architect's breezeway, the same thing. Down in the original home of the American cow-ranching business, along the Nueces and the Bravo, where it gets right hot on occasion, you'll still find the ranch houses with their dog-trots set for the prevailing winds.

Going north, in North Texas and the Indian Nations, you would find the same style. But here, quite often, the back or north side of the hall would be closed in, because it sometimes gets cold up there and stays cold. Or perhaps both sides would be more or less closed in. Going still farther up the trail, more and more often you'd find the dog-trots closed in at both sides because of the climate. But even in Montana and Wyoming the pioneer ranch houses, built by emigrant Texans or by cowmen influenced by Texas styles, would be typically two log cabins, end to end, with that covered hall in the middle. Saddlebag houses, as they used to say. Incidentally, a house with the rooms in line, like beads on a string, was and is a shotgun house.

Down south the ranch houses were likely to be adobe. But farther north they were usually of lumber or logs, since the cowman had got there first and had always settled near water, which ordinarily meant timber as well. Building, or rather raising, a log house was an art, and also a tall chore. It took strong backs, because you have to lift and push plenty. You would snake in the logs, cornermen would notch the ends to make them fit flat (nothing to prevent you from being your own cornerman, of course!), then you'd push the logs up skids, or just lift them into place in the walls. With wood plentiful you'd make your roof of shakes or clapboards, much better than sod. Down south you'd maybe rive cypress, which lasts forever, or use cedar to make your shakes; up north you might use oak. But, either place, once you got through splitting your shakes from a 3-foot chunk of log, you'd have a little triangular core left, which you'd use to help chink up the cabin; that is, to fill the spaces between the logs. You'd use clay for the rest of your chinking, sealing carefully. If you did a good job, you'd have a pretty warm house.

At one end you'd build a huge fireplace and chimney, as we've described, and it could be that you'd put in a ceiling and have a loft or attic up under the eaves, just high enough to crawl into on hands and knees. But people could sleep up there, getting up by a ladder. One of your cabins, on one side, would be the living quarters or bunkhouse, with bunks built in along the walls, a rawhide lumber table or two, some benches, three-legged stools, and so on, all homemade. The cabin on the other side of the dog-trot would be the cookhouse or dining hall. It, too, would have a huge fireplace, and maybe an iron cookstove too if this outfit was up-and-coming, plus the cookie's pots and pans, his work table, and another long table for eating, usually with benches. Eating tools and dishes would be here too, probably iron knives and forks, and heavy ironstone plates; cups and saucers, maybe white, but often blue, brown, or mulberry in color. In brief, here is the genesis of the cowboy bunkhouse on one side and cookhouse on the other. Saddles, ropes, bridles, dogs, and so on were kept in the dog-trot between.

Later on, as the ranch prospered, perhaps you'd build a separate residence, a big house for the owner and his family, and you might separate sleeping quarters and dining hall for the hands. But bunkhouse and cook shack would always be there.

For light you had the fireplace; maybe candles which you made yourself, either by dipping, or molding in a candle mold; or maybe a coal-oil lamp or two; or you could even make yourself a pretty fair light if you just had a 'possum, some lard oil, or even a skunk. A nice dead skunk, of course, who hadn't had time to advertise. From either of these animals, and from others as well, you could render oil, and you could make the lamp too, by filling a cup or bowl half full of sand, then imbedding a nail, point up, in the middle and hooking a wick—almost any old kind of rag would make one—on the point. Pour the oil in the sand, taking care to soak the wick too, and light it, and you had a kind of Betty lamp! Betty or Phoebe lamps were simply fat- or grease-burners, not very different from the lamps of ancient Greece and Rome. When you bought them, they were somewhat like a covered gravy dish, often with a hook or chain on the handle so you could hang them up. The wick came out the spout of the dish. They were made of 'most anything—iron, brass, copper, pottery, stone.

Rush, or rushlight, holders, even more primitive, were a crude kind of clamp, to hold fat-soaked rushes, which you pulled from the creek banks, for candles. Usually the rushlight holder had a spike to stick in the wall and hold the light up. They were used in the West, by some folks at least, right up to the eighties.

Of course there were all sorts of candlesticks and candelabra. I suppose anyone can visualize, from the modern electric versions, a real fancy Western chandelier made out of an old wagon wheel, or a doubletree, or even a singletree, and a colorful lamp that was once a wagon hub. You saw some of these with coal-oil lamps in ranch houses on the frontier. Some lamp oil had actually been made from coal in the fifties, real "coal oil," and the name persisted when kerosene, made from petroleum, took

WROUGHT-IRON LIGHTING ARRANGEMENTS

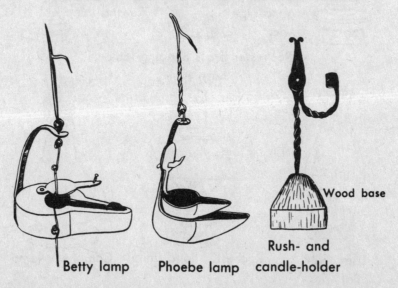

Betty lamp   Phoebe lamp   Wood base

Rush- and candle-holder

over in the sixties. Before the "coal-oil" lights came along, lamps burning whale oil (expensive, too, brought in by whalers from South Pacific whales, $2 and up a gallon) or camphene, made from alcohol and turpentine, were also in use. You'd see some of them in pioneer areas, of course.

But "coal oil"—kerosene—was lots cheaper, so they used it when they could. There were two basic kinds of kerosene lamps in the period we are covering, the flat-wick variety, which didn't give too much light, and the round-wick or Argand type, which produced a circle of flame and

LAMPS

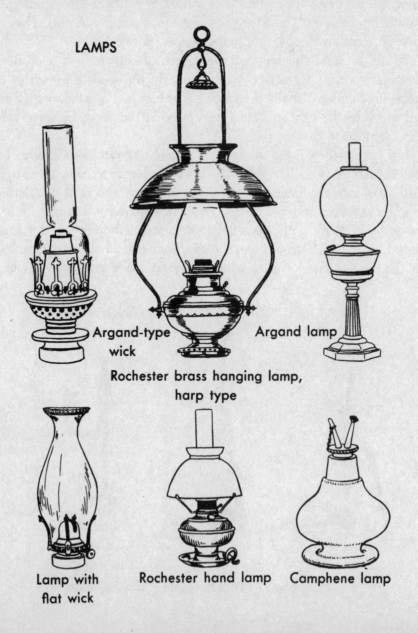

Argand-type wick

Argand lamp

Rochester brass hanging lamp, harp type

Lamp with flat wick

Rochester hand lamp

Camphene lamp

considerably more illumination, maybe 10 or 12 candlepower anyway; people worried about its being so bright it would ruin your eyes. The Rayo and Rochester brass bowl lamps, which perhaps you can remember Grandpa and Grandma using out on the old farm, were Argand round-wick lamps, the ones with the green, white, or red shades you see in the Western movies. And while we're at it, we might note also that the very fancy cinema lamps, the *Gone with the Wind* kind with flowers and designs on round, street-lamp-style shades, didn't come along until the opulent eighties.

You could buy lamps by mail, and practically anything else too, even in the sixties. You could order anything from anvils to zithers, and though most of it had to come by express or freight, still small articles galore could be mailed. But there was no parcel post, not until 1913. And rural free delivery, R.F.D., the farmer's famous friend, started only in 1896, practically at the end of the frontier period. Before that you had to go into town to the post office to get your mail.

From the Civil War to 1883 letter postage was 3 cents. But in 1883 Congress reduced it to 2 cents for half an ounce, and in 1884 decided you could mail a full ounce for your 2 cents. Three-cent postage did not come back until 1917, one of those "temporary war emergencies" that sometimes last forever. You could get postal money orders after 1864, penny postcards from 1872 on, special delivery after 1885. And registering letters had been possible since the mid-1850s.

Where railroads or steamboats could not deliver mail, the Post Office Department from 1845 on let contracts to the lowest bidders offering other means of transport—stagecoaches, mail hacks, horseback carriers, dog sleds, or whatever—requiring only a guarantee of "due celerity, certainty, and security." This proviso was usually indicated in advertisements and contracts by three stars, hence the name "star route" for this kind of mail service, which served huge areas of the Old West. But a star route was not an R.F.D. route; it served only post offices.

If you were a farmer, you could have bought a Kirby Patent Harvester on your way home from the Civil War. It cut your wheat, oats, or whatever, but did not bind the stalks into bundles. That you still had to do by hand. But by 1880 the harvesters had been improved to do their own binding, and McCormick and Deering were putting out just such machines—binders, as the combined binder-harvester soon was called. Threshing machines, probably with J. K. Case as the pioneer maker, were machines worked at first by horses, four or five teams circling 'round and 'round to turn a big wheel called a power, which in turn operated a separator, which separated the grain from the chaff. But even before the end of the seventies, this

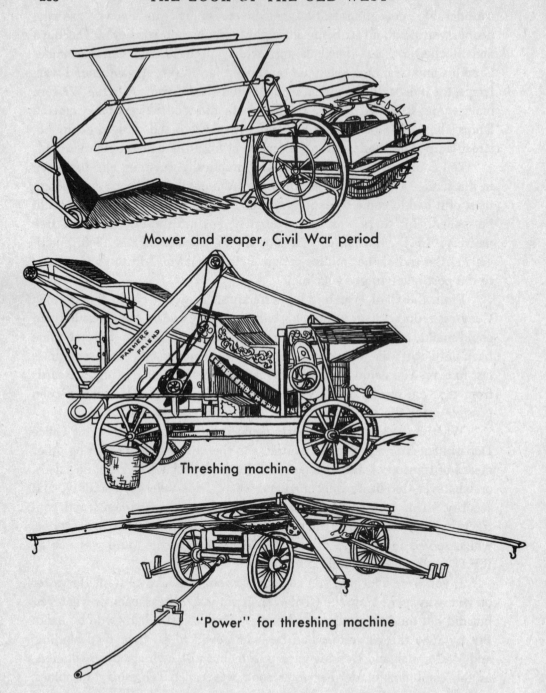

Mower and reaper, Civil War period

Threshing machine

"Power" for threshing machine

primitive method was being succeeded by the steam engine, mounted on a wagon and requiring horses to move it around. By the mid-eighties, the horses were displaced by a self-propelled traction engine, roaring and

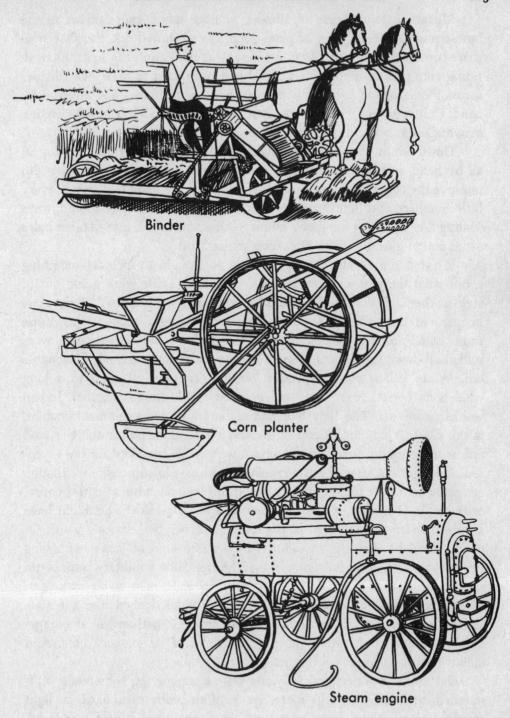

Binder

Corn planter

Steam engine

lumbering along on its steel wheels (at about 3 miles an hour) and towing the separator.

Meantime John Deere of Illinois, another name long famous in the farm-equipment field (the original John Deere turned out the first steel share-breaking or turning plow in 1837), was perfecting the first practical, riding corn planter. Before that a sled had been used to make the furrows across the harrowed field, and the corn had been planted and covered by hand. Cultivators, of various sorts, had been on the market since the sixties, mowing machines and gang plows from the middle seventies.

Down South, they'd still be planting cotton, chopping and picking it, all by hand, just like their grandfathers, almost up to now. But they did improve the cotton gin, which used to be one of the main features of every little Southern and Southwestern country town, some one of them always "baling fire" in one of the great, clumsy, burlap-wrapped, iron-banded bales —and cotton gins did make fine, spectacular fires!

We've had a lot about men's clothes, so I ought to include something about what the pioneer women wore, too. Hoop skirts were going out of style as the Civil War ended, crinoline was being used instead of the steel hoops, and tight corsets were coming back. Around 1868-70 the bustle came back, and by the 1880s it was a darb. A lady's petticoats were ruffled all down the back and even had an extra, long, ruffled, detachable tail! White ladies wore suspender garters, generally attached to a long whalebone corset, from the late seventies on—I dunno whether Indian women wore 'em. The lady had had elaborate drawers (unmentionables, in the chaste Victorian lexicon of the Old West) since before the war, and red flannel ones, by Jove, for the winter weather in the West, in the seventies and eighties. After about 1875 she could have a princess slip, though generally her upper undergarment would still be a chemise, a "corset cover" or camisole. Over that, if she was wearing a balmoral skirt, she might have a muslin waist (it says here in the old ad) or maybe a basque waist. Or maybe she'd be wearing a paletot, which was a kind of jacket with long sleeves and high neck, buttoning down the front like a military tunic. Or a sacque, which was a female version, with doodads, of a man's sack coat; though you could also have a long sacque, which looked like a female version with doodads of a man's cutaway coat. Or perhaps, in the stagecoach, madam would prefer a traveling dress of serge, very chic. And milady's hat was usually a bonnet.

Out on the frontier, generally she wore a sunbonnet, homemade, stiff-starched, and stiffened still more, quite often, with cardboard or light wooden inserts which were taken out when the bonnet was laundered. You could make your own starch, from the settlings of potato water, or by soaking wheat in water, straining it, and then pouring off the water after

MODES OF THE 1880s

Underskirt

Dress with paletot (coat)

Basque

Dress

Hat

Mitt

Purse

Waist

Sacque

its starchy dregs had settled. She had a calico dress, our frontier woman, long sleeves and high neck, and her efforts to beautify it, and herself, were often wistful and pathetic. Not even any face powder, imagine! And she did *not* wear men's pants, nor did she ride astride, ever!

The divided riding skirt came along with the Wild West shows and the rodeos, and riding breeches for women developed in this century. They were no part of the early West. Indian women rode astride, yes. But a white woman rode a side saddle, which was an atrocity with a curved, padded bar for a horn, sticking out on the upper left side. The rider hooked her knee over this and rode with both legs on the same side of the horse, demurely covered, furthermore, with about yea yards of riding skirt. Sometimes, on a jumping saddle, there would be a down-curving horn too,

Gray serge traveling costumes of the 1870s

ACCESSORIES, EARLY 1890s

Drawers and petticoat
of embroidered flannel

Bust pads

Small bustle

Hip bustle

Sack

Curling iron

Shell and amber hairpins

Diamond earrings

Afternoon hat

Long-skirt chemise

Lady's garter

Dusting cap

Kid-and-cloth shoe

Sunbonnet

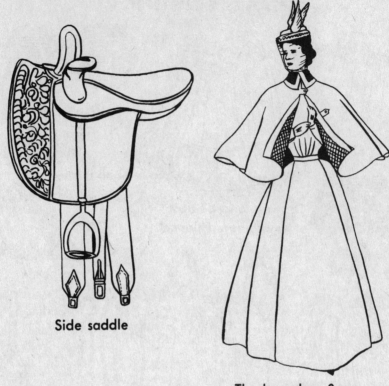

Side saddle

The hourglass figure

this to hook the left knee under. It was a heck of a way to have to ride. Nevertheless, there were many amazingly skillful feminine riders.

The hourglass figure, by the way, was a figure of speech, as well as fashion, in the nineties, but even in the sixties and seventies, for a mere dollar or so you could buy such female comforters as Peerless Bust Developer, complete with exerciser.

We started with the Army; let's go back to it, for a final look. In 1890 the brief, brutal battle of Wounded Knee, South Dakota, with 200 Indians and 60 soldiers casualties within a few minutes, ended the Indian Wars. And when the Cherokee Outlet was opened September 16, 1893, with 30,000 white adventurers racing for claims, the Old West was practically gone. Let's take a look at the little Army that fought that last Indian battle and supervised that final mass stampede. They did look like the frontier troopers we see in the movies, because they wore just about the last of the old Army blue.

In 1881 the infantry dress shakos were abolished and everybody got helmets, with spikes for infantrymen, although their field officers drew white buffalo or yak-hair plumes. In the cavalry officers and enlisted men already had yellow plumed helmets, everybody in artillery had red plumes, and now there were new orange plumes for the Signal Corps. And the same year knit undershirts and blue overshirts for everybody came in.

In 1884 gauntlets were issued to all mounted men. In 1885 the drab-colored fatigue hat was authorized. In 1889 an issue of one pair of suspenders to each enlisted man was ordered, and the Signal Corps got the straight-sided conductor's-type cap that eventually would replace the old forage cap for the entire Army. Brown cotton-duck leggings were ordered for all foot troops, and the change was on the way.

In 1894 the faithful old .45-70, black-powder Springfield was replaced by the Krag-Jorgensen, a Danish invention, bolt-action, .30 caliber (in the model adopted by the U. S.), five shot, smokeless, with a peculiar magazine on the right side, a sort of swinging box you flipped open to insert the cartridges, one at a time. It did not use clips. But it was a repeater and a high-powered weapon, sighted for 2000 yards. It was made both in rifle, 30-inch barrel, and carbine, 22-inch barrel, styles, and it was the weapon that fought the Spanish-American War, with the doubtful help of some obsolete .45-70 Springfields, mostly in the hands of state troops, who soon discovered that their old charcoal burners weren't much more than a fine smoke signal to the Spaniards, armed with smokeless Mausers.

The Krag-Jorgensen cartridge, at first called the .30 Army and then the .30-40, is *not* the .30-06 Springfield cartridge, which is a hull of another hue altogether. For one immediate distinction, the Krag shell is rimmed, the .30-06 is not. The odd designation of the latter cartridge came about because of an ammunition change. In 1903 the U. S. discarded the Krag in favor of a new bolt action, the famous Springfield Model, which had '03 cartridges made for it. But in 1906 the bullet and the cartridge were improved, the chambering of the rifle was altered slightly, and the piece

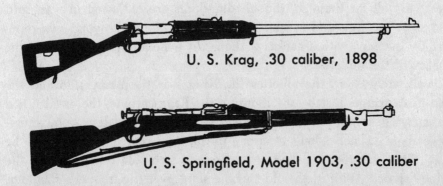

U. S. Krag, .30 caliber, 1898

U. S. Springfield, Model 1903, .30 caliber

became the Springfield .30-06. So the last figure this time refers to the year. This rifle, with the modified Enfield, Model 1917, which also took the Government .30-06 ammunition, was the principal weapon in World War I.

But back to the Krag. It was a good gun and riflemen still swear by it. It was much more powerful than the old .45-70 and produced no betraying clouds of white smoke. Its bullets were "patched"; that is, the lead core was covered with a thin layer of cupro-nickel or gilding metal, thus making them what soon came to be called "steel-jackets," which, of course, they were not. A bullet actually coated with hard steel would wreck a rifle barrel.

There were two reasons for this change, or rather a reason and a happy result. Smokeless powder, which does produce some fumes, for all its name, is made either from guncotton or from a combined guncotton-nitroglycerin base, the first being called a single-base, or bulk, smokeless powder, the second a double-base, or dense, powder. Guncotton was discovered in 1845 and nitroglycerin in 1846 (dynamite was not invented by Alfred Nobel until 1866, for the benefit of some authors who have been trying to win the Civil War with it). Both guncotton and nitroglycerin are very violent in their effects, and it was not until the eighties that chemists found out how to slow down the explosions enough to make rifle powders possible.

When they did, they discovered that the new powder slammed the old lead bullets through the barrel so fast that the bullet was virtually torn apart, especially in the smaller, higher-twist rifling barrels of the new weapons. When the experimenters fixed this, with a harder bullet, they found that the penetration in the target was much greater, but that was not an unmixed blessing, because now the slug would sometimes go right on through, carrying with it much of its knock-down force.

So they fixed this with hard-jacketed but soft-nosed bullets, the earliest including some with two slits cut in the point of the bullet. These were the so-called dumdums which every nation at war around the turn of the century accused its enemies of using. But the poor game animals had nobody to yell for them so, though dumdums are outlawed in war, soft-nosed slugs are still used in sporting rifles. You can make your own dumdums, by the way, with a hacksaw, though it generally plays hob with the accuracy of the bullets.

Well, anyway, in the nineties the Krag was the Army rifle and the .30-40 its cartridge. Just before adopting the Krag carbine, the cavalry had been carrying its single-shot Springfield carbines in a leather boot, brass-tipped, about 14 inches long, strapped to the right rear quarterstrap of the saddle. This was the so-called short boot, which left the barrel of the carbine exposed. With it, the old carbine sling over the trooper's shoulder, snapping into a ring on the small of the stock, was still being used. But with the adoption of the bolt-action Krag, which has a much thicker breech than the old Springfield, a long boot came into use, covering the entire carbine, up to the stock. This was slung from the right pommel ring, so that the carbine butt slanted to the front, near the horse's neck, and the scabbard was under the rider's leg. This was a necessary but not very happy arrangement, since the rifle under the leg interfered with the rider's seat, there was too much weight on the pommel, and the carbine could no longer be carried slung to the trooper.

That was important for cavalry, because bitter experience had demonstrated that a cavalryman had better have that piece tied to him. The saber didn't matter; he wouldn't need that afoot, so it was slung on the left front side of the saddle, hilt canted forward, and the scabbard steadied with a strap through the cinch ring. But he would need the carbine, and now he had to be trained to grab for it. His pistol, of course, he still wore with the butt to the front, in a flap holster on the right side of his belt, and this holster now had a squared flap, buttoning directly to the stud, rather than the rounded flap and strap arrangement of the Civil War holster.

In 1894 or thereabouts, the pistol had become a double-action, swing-out-cylinder .38, either a Colt or a Smith & Wesson, very much like our modern double-actions.

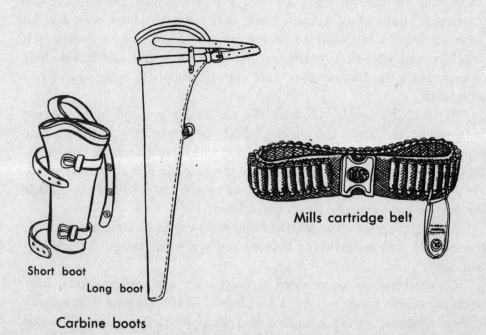

Mills cartridge belt

Short boot

Long boot

Carbine boots

That wide web cartridge belt around the trooper's middle, which had been a Prairie belt, was now generally called a Mills belt. General Anson Mills, long of the Tenth Cavalry, had devised the way to weave in the cartridge loops, in 1867, and the Army had adopted his improved belts in 1879. There was no sewing in the entire belt, which was also called a thimble belt, since it carried loops, or thimbles, for the individual cartridges. It held various quantities of cartridges, forty, forty-five, or fifty, though later models, for the Krags, would have a double row of loops, one atop the other, accommodating one hundred cartridges. It adjusted in front by folding back through brass keepers, and buckled with a simple brass loop, or a brass belt plate carrying the U. S. in an oval. It was dark blue or gray, changing to drab as the khaki came in. Mills belts were also made commercially, and were used by many sportsmen for everything up to and including shotgun shells.

The trooper would now be wearing a drab campaign hat, creased fore and aft, a blue woolen shirt, blue single-breasted blouse with turndown collar (the old fatigue coat), lighter blue trousers, and black cavalry boots, or drab sidelace leggings. For dress he still had the fancifully trimmed blouse, or rather uniform dress coat, much as in the seventies; a dress helmet, complete with yellow plume, brass scale chin strap, huge brass eagle on the front, and yellow braided helmet cord. The trumpeters still wore rows of braid plastered across their chests. The trooper still had a forage cap for undress wear. He had a brown canvas fatigue coat and trousers for stable duty, a stable frock, and maybe a winter campaign kit which included a blanket-lined canvas overcoat, fur cap and gauntlets, felt leggings, and wool-lined overshoes. Many of these still had buffalo-hide uppers, which was the way they were until the supply of buffalo hides was exhausted.

He probably would still have the old double-breasted blue overcoat with yellow-lined cape, though the officers were switching now to a new ulster coat, with no cape but instead a hood which hung down on the back— this became the universal model when the new olive drab was adopted. He wouldn't have all this stuff on him, of course, but he'd have it. This is the trooper you generally see in the cinemas.

With appropriate changes, the other arms would be similarly arrayed, the infantry with spiked dress helmets and white trimmings, the artillery with scarlet trim.

On the horse, as we've noted already, saber and carbine would now be on the saddle, which was still a McClellan but now covered with smooth leather. Overcoat would be rolled and strapped to the pommel, while blanket, dog-tent half, underwear, and a nosebag for feeding the horse made up the cantle roll. A short-strapped, round canteen with its strap passed through the handle of a big tin cup fastened to the near cantle ring. In the saddlebags now, along with the extra ammunition, spare horseshoes, rations, and so on, would be a meat can, a covered mess kit somewhat like the one used today, except that it was round, made of tinned iron, and lacked the fancy compartments. Its long handle folded over the cover much as now and you used it for a frying pan, as well as plate. Halter would be on the horse, under the bridle, and the lariat was carried coiled and dangling, like a hangman's knot, over the near saddlebag.

Such would be the trooper of the nineties, soon to fight in the brief Spanish-American War. There were so few of him that you could scarcely say we'd even kept sufficient samples for a Regular Army. In the long period from Appomattox to the sinking of the *Maine* the United States had almost let its Army lapse, sending the soldier after the free land and the buffalo.

The Fifth Corps, the little army that sailed from Tampa, Florida, for

Rough Rider   Regulation Infantry, 1898

Santiago, Cuba, in June 1898 to subdue the Spaniards, numbered less than 17,000 men. We'd just about consider it a good strong patrol today. In that little force was more than half of the Regular Army, all but seven of the twenty-five infantry regiments, five of the ten cavalry, and elements of a sixth (the Second Cavalry), plus batteries from three of the five artillery regiments! Not many regulars, but among them a lot of darn good men.

There were volunteers, too, some of whom would disgrace themselves, while others would put on a rip-roaring Wild West show, practically stealing all the glory of the entire war—that outfit, of course, was the First Volunteer Cavalry, Teddy Roosevelt's famous Rough Riders.

They were a rootin' tootin' outfit, too, whose like will not be seen again in an American army. With Doctor (later Major General) Leonard Wood, President McKinley's personal physician, as colonel and Theodore Roosevelt, who had been Assistant Secretary of the Navy, as lieutenant colonel, the regiment was raised in Oklahoma, Indian Territory, New Mexico, and Arizona, and trained in San Antonio. It had cowboys, bronc busters, sheriffs, gamblers, Indians, the mayor of Prescott, Arizona, doctors, lawyers, actors, writers—oh yes, and a small but select bunch of dudes from Princeton, Harvard, and Yale! I am happy to report they liked one another and got along well.

But if you think they were military, hah! They had to know how to shoot and ride before they could get in, but they were probably as unmilitary a regiment as was ever mustered, and they didn't get much help. The horses, eventually supplied by a somewhat shell-shocked government, were mostly unbroken broncs; the unfamiliar Krag carbines didn't arrive until shortly before the outfit departed for the front; and they never got any real uniforms during the war. *De nada*—so what? They already knowed how to fight, even on foot.

That uniform detail maybe needs elucidating. The Army, restless in the thick old Army blue, was casting an inquiring eye at the British Army and its campaigns in North and South Africa. Some of the British units were using a stout, brownish, cotton cloth they called "cock-ee," or "kack-ee," or something like that from a Hindu word meaning dust-colored. The vaunted "thin red line" had been finding out the hard way that when a real marksman, say a keen-eyed Boer, is shooting at you, you'd better look like dust, or your name is very likely to be mud. So, "for tropical service," the American Army also was flirting with khaki, which was cool, too—well, anyway, cooler than inch-thick wool.

But with the niggardly appropriations of the period about all the trend toward khaki had amounted to was brown-colored fatigue clothing,

stable garments, mainly pants, plus drab fatigue hats, now termed campaign hats, and drab leggings. There were a few khaki blouses, mostly for
officers and on the British style, high standing collar, two breast pockets,
the cuffs, shoulder tabs, and sometimes the pocket flaps in the color of the
arm—yellow, red, or white. But most of the uniforms were still the old
Army blue, shoulder straps still worn crosswise, chevrons points down. And
of course that old Army shirt, thick enough to stop a Dakota blizzard.

That was what the Rough Riders got. Brown canvas fatigue clothes.
Canvas pants, brown leggings, blue wool shirts with the collar open and
sleeves rolled up (you can imagine why!), a red cotton bandanna about
the neck, and a campaign hat, creased any and every old way, including
the new Montana Peak, which presently the Army would adopt. With no
horses in Cuba, they fought on foot; they carried their gear in a flopping
canvas haversack slung on the left hip, and in a blanket roll curled over
the left shoulder. Out of the grave, the old butternut brown and blanket
roll of the Confederate Army, serving now with the blue!

They looked like tramps and admitted it; they fought like regulars;
but they were civilians to the end, citizens in the service of a civilian
nation. Horsemen, they went up San Juan Hill on foot. But in that charge,
laced under the clumsy leggings, was at least one pair of high-heeled
cowboy boots.

BIBLIOGRAPHY

ARMY; CIVIL WAR

American Heritage (magazine). New York, N. Y.

Army Navy Journal (now *Army, Navy, Air Force Journal*). Washington, D. C.

Cavalry Journal (now *Armored Cavalry Journal*). Washington, D. C.

Davis, Gherardi. *The Colors of the United States Army.* New York: Gilliss Press (privately printed), 1912.

Downey, Fairfax. *Indian Fighting Army.* New York: Scribner, 1941.

Flags of the Army of the United States Carried During the War of the Rebellion. Washington, D. C.: Quartermaster's Department, 1887.

Ganoe, William Addleman. *History of the United States Army.* New York: Appleton, 1924.

Meredith, Roy. *Mr. Lincoln's Camera Man.* New York: Scribner, 1912.

Miller, Francis T., ed. *Photographic History of the Civil War.* 10 vols. New York: Review of Reviews Co., 1912.

Quaife, M. M. *The Flag of the United States.* New York: Grosset & Dunlap, 1942.

Rodenbaugh, T. F., and Haskin, W. L. *The Army of the United States.* New York: 1896.

Thruston, R. C. B. *Origin and Evolution of the U. S. Flag. Sons of the American Revolution Yearbook,* 1915.

WEAPONS: MILITARY AND CIVILIAN

The American Rifleman (magazine). Washington, D. C.

Amber, John T., ed. *Ten Rare Gun Catalogs.* New York: Greenberg, 1952.

Cunningham, Eugene. *Triggernometry.* Caldwell, Idaho: Caxton, 1941.

Fuller, C., and Steuart, R. D. *Firearms of the Confederacy.* Huntington, W. Va.: Standard, 1948.

Gluckman, Arcadi. *United States Martial Pistols and Revolvers.* Buffalo, N. Y.: Ulbrich, 1944.

Gluckman, Arcadi. *United States Muskets, Rifles and Carbines.* Buffalo, N. Y.: Ulbrich, 1948.

Gun Digest (annual). Chicago, Ill.

Guns (magazine). Chicago, Ill.

Hatcher, J. S. *Textbook of Firearms Investigation, Identification, and Evidence.* Georgetown, S. C.: Small-Arms Technical Publishing Co., 1935.

———. *Textbook of Pistols and Revolvers.* Georgetown, S. C.: Small-Arms Technical Publishing Co., 1935.

Haven, Charles T., and Belden, Frank A. *A History of the Colt Revolver.* New York: Morrow, 1940.

Hobbies (magazine). Chicago, Ill.

Holloway, Carroll C. *Texas Gun Lore.* San Antonio, Texas: Naylor, 1951.

Karr, C. L. and C. R. *Remington Handguns,* 2nd ed. Harrisburg, Pa.: Stackpole, 1951.

Logan, H. C. *Hand Cannon to Automatic.* Huntington, W. Va.: Standard, 1944.

Official Gun Book (annual). New York: Crown.

Parsons, John E. *The Peacemaker and Its Rivals.* New York: Morrow, 1950.

Rywell, Martin. *Samuel Colt.* Harriman, Tenn.: Pioneer Press.

———. *Smith & Wesson.* Harriman, Tenn.: Pioneer Press, 1953.

Satterlee, L. D., ed. *Fourteen Old Gun Catalogs.* Privately printed.

———. *Ten Old Gun Catalogs.* (Privately printed)

Sawyer, Charles W. *Our Rifles.* Boston: Williams Book Store, 1941. (Reprint of vol. III of *Firearms in American History,* 1910-1920.)

Serven, James. *Colt Cartridge Pistols.* Santa Ana, Calif.: Author, 1952.

———. *Colt Dragoon Pistols.* Dallas, Texas: C. Metzger, 1946.

———. *Colt Percussion Pistols.* Dallas, Texas: C. Metzger, 1947.

———. *Paterson Pistols.* Dallas, Texas: C. Metzger, 1946.

Sharpe, Phil. *The Rifle in America.* New York: Funk & Wagnalls, 1935.

The Shotgun News (magazine). Columbus, Nebr.

Smith, Winston O. *The Sharps Rifle.* New York: Morrow, 1943.

Thorp, Raymond W. *The Bowie Knife.* Albuquerque, N. M.: University of New Mexico Press, 1948.

Williamson, Harold F. *Winchester,* Washington, D. C.: Combat Forces Press, 1952.

TRAILS AND TRANSPORTATION

Cole, Harry E. *Stage Coach and Tavern Tales.* Cleveland, Ohio: A. H. Clark Company, 1930.

Dodge, Grenville M. *How We Built the Union Pacific Railway.* Council Bluffs, Iowa: Monarch Printing Co., no date.

Heckman, William L. *Steamboating.* Kansas City, Mo.: Burton, 1950.

Hereford, Robert A. *Old Man River.* Caldwell, Idaho: Caxton, 1943.

Hunter, J. Marvin, ed. *The Trail Drivers of Texas.* San Antonio, Texas: Old Trail Drivers Association, 1920.

MacMullen, Jerry. *Paddle Wheel Days in California.* Stanford, Calif.: Stanford University Press, 1944.

Ormsby, Waterman L. *The Butterfield Overland Mail.* San Marino, Calif.: Huntington Library, 1942.

Reck, Franklin M. *The Romance of American Transportation.* New York: Crowell, 1938.

Sabin, Edwin L. *Building the Pacific Railway.* Philadelphia: Lippincott, 1919.

Santleben, August. *A Texas Pioneer.* New York: Neal, 1908.

Winther, Oscar Osburn. *Express and Stagecoach Days in California.* Stanford, Calif.: Stanford University Press, 1931.

HORSES AND CATTLE

The Cattleman (magazine). Fort Worth, Texas.

Carter, William Giles Harding. *The Horses of the World.* Washington, D. C.: National Geographic Society, 1923.

———. *Horses, Saddles and Bridles,* 2nd ed. Baltimore: Lord Baltimore Press, 1902.

Denhardt, Robert Moorman. *The Horse of the Americas.* Norman, Okla.: University of Oklahoma Press, 1948.

Dobie, J. Frank. *The Longhorns.* Boston: Little, Brown, 1941.

———. *The Mustangs.* Boston: Little, Brown, 1952.

Graham, R. B. Cunninghame. *Horses of the Conquest.* Norman, Okla.: University of Oklahoma Press, 1949.

McCoy, Joseph G. *Historic Sketches of the Cattle Trade.* (Ralph P. Bieber, Ed.) Glendale, Calif.: A. H. Clark Company, 1940.

Speed, John G. *The Horse in America.* New York: McClure, Phillips, 1905.

Wallace, John F. *The Horse of America.* New York: privately printed, 1897.

Wellman, Paul I. *The Trampling Herd.* New York: Carrick & Evans, 1939.

FRONTIER LIFE

Adams, Ramon F. *Western Words.* Norman, Okla.: University of Oklahoma Press, 1946.

Brooks, Jerome E. *The Mighty Leaf: Tobacco through the Centuries.* New York: Little, Brown, 1952.

Chronicles of Oklahoma (magazine). Oklahoma City: Oklahoma Historical Society.

Coolidge, Dane. *Arizona Cowboys*. New York: Dutton, 1938.

———. *Old California Cowboys*. New York: Dutton, 1939.

———. *Texas Cowboys*. New York: Dutton, 1937.

Dick, Everett. *Sod House Frontier*. New York: Appleton, 1937.

Dobie, J. Frank. *A Vaquero of the Brush Country*. Dallas, Texas: Southwest Press, 1929.

Frontier Times (magazine). Bandera, Texas.

Hendricks, George D. *The Bad Men of the West*. San Antonio, Texas: Naylor, 1941.

Hough, Emerson. *The Story of the Cowboy*. New York: Appleton, 1897.

———. *Story of the Outlaw*. New York: Grosset & Dunlap, ca. 1907.

Humfreville, J. Lee. *Twenty Years Among Our Savage Indians*. Hartford, Conn.: Hartford Publishing Co., 1897.

Mora, Jo. *Trail Dust and Saddle Leather*. New York: Scribner, 1946.

Raine, William MacLeod. *Famous Sheriffs and Western Outlaws*. New York: Doubleday Doran, 1929.

Robert, Joseph C. *The Story of Tobacco in America*. New York: Knopf, 1949.

Rolling, Philip Ashton. *The Cowboy*. New York: Scribner, 1922.

Texas Almanac (annual). Dallas: *The Dallas News*.

Tilghman, Zoe A. *Marshal of the Last Frontier*. Glendale, Calif.: A. H. Clark Company, 1944.

Vestal, Stanley. *Dodge City, Queen of Cowtowns*. New York: Harper, 1952.

Wright, Muriel. *A Guide to the Indian Tribes of Oklahoma*. Norman, Okla.: University of Oklahoma Press, 1951.

INDEX

(Page numbers in italics refer to the illustrations)